75th SCOPES TRIAL Anniversary 2000

Court House, Dayton, Tenn. Where the Scopes Evolution Case was Tried, July 1925

Introduction

The conflict didn't begin in Dayton. Nor did it end there. But battle lines were drawn in 1925 when the 30 year old courthouse on the village square nestled between the Cumberland Ridge and the Tennessee River hosted the Trial of the Century and it played out in front of the whole world.

Before the Depression, before TVA, Dayton was in a region where God fearing, honest people eked out their living on a scrap of hillside or bottomland. A living that consisted with what we know of frontier life.

Schools were scattered and small. Children attended when they weren't needed at home for planting or harvest. Girls usually attended longer than boys. There was a strict moral code instilled in the children, passed down and upheld by an extended family. The jurors in the trial came from this group of hard working people.

The sleepy little town of Dayton came alive with visitors from across the nation. Its hospitality committee organized the overwhelming influx of reporters and visitors and miraculously averted chaos. In the crowded courtroom, where temperatures soared, a 'fan' meant a utensil with a handle that an individual waved to stir overheated air and cool perspiration laden faces. In the middle of the trial, the pervasive heat caused the proceeding to be moved into the open air of the courthouse lawn.

A noted lecturer of the day, thrice nominated for president of the United States, champion of the common man, assisted in the prosecution. He upheld the people's Christian standards, spoke in their behalf, saying what they would want to say but couldn't. They supported him with their presence and cheered in his behalf, oblivious to the big city critics who were calling them ignorant or making fun of the isolated lives they led.

On the other side came the champion of the 'philistines', 'Goliath.' A noted defense attorney from the north, self-proclaimed agnostic, determined to try Christianity and prove its God did not exist.

The characters were in place, the town was upholding the standard of southern hospitality, the courtroom began to fill.

What really happened in the days leading up to the trial? During the trial? In the aftermath?

The following pages relate verbatim every article about the trial, its participants, or the issues being debated, as printed in the Des Moines (Iowa) Register from July 1 to August 9, 1925. On this 75th Anniversary year of the trial, I challenge you to let the newspaper record take you back in time and see if the issues have changed? Situations gotten better or worse? YOU be the judge.

Janet M. Cruver
Timothy C. Cruver

The Scopes Trial Festival
is held annually in the month of July, presenting a reenactment of select portions of the original trial transcript to the public. The courtroom where the trial took place in 1925 becomes the stage for this production and local volunteers and professionals portray characters. For information contact:

Dayton Chamber of Commerce
107 Main Street
Dayton, TN 37321
PH 423-775-0361

Editor's Note: This transcript was taken from the original printed Des Moines Register. Punctuation, spelling, capitalization, etc. have been copied verbatim from the original to preserve the historical integrity of the work.

The text should be read as one would read the evening paper. Articles are copied consecutively from the original papers and differ in subject content. They are separated by ** so the reader can tell where one article stops and another begins.

YOU Be The Judge

Compiled by

Timothy C. Cruver

Edited by

Janet M. Cruver

Printed by The College Press

IBSN
0-9704900-0-3

Contents

Days, Dates **pages**

Wednesday, July 1, 1925..........**Pre-Trial**.................8

Thursday, July 2, 1925.. 9

Friday, July 3, 1925..12

Saturday, July 4, 1925..19

Sunday, July 5, 1925.. 23

Monday, July 6, 1925...25

Tuesday, July 7, 1925...27

Wednesday, July 8, 1925...30

Thursday, July 9, 1925...36

Friday, July 10, 1925...42

Saturday, July 11, 1925..45

Sunday, July 12, 1925...52

Monday, July 13, 1925...........**Trial Begins**............66

Tuesday, July 14, 1925...76

Wednesday, July 15, 1925.......................................89

Thursday, July 16, 1925..99

Friday, July 17, 1925..119

Saturday, July 18, 1925....129

Sunday, July 19, 1925....139

Monday, July 20, 1925....155

Tuesday, July 21, 1925....160

Wednesday, July 22, 1925....185

Thursday, July 23, 1925....198

Friday, July 24, 1925....199

Saturday, July 25, 1925....207

Sunday, July 26, 1925....212

Monday, July 27, 1925....**Bryan's Death**....215

Tuesday, July 28, 1925....253

Wednesday, July 29, 1925....271

Thursday, July 30, 1925....312

Friday, July 31, 1925....327

Saturday, August 1, 1925....343

Sunday, August 2, 1925....357

Tuesday, August 4, 1925....369

Wednesday, August 5, 1925....374

Thursday, August 6, 1925....375

Sunday, August 9, 1925....381

Wednesday, July 1, 1925
The Des Moines Register

TEACHERS TAKE ACTION AGAINST TENNESSEE LAW

Chicago. June 30 (A.P.) — A resolution deploring "unenlightened legislative dictatorship" and denouncing the Tennessee anti-evolution law was presented today at the convention of the American Federation of Teachers.

The resolution declared that "the reactionary Lusk school laws in the state of New York, abolished in 1923 after a trial of two years, the Greene law of California, proposed in 1921 and dealing with the matter of controlling the opinion of teachers as well as numberous bills in several other states that have been designed to censor the writing and the teaching of history in the schools—all reflect the same unfortunate suspicion and mistrust of educational intelligence which the Tennessee anit-evolution law does."

Deny Publicity Charges.

Dayton, Tenn., June 30 (A.P.)—Dr. George W. Rappleyea today told The Associated Press there is "absolutely no foundation" for a published report that he had originated the Scopes evolution test case for publicity purposes.

No report to this effect has been carried by The Associated Press.

"While I originated the case and served at first as prosecutor in the matter, I did it from no ulterior motive," Dr. Rappleyea said. "My only object in the matter was to bring about a test of the evolution law.

"No person in Dayton thought the matter of any interest when first it was instigated and even after it was started and the warrant decided upon after the drug store argument, so little was thought of it that F. E. Robinson, proprietor of the drug store and correspondent of the Chattanooga Times was undecided whether or not he should call the paper and tell them of it."

Thursday, July 2, 1925
The Des Moines Register

EDUCATORS DROP DISCUSSION ON EVOLUTION LAW

Indianapolis Meeting Says Action 'Inadvisable.'

Indianapolis, July 1 (A.P.)—Although several resolutions condemning legislative restrictions on the teaching of evolution were submitted to the resolutions committee of the National Education association, none will be presented to the convention, according to U.W. Lamkin of Maryville, Mo., chairman. He said today the committee deemed it "inadvisable" for the association to express an opinion on the subject.

Mr. Lamkin declared that the theory of evolution was capable of so many different phases of interpretation that any resolution bearing upon the subject with directness would arouse opposition, whatever its wording and that the committee deemed a vague expression of the position as no value in establishing a policy.

The committee also desired, Mr. Lamkin said, that it should not appear to be making capital of current agitation over evolution.

"The National Education association must resist, with all its power, the attempt that is being made to put an iron band around the growing tree of education," Francis G. Blair, state superintendent of public instruction of Illinois, declared.

"In addition to the fixing, by law, of the specific subjects which shall be taught, we now are faced with a more dangerous proposal to prohibit by law the teaching of certain subjects," Mr. Blair said. "This proposal may close the door to free and open investigation of the truth and padlock the door with a statute."

"Every good idea, every good emotion, every worthwhile thought of the past is just as living and vital today," he added.

Indefinite or permanent tenure of office for teachers "is in the interest of schools and children" Frederick M. Hunter, superintendent of schools, Oakland, Cal., and former president of the association, declared.

"Indefinite or permanent tenure protects the great body of good teachers from political attack and from dismissal for petty personal and political reasons, Mr. Hunter said. "It is in accordance with the American principle of civil service and against a political spoils system in the schools."

More competent young people are attracted to the profession when they are assured that worth alone will determine their employment, the Californian asserted.

"A sound tenure law provides for the easy dismissal of incompetent or subordinate teachers where just cause can be shown." he concluded.

**

Support Scopes.

Chicago. July 1 (A.P.)—Support of John T. Scopes, the Dayton, Tenn., teacher charged with violation of the Tennessee anti-evolution law, and censure of "the spirit of unenlightened dictatorship" were expressed in a resolution adopted here today by the American Federation of Teachers.

Resolutions condemning religious education and military training in public schools also were adopted by the teachers.

**

Deny Sister Job

Paducah, Ky., July 1.—Miss Lela V. Scopes, sister of John T. Scopes, who will be tried this month at Dayton, Tenn., for violating the Tennessee evolution law, has been denied a position in the Paducah schools, because she declined to repudiate the theory of evolution.

Miss Scopes, who is now studying in the University of Kentucky at Lexington, filed application for a position as instructor in mathematics in Paducah.

Z. A. Bennett, a member of the Paducah board of education, said today that L. J. Hanifan, superintendent of schools, acting under authority of the board, had told Miss Scopes that her services would not be required because she was unwilling to say that she would not advocate the theory of evolution.

"It was the sense of the board that Miss Scopes' services would not be desired unless she renounced the theory of evolution," Mr.

Bennett said, "as it might be embarrassing to the public school system to become involved in the publicity resulting from the Scopes discussion.

"Superintendent Hanifan saw Miss Scopes after the board meeting and informed her of the decision," Mr. Bennett said. "All of the members did not express themselves, but two or three were very decided in the stand they took." The young woman told Superintendent Hanifan she indorsed her brother's views in their entirety, Mr. Bennett stated.

**

Want Goldsmith at Trial.

Dayton, Tenn., July 1 (A.P.)—William N. Goldsmith, Ph. D., professor of biology at Southwestern college, today was asked by Dr. George W. Rappleyea to serve as a witness for the defense in the case of John T. Scopes, charged with violation of the Tennessee law against the teaching of evolution in public school. Dr. Goldsmith's publishers at Anderson, Kan., have assured Dr. Rappleyea that he will serve as a witness if summoned.

The request for Dr. Goldsmith's presence strengthens the assumption that scientists will be brought to Dayton to oppose the views of W. J. Bryan. A portion of one of Dr. Goldsmith's recent books is devoted to a discussion of Mr. Bryan's ideas.

Dr. Goldsmith is the author of several books and is a member of the American Association of Zoology, the British Association for the Advancement of Science, the Eugenics Research association, the Eugenics Society of the United States and a fellow in the American Association for the Advancement of Science.

**

Calls Evolution a Guess.

Lafayette, Tenn., July 1 (A.P.)—Representative J. W. Butler, of Macon county, declared today to The Associated Press that he introduced the anti-evolution bill in the Tennessee legislature to safeguard the principles of government and "to protect our children from infidelity."

This test case at Dayton is not a controversy between science and the Bible," he said. "There is no controversy between true science and the Bible.

"Evolution which teaches that man has descended from a lower order of animals is not true science, but only a guess."

Friday, July 3, 1925
The Des Moines Register

DARWIN REFUTES OWN THEORY IN SPIRIT MESSAGE

Lord Northcliffe's Former Secretary Gets Views

London, July 2 (U.N.) — Charles Darwin, the man who started it all, is on the side of the Tennessee law and the fundamentalists in the forthcoming trial of John T. Scopes for preaching the doctrine of evolution.

In a spirit message—his first—to Miss Louise Owen, leading British spiritualist and collaborator of Sir Arthur Conan Doyle and other psychic experts, Darwin declared that he was wrong in ascribing to man and the lower animals a common origin.

It was through her connection with Lord Northcliffe as secretary that Miss Owen received the Darwin message. Northcliffe, she declares, caused her to devote her life to spiritualism.

Receives Spirit Message.

Miss Owen was sitting in a country cottage talking about the Scopes trial with Miss Rowe, her secretary, when the secretary began an automatic writing through which she receives spirit messages. Miss Owen said the following message came through:

"Darwin is here and he wishes to tell you and Louise that his message must be broadcast. You must give to the world and you must propagate the truth, not of the origin of species but of the origin of man's divinity. It was for the individual source, not the true source of all, and I ruled out the divinity—the source of all. I was the originator of the cult called Darwinism.

"The ape is the anithesis of man. How could I—a mere man—

dissect the divine plan, question his wisdom who created them both, the one of the animal kingdom, the other of the human and divine kingdom.

"The reason for the similarity is that God intended the ape as a forest denizen, as a creature with human intelligence up to a certain point as a safeguard.

Ape Is Mere Imitator.

"Your domestic pets have just as much intelligence as the monkey, save that the one is a friend of man and the other is simply an imitator of man's characteristics. Let me illustrate. The ape is designed on similar lines. His body is designed to climb, to execute the difficult work of supremacy over the animal kingdom. He is born with a cunning equal to that of some of the lower orders of humanity. He needs the constant vigilant eye of the hunter because he is hunted from his native haunts ruthlessly and the mimicry of the monkey is just one of the ever marvelous wonders of the universe.

"Let me say how difficult it is to explain my point of view.

"No member of the animal kingdom is to be even classed with the human race, and that is where I made my great mistake.

"The centuries have rolled on, the pages of history have been turned over and over in the vain attempt to solve the mystery of creation, the mystery of the universe.

"The lighted firmament, how it glows with the mystery of God, how it sheds mystery upon mystery on the struggling world beneath! How can we poor spirits criticize and try to explain even a blade of grass?

"God Knows Why."

"Let me ask Louise to mention by return at every meeting; in every drawing room; at every public function; because the scientists are forgetting the fundamentals in their vain search for a reason—God knows why, God knows why!

"I feel this so deeply that I am constrained to utterances that may seem stranger than you usually receive from your spirit friends.

"The American press is giving greater publicity than ever to my exploded theories. Yes, and the pioneer—how he suffers! How he wishes he could undo the incalculable harm he has caused by ruling out the creator of both—and the ape—what is he but the poor travesty of the humblest member of the human race? Mimicry and senseless action—that is all he is.

"Go to the ant for wisdom, but never compare the wisdom of the animal kingdom with that of God's crowning glory—man."

**

TALK OF MOVING SCOPES' TRIAL TO NASHVILLE

Defense Determined Case Shall Have Dignity.

New York. July 2 (U.N.)—Insisting that levity and modern ballyhoo have no place in a trial upholding the evolution theory, the imposing legal talent for the defense is determined that the case of Prof. John T. Scopes shall be restored to a dignified basis.

To accomplish this, attorneys for Scopes may even seek to transfer the forthcoming trial from Dayton to a federal court in Nashville. This became known Thursday after a conference here in which Clarence Darrow, Bainbridge Colby, Dudley Field Malone and John R. Neale, all attorneys for the defense, participated.

"We are much exercised," Clarence Darrow said in a statement after the conference, "over the fact that so many of the public do not appreciate the importance of this prosecution. The freakishness of the law and the campaign for its enactment caused a general feeling that the case was absurd."

Darrow's statement pointed out that the issues of the trial would have tremendous importance upon the future of educational liberty in the United States and should be taken with the seriousness it deserved.

None of the attorneys would confirm the report that they might seek to remove the trial to Nashville but it was admitted this was suggested. To do this, according to Darrow, it would be necessary to first ask the federal court for an injunction against prosecution in the state court. If this were obtained the attorneys would ask for the transfer of the case to federal jurisdiction.

DAYTON TURNS THE MONKEY INTO MONEY

BY W. A. MACDONALD IN BOSTON TRANSCRIPT.

There is something admirable about the way Dayton, Tenn., is approaching its opportunities which arise from the imminent trial of John T. Scopes, charged with violating the anti-evolution law which forbids teaching any theory of creation in schools of the state which are supported in whole or in part by taxation. Dayton is making the most nationwide interest in the case. Moreover, it is so ordering its preparations as to do the most possible for those visitors from whom it expects to benefit. There is an efficiency about its methods which the north does not always associate with the south.

The newspaper man who telegraphs for his reservation at the press table is answered on the same day by whatever official he directs his message to. He is informed that arrangements are in the hands of Whitney W. Morgan and he is furnished by mail with his ticket, information about his living accommodations, his wire facilities and any other matter about which he inquires. The letterhead of the committee was printed for the business in hand. "Entertainment Committee for Scopes Trial" is the line across the top. The press table ticket is signed by the county judge, numbered and assigned to him in his name. He is informed that the Western Union has made arrangements for a dozen extra operators to handle press matter. There is a room fitted with accommodations for news men. The courtroom has been reseated to take care of approximately 1,200 people. The trial will be broadcast by radio by Station WGN, the Chicago Tribune, by remote control equipment for which is being installed. The courthouse lawn has a seating capacity of 5,000 who will be able to hear the trial by means of loud speakers. Amplifiers are being installed in the city auditorium and other halls and public buildings which have a capacity of 4,000 people.

—

Dayton has a population of 2,200. The entertainment committee has estimated that there are living accommodations in the town and vicinity for at least 5,000 persons. A canvass has been made and the best homes listed. About one-fourth of the rooms available have been taken up already. The committee has fixed a maximum rate of $5 a day for room and board. The Tennessee health commission has established an office in Dayton. Concessionaires are required to conform to fixed prices. Their stands must be screened and sanitary, their tableware sterilized. Traffic regulations and police protection are being worked out by Commissioner James S. Frazier. The city commissioners have obtained from the high school board the use of the high school building as an emergency hospital. This building is two blocks off the main thoroughfare and with its cafeteria is considered ideal for the purpose to which it is to be put.

The baseball park and an adjacent field are reserved for parking automobiles and it is estimated that they have capacity of 50,000 cars. Half a dozen or more tourist camps will be established just outside the city where excellent springs are said to be available for water supply. A field is being reserved for airplanes one mile north of the town. Arrangements have been made with the Southern railway to operate a shuttle train between Dayton and Chattanooga, thirty-nine miles away, to take care of the overflow. Chattanooga has the facilities that go with a city of 45,000.

—

Requests for reservations have come in from all over the country. Press tables have been installed to take care of 300 reporters and 100 press men have thus far made reservations. Their applications have come from all parts of the country, from Boston, New York, Chicago, San Francisco. In one day the requests included those from one of the press associations, Arthur Brisbane, a woman reporter from the San Francisco Examiner, a man in New York, and two in Baltimore. The public will not need to worry about not being informed. There will be bus service as well as rail services to Chattanooga. Among the thousands of outsiders expected are several presidents of universities and some of the other prominent educators of the country.

Nor will entertainment be missing. The Rhea Central High school band will give concerts in the evening. Arrangements have been made to have talks by William Jennings Bryan and Clarence Darrow and other visiting notables in various public buildings so that everyone may have a chance to see and hear these men.

The town has three hotels and several boarding houses. The inquirer is likely to be informed that one of these hotels is on high land looking to the mountains, that it has a mineral spring, a swimming pool and road connection with the Dixie highway. It is said that Mr. Darrow of counsel for the defense will be provided with a private house for himself and his family. Just where Mr. Bryan will put up does not yet appear, but probably his comfort will be no less than that of Mr. Darrow. The city is said to look much larger than it is and to "compare favorable with towns three times the size."

—

One complaint of those in charge of arrangements has been that requests for accommodations have been directed to various persons with the result that they failed to arrive quickly in the proper hands. Anybody seeking information from the entertainment committee must be impressed by the anxiety of this body to do everything it can toward hospitality. Some weeks ago there was a story to the effect that the war department had been asked for army tents to help house the expected crowds and that the Pullman company had been requested to provide a rolling city for those who could be accommodated in its cars. There is no late information to show whether these facilities are still expected. Mr. Morgan of the entertainment committee is evidently preparing against any emergency, however, because he has issued a warning request that all who contemplate going to Dayton for the trial make their reservations at once "in order that we may not be swept off our feet at the eleventh hour."

All over the United States and in Europe the forthcoming trial, which will begin on July 10, has been advertised. Newspaper articles on evolution, on the personalities of counsel for prosecution and defense, the origin of the case, the law in the case, the views of scientists and fundamentalists have appeared north, south, east and west. Popular articles on evolution have been printed; the observations of Wolfgang Kohler, whose work with apes on the island of Tenerif were first chronicled in the Transcript on Dr. Kohler's arrival in this country last February, have been reprinted east, south and west. Magazines of national circulation have supplemented the information in the daily press. In England George Bernanrd Shaw has paid his respects to Mr. Bryan; and on the continent French and German scientists have had their say about freedom of teaching and merits of evolutionary theories.

—

A few days ago the dispatches carried the news that a man in Dayton had sued the entertainment committee, alleging that he originated the idea of the trial as a commercial publicity stunt. He sued for $1,500 and it has since been reported that he has settled for $300. The state authorities took occasion to reply, however, that the trial was thoroughly sincere. It is a good deal more than doubtful if any man could have foreseen when it was decided to make a test case that any such interest would develop as that which is apparent a fortnight before young Mr. Scopes is due to go on trial.

**

THE DAYTON "SHOW."

The New York Times, announcing special features from Dayton, Tenn., publishes this announcement:

EVOLUTION ARENA AT DAYTON.

Circus sideshows and curious visitors descend upon Tennessee mountain town as the time draws near for the trial of John T. Scopes, instructor in science in the Rhea County High School for violation of anti-evolution statute. A native Tennessean describes the place which the "sportive gods of news" have made famous, tells of the number of "Darwinians" in the town and gives an idea of the character of the man on trial, the judge and counsel.

—

Of course thousands of people all over the world are going to read up on evolution who would never hear of it but for the "show" features of this trial.

But just what effect are the show features going to have on our American notions of law administration and on the law itself, to say nothing of the measure it puts on American intelligence.

This whole debate was gone over fifty years ago and settled for those who study. Religion, instead of losing ground, has gained in the fifty years.

Does anybody believe a pios man as Bishop Bashford of the Methodist church was conspicuously, would come to Des Moines to preach evolution if it contained a concealed attack on religion?

Saturday, July 4, 1925
The Des Moines Register

SEEK FEDERAL WRIT TO HALT SCOPES TRIAL

Defense Would Take Case Out of State Court.

Chicago. July 3 (A.P.)— Announcement today of a sudden shift in plans of the defense brought about the possibility that John T. Scopes, principal in the case to test Tennessee's anti-evolution law, may never face trial at Dayton, where it is scheduled for next Friday.

Under plans announced today by Clarence Darrow, associate counsel for Scopes, the case will be carried directly to the federal courts, either at Knoxville or Chattanooga, through proceedings seeking to restrain state enforcement of the law. This action would bring the law's constitutionality before the federal courts., where it is agreed by all parties it must eventually go.

Dr. John R. Neal, of Knoxville, senior defense counsel, has data on which to base application for the injunction. Petitions will be filed Monday or Tuesday of next week in a court to be selected by Dr. Neal.

Should the defense obtain a federal injunction the Dayton trial would be blocked pending appeal by the prosecution. Should the injunction be sustained by the United States Supreme court on the ground the law is unconstitutional, further prosecution of Scopes would be blocked.

Would Avoid Dramatics

Desire to avoid the sensational and dramatic potentialities of the Dayton trial influenced the defense attorneys in their move. Of equal weight was the promise of a shorter route to the supreme court.

While Dayton was obviously perturbed by reports it might be deprived of the trial, after elaborate arrangements to care for those it would attract, attorneys for the prosecution scouted the ideal of the trial in the federal court.

"In my opinion," said Herbert Hicks, one of the prosecution counsel, "the rumor is another part of the advertising program the defense has been carrying on.

"I do not doubt the defense is considerably worried and would like to find some way of avoiding the procedure at Dayton."

Continue to Map Plans.

Despite defense plans, authorities at Dayton indicated tonight arrangements for the trial will be carried out. Fifty veniremen will be chosen Monday in the Rhea county circuit court from whom the Scopes jury would be selected.

Leading citizens of Dayton, it was announced, telegraphed to Dr. Neal protesting against the new defense move.

Restraining action probably will be started either in Knoxville or Chattanooga, which are favored by Dr. Neal. Decision in the matter is understood to rest with him.

Two complaints will be filed in the federal court determined upon by Dr. Neal, said Mr. Darrow. One will be filed by Scopes and the other by a property holder as yet not determined upon.

Two major considerations are involved in the proposed step: To obtain a short cut to a determination of the constitutionality of the measure, and to remove the sensational element from the case. Also it is desired to bring home to the people the really serious aspect it has assumed.

"This is an increasingly serious matter," said Mr. Darrow upon his arrival here from New York. "Tennessee is not the only state which has this law. It is in effect in Oklahoma and South Carolina as well, and it is pending in twenty other states, I am informed, including California, Kansas, Texas, North Carolina, Kentucky and Florida."

"It is supported by a strongly organized element. The Dayton trial has been treated with levity, and it is not a matter for joking."

Their Only Recourse.

Should the federal injunction not be granted Darrow and his three associates would have no recourse but to proceed with the Dayton trial.

Should the federal judge grant the petition, the evolution case would lose all its appeal as a great drama, with its nationally known witnesses appearing upon the stand and expounding their views of the creation of man.

Instead the lawyers themselves would argue the matter of the legality of the Tennessee law.

A federal decision would have far more weight in determining the status of the proposed legislation in other states," said Mr. Darrow, "than would a decision by the Tennessee Supreme court. It also would be quicker. One reason we want to take the matter into the federal court is to obtain a short cut to a decision as to the law's constitutionality.

"We think there is a federal question involved, and that the proposed step is the proper way to handle it.

"The case probably would never be determined to the satisfaction of all were it fought through the state supreme court, and even if it took that course there is at least considerable prospect of it winding up in the federal court."

**

New York. July 3 (A.P.)— Although there has been no friction among members of the legal forces, for the defense of John T. Scopes, in his evolution trial, "an honest difference of opinion" has manifested itself, it was learned tonight as to the value of the move to have the case taken from the state to the federal courts.

Dudley Field Malone and John R. Neal are opposed to seeking a federal injunction and a temporary restraining order against the state trial. Clarence Darrow and Bainbridge Colby, on the other hand, are of the opinion that it is both wise and possible to have the case taken from the state to the federal courts.

Scopes Not Consulted.

Scopes himself has not been consulted nor has he given his permission to the federal court move, Mr. Malone said tonight. Mr. Malone is remaining in New York to prepare to go ahead with the state trial if the federal injunction fails to be obtained.

Mr. Malone will leave for Dayton on July 6.

One benefit of continuing the case in the state courts is the educational good that will result, Mr. Malone thinks, with the american people fully aroused.

The opinion of counsel opposed to the federal court attempt is that it will fail and the case go to trial at Dayton according to schedule.

**

Knoxville, Tenn., July 3.—Dr. John R. Neal, senior counsel for John T. Scopes, defendant in the evolution trial at Dayton, Tenn., persistently declined to issue any statement for publication, relative to the intention, announced from Chicago, of seeking to transfer the Scopes case by injunction to a United States court, since his arrival here today from New York at 1:10 p.m.

Dr. Neal gave as his reasons for refusing to state what his plans are that the newspapers had treated the case so as to ridicule it and that he had decided to let newspapers suffer a while.

Dr. Neal stated he was senior counsel and Mr. Darrow is junior counsel and his declarations were not official. "I am not responsible for Mr. Darrow's statements," he said.

Sunday, July 5, 1925
The Des Moines Sunday Register

ASSAIL MOVE FOR WRIT IN SCOPES CASE

Three Lawyers Criticize Injunction Threat of Defense.

Dayton, Tenn., July 4 (A.P.)— Three local attorneys associated in the prosecution of the Scopes evolution case declared in a statement issued today that the state of Tennessee is sovereign and not subject to control of the federal government in regard to its local affairs and the enforcement of the criminal laws.

This declaration came on the heels of the announced plan of defense counsel to seek removal of the trial of John T. Scopes, teacher, from state courts to United States courts by means of a federal injunction which would procure an earlier decision on the constitutionality of the Tennessee statute forbidding the teaching of evolution in public schools.

Local counsel for the prosecution ridiculed the latest move of defense counsel and characterized it as "an effort to make a sensational display of the trial of a simple case."

Residents of Dayton, where the trial is scheduled to begin July 10, perplexed yesterday by the announcement in Chicago by Clarence Darrow of Scopes' counsel, that the defense would seek to remove the proceedings to federal court were confident today that the test of the evolution law, long planned for, would be held in this little town.

Neal Reaches Dayton.

The arrival here today of Dr. John R. Neal, senior defense counsel, who is expected to file application for the injunction with a federal judge, is awaited with keen interest. Dr. Neal in Knoxville last night, declined to discuss Mr. Darrow's statement regarding the injunction move. He told reporters that Mr. Darrow's statements were not official and that he (Neal) was not responsible for them.

Mr. Scopes, who returned to Dayton late yesterday after a visit to his Kentucky home, indicated last night that he knew little of the proposed injunction proceedings and was not concerned over the location of the trial. Declaring he had signed no injunction application he said he would do so if his attorneys thought proper.

The statement by local prosecution counsel said:

"As attorneys for the state we have attempted to maintain a dignity commensurate with our duty and responsibility to Tennessee as officers of the law.

"We have kept the state's case on a plane of dignity and regularity. We regret that the defense has made such widespread effort to make a sensational display of the trial of a simple case.

Says Defense Move Ludicrous.

"The latest effort at sensationalism is so foolish and ridiculous as to be ludicrous.

"The defendant Scopes is being prosecuted in good faith and will be tried in the circuit courts of Rhea county. The prosecution will be ready for trial July 10 and will insist on the trial at that time.

"There is no danger of the United States courts issuing an injunction or otherwise interfering with the state courts.

"If any question is to be made as to the regularity of the proceedings or as to guilt, it must be made in the state trial courts. Such questions may be taken into the supreme courts and later into the supreme court of the United States, provided there is a federal constitutional question involved. The local federal courts cannot review the action of the state courts."

Should the federal court take jurisdiction the case would go to Chattanooga in which jurisdiction Dayton lies.

Walter White, superintendent of the Rhea county schools, is still awaiting a reply to his invitation to Evangelist "Billy" Sunday to appear as a state witness.

First Step Monday.

The first step in the Scopes trial is scheduled for Monday when the Rhea county circuit court convenes. Fifty veniremen will be chosen from the county roll and from these the trial jury will be selected later.

Reports from New York told of a difference of opinion among defense counsel as to the wisdom of the injunction move. Dudley Field

Malone and Dr. Neal believe it is too late to expect a federal court to assume jurisdiction and they opposed in the conference the proposal to ask a federal injunction and a temporary restraining order against the state courts. Their associates, Clarence Darrow and Bainbridge Colby advocate the injunction proceedings as both a wise and a possible means of taking the case from state to federal courts.

Louisville public school authorities announced that Miss Lela V. Scopes, sister of the defendant, could obtain a place in the public schools of that city upon satisfying educational requirements. Miss Scopes' application for a position in the Paducah High school recently was rejected when she declared her disbelief in the theory of evolution.

Monday, July 6, 1925
The Des Moines Register

RELIGION AND SCIENCE WALK HAND IN HAND

Waters Says Evolution Helps Understanding

Science and religion both go hand in hand Rev. Wayne L. Waters, pastor of the Waveland Park Congregational church told the congregation at the morning service yesterday. He talked on evolution as a friend or foe of religion.

"There should be no conflict between religion and science," the speaker said. "Both have made wonderful contributions to modern civilization. We are indebted to both for all that the world possesses today."

"Science and religion are both vitally necessary to the present scheme of things. Without one there could not be the other. They are closely interwoven. Science has helped religion and religion has helped science."

"Evolution has helped many in an understanding of God," he continued. "I would define evolution as a study of God's way of doing things. Evolution is growth. Every form of life known in the world is what it is today, due to growth. Growth is essential to bring things to full maturity. Growth in turn is the living purpose and presence of God which links science, evolution, and religion into one."

Medbury Talks on Man.

Man does not hold the value of his life above everything else. Rev. Charles S. Medbury of the University Church of Christ said in his sermon.

"It is often said and believed by many that man holds his life as a priceless possession. While this is true in a sense, there are many instances to contradict the purported fact," he declared. "Life is precious but there are other things more precious. This is proven in scientific research, in discoveries of other lands and in missionary work not only of the church but of other agencies."

"In times of war men let their lives be snuffed out without so much as combating the idea of death. Death passes out of their reasoning entirely and other things are uppermost. In scientific research men constantly lay down their lives for the benefit of humanity. They don't pause to consider that they are losing life. Discoverers die in foreign lands far from home in making discoveries. Their last thought is of sending information back to civilization."

Says Churches Must be Lively

Rev. E. T. Aldrich, pastor of St. Andrews United Brethren church spoke on "dead" churches. A church should be a living and lively institution, he said.

"Churches that bury themselves, that live within their own sphere and have not a contact with the outer world, are useless," Rev. Mr. Aldrich asserted.

"A church must take a lively interest in the doings of the world. They must make themselves part of the world and work on a footing with others to accomplish real things. There are too many churches that are content to be self-centered."

Bishop Harry Longley preached at the morning service at St. Paul's Episcopal church. He urged a closer relation between members of the church and the clergy.

"Close co-operation is necessary between communicants and the clergy. Neither can exist without the other. The closer the two groups are brought together the more successful will religion be," he said.

Tuesday, July 7, 1925
The Des Moines Register

SCOPES LOSES PLEA FOR TRIAL IN U.S. COURT

—

Federal Judge Refuses to Restrain State Prosecution of Case.

—

Cookeville, Tenn., July 6 (A.P.)—John T. Scopes, public school teacher, must stand trial by jury in the state court at Dayton, Tenn., on Friday on a charge of violating the Tennessee statute prohibiting the teaching of evolution in the public schools, as Federal Judge John J. Gore today refused to grant the pedagog a restraining order to stop the criminal case. The appeal for an injunction asserted that Scopes' constitutional rights would be violated by his trial in the state court.

John R. Neal, leading counsel for Scopes, said no appeal would be taken from Judge Gore's ruling now, but that he would soon apply to Judge Hicks, federal judge for eastern Tennessee, now in Detroit, for a federal court order in the case.

In his lengthy ruling, Judge Gore did not discuss the constitutionality of the Tennessee statute under which Scopes was indited, but gave his decision on the question of his territorial jurisdiction. He cited the United States constitution and statutes, and numerous precedents to uphold his belief that he did not have jurisdiction in the case.

Listening to the decision of Judge Gore, Scopes seemed unperturbed. He said he expected the trial at Dayton to begin next Friday, according to schedule.

Holds Writ Unjustified.

Judge Gore at the outset of his decision pointed out that the petition showed that the petitioner is under indictment in Rhea county and that the case is pending undetermined. He stated that he was of the opinion that he was not justified in granting the writ.

Two petitions were presented, one in the name of John T. Scopes and the other in behalf of Robert M. Wilson. Both were directed at Gov. Austin Peay, Atty. Gen. Frank Thompson and A. T. Stewart, attorney general for the eighteenth judicial circuit of Tennessee, as defendants.

Scopes' petition advanced the claim that he was deprived under the Tennessee law of liberty and property without due process of law. Wilson's plea contended that the law deprived him of the right to properly educate his children. Both contended that enforcement of the law is not a valid exercise of the police power of the state.

Referring in his decision to the contention of counsel that it was the court's duty to grant a temporary restraining order to remain in force until a hearing and determination of an application for an interlocutory decree, Judge Gore said that even if he had the power to grant a temporary restraining order he was of the opinion that he should not do so upon the allegations made in the petition.

Trial According to Law.

"The object of the injunction sought in this case is to restrain the officers of the state from prosecuting the petitioner for violation of an act which said officers are expressly charged to enforce in the only way in which they are authorized to proceed—by bringing criminal prosecution in the name of the state. This is virtually to enjoin the state from proceeding through its duly qualified and acting officers."

The petitions were signed by John R. Neal, Clarence Darrow and Bainbridge Colby, of counsel for Scopes.

Dr. Neal's suggestion that the case will finally reach the Supreme court, made before the courts' decision was announced today, was a statement for his client in case of conviction in the Rhea county court. It was assumed that the state of Tennessee would have filed an appeal had Judge Gore's decision this afternoon been in favor of the plaintiff.

**

Portland, Ore., July 6 (A.P.)—In a telegram to The Associated Press today, Rev. William A. (Billy) Sunday announced he would be unable to go east in connection with the Scopes evolution trial, but that he indorsed any views expressed by William Jennings Bryan, who is on his way to Dayton, Tenn., for the hearing.

Asks Dean to Be Witness.

Chicago. July 6 (A.P.)—Dean Shailer Mathews of the divinity school of the University of Chicago, has been invited by Clarence Darrow, associate counsel for John T. Scopes, to appear as a witness for the defense in the Tennessee evolution trial, in the event the criminal proceedings in the state court begin next Friday, as originally planned.

Dr. Mathews was out of the city today and his answer to the invitation will not be known until his return tomorrow. As dean of the Chicago Theological school and a public lecturer and preacher, Dr. Mathews has won note as a champion of the liberal forces in the Baptist church.

***

MAN AS "ANIMAL"

In some of the discussion of evolution which has grown out of the Scopes' trial there is an attempt to distinguish between evolution of "animals" and evolution of man. This is like common references to "animals and fish" or "animals and insects." Fish are animals, insects are animals, men are animals. The basic classification of like forms is between animal and plant.

Linne said that plants grow and live but that animals grow, live and feel, yet this is only an attempt to define the two forms. In their simplest forms animals and plants are not fundamentally different. Both are constituted of protoplasm, "the physical basis of life." The strictest definition possible is that an animal is a living organism the protoplasm of which does not secrete a cellulose cell-wall and the existence of which requires proteid material obtained from the living or dead bodies of existing plants or animals.

Webster defines man as "the highest type of animal existing or known to have existed, but differs from other animals more in his extraordinary mental development than in anatomical structure." In expanding the definition the statement is made that "modern zoologists find his structural peculiarities at most sufficient to justify separating him from the anthropoid apes as a separate family, Hominidae, though older zoologists regarded him as constituting a separate order, Bimana." It is pointed out here too that no scientists classify man as a descendant of the ape but both as descendants of a common ancestor.

In the Americana encyclopedia this statement is made: "A great many people in our time are of the impression that it was not until the serious discussion of the theory of evolution came up that man's intimate relations to the animals were recognized. It has been the teaching of Christian philosophers from the very beginning that man is an animal, and the definition for man adopted from the Greeks by all Christian writers was that he is a rational animal."

Further it may be said that Saint Augustine, whose teachings, centuries before Darwin, became the scholarly Christian tradition, suggested that the original creation was of "semina rerum"—the seed of things. Wasmann added that any objection to this theory may be met by a reminder that man's body even now is produced by germinal development from a fertilized ovum. This has no application to the present discussion except to show that the idea of man developing as an animal is neither particularly new nor contrary to early Christian teachings. The point is that no scholar denies man's classification as an animal.

Wednesday, July 8, 1925
The Des Moines Register

TERMS SCOPES HEARING DUEL TO THE DEATH

Citizens in Readiness As Hundreds Begin to Invade Town.

Dayton, Tenn., July 7 (A.P.)—William Jennings Bryan, connected with the prosecution of John T. Scopes, charged with violating Tennessee's anti-evolution law arrived here late this afternoon.

Mr. Bryan was met at the train by prosecution attorneys, defense attorneys, newspaper men and a host of Dayton citizens. He was escorted to the home of Richard Rogers, where he will remain until the conclusion of the evolution trial.

"Duel to the Death."

The contest between evolution and Christianity is "a duel to the death," Mr. Bryan declared tonight in an address at a dinner given in his honor by the Progressive Dayton club.

"It has been in the past a death grapple in the dark," said Mr. Bryan, "but from this time on it will be a death grapple in the light."

Mr. Bryan, who is associated with counsel for the prosecution of the young high school instructor was a guest of the club which two weeks ago entertained Clarence Darrow of defense counsel in the same dining room. The arrival of Mr. Bryan shortly after noon followed the return of John Thomas Scopes and Dr. John R. Neal, chief defense counsel, from Cookeville, where yesterday they filed a petition for an injunction to remove the case from the state to the federal courts, only to have it refused.

Scopes Attends Dinner.

The dinner was attended by John T. Scopes, members of counsel for both parties to the suits, leaders in Dayton's civic life and newspaper men. Mr. Bryan avoided details of the Scopes case, saying the case would not be tried in the newspapers but in court.

He inquired into the causes of the widespread interest in the case and pointed out that the severest punishment possible could not be more than a fine of $500.

"The secret of the world's interest in this little case is found in the fact that this trial uncovers an attack which for a generation has been made more or less secretly upon revealed religion, that is the Christian religion," he asserted.

"We have no knowledge of it outside the Bible, which Christians regard as the revealed will of God. It gives us our only conception of God and our only knowledge of Christ.

"Anything that attacks the Bible attacks revealed religion. A successful attack would destroy the Bible and with it revealed religion.

"The contest between evolution and Christianity is a duel to the death. This trial is going to give information or be the means of bringing out information upon which this controversy will be decided.

"If evolution wins, Christianity goes—not suddenly, of course, but gradually, for the two cannot stand together. They are as antagonistic as light and darkness: as antagonistic as good and evil."

Christians Wage Fight.

Christians, he said, believing that "revealed religion offers mankind the only abiding truth. . . .will fight evolution as their only great foe."

"If information furnished at the trial shows evolution to be unproven and therefore unworthy of acceptance, science will have to fall back upon demonstrated truth, which has no terrors for Christianity."

Mr. Bryan insisted that the basic principle of the Tennessee anti-evolution law was the theory that the people, speaking through the legislature have a right to control the public schools.

"Some irreligious editors have scoffed at the idea of the schools being controlled by those who support them, but they have not yet pointed out any other control than control by the public," he said.

"Our constitutions may place restraints upon legislatures but the people make the constitutions and can change them. Our courts may temporarily restrain legislatures, but the people create our courts and can change them.

"Arguments must therefore be addressed to the people. Expressions of contempt for the people are not sufficient and they do not show the spirit that we have a right to expect in Americans."

During the course of his address, Mr. Bryan especially emphasized what he termed the right of the people to control the schools they create and maintain.

People to Decide.

"The jury will not settle the question in the Scopes case finally but the people will. Throughout the case we should be interested in giving the people a thorough understanding of the principles involved. That is what makes this case as important as it is."

He touched briefly upon charges that people of Tennessee were illiterate and was loud in praise of Tennesseeans.

"Character is better than education," he said, "and I will put the character of the people of Tennessee against that of the people of any state in the country."

As he opened his address, Mr. Bryan remarked on the broadmindedness of the Progressive Dayton club in extending the same welcome to the attorneys on both sides.

Introduced to Scopes.

Before entering the dining room Mr. Bryan was introduced to Scopes as a crowd filled the hotel lobby.

For some minutes the two stood talking and several times during the course of his talk Mr. Bryan spoke favorably of the defendant.

As Mr. Bryan stepped from the train this afternoon he was greeted by the clicking of cameras. A crowd rushed forward to greet him and he was surrounded by his Dayton admirers.

Discards Wide Hat.

Mr. Bryan wore a very wide brimmed helmet which he doffed as soon as he alighted from the train. He was surrounded by a crowd and declared that he was glad to be in Dayton. As the train left the station the persons sitting on the observation platform cheered and one lusty voiced man cried, "Good luck, Bill." Mr. Bryan acknowledged this with a smile.

A woman who refused to give her name pushed her way to the front of the crowd and seizing Mr. Bryan's hand said, "Welcome to Dayton, Mr. Bryan. This is the day I have looked forward to."

Mr. Bryan spoke for a few moments to newspaper men, saying that he was pleased at the decision of Judge Gore in refusing to issue a federal restraining order. He added that he expected to remain here until the trial ends.

"Are you ready for the fight?" some one asked.

"It would be better, perhaps, to say that I am ready for the trial," Mr. Bryan replied.

Meets Opposing Counsel.

Soon shedding his coat and joining the shirt sleeved majority in Dayton, Mr. Bryan appeared in the streets and was introduced to John R. Neal, chief counsel for Scopes. Mr. Neal said, "Welcome to Rhea county, Mr. Bryan."

"But you are from Knoxville," suggested the prosecution counsel."

"Only occasionally," said Dr. Neal. " I am really from Rhea county."

"But you are on the other side of the case," persisted Mr. Bryan.

"Oh, yes," said Dr. Neal.

"Then we'll meet often," Mr. Bryan said with a smile.

Chats with Crowd.

Mr. Bryan then chatted with a crowd that surrounded him.

"This case is not a joke," he said. "I think everyone is rapidly coming to understand that there is no joke connected with it."

Scopes departed for Chattanooga late today to meet his father who will come from Paducah, Ky., to attend the trial.

Dr. Neal, discussing the failure of defense attorneys to obtain a federal injunction yesterday in Cookeville, said no further efforts would be made to interfere with the trial of the Scopes case.

The filing of a petition for injunction to prevent state authorities from enforcing the anti-evolution teaching law will give the defense an indisputable road into supreme court, he said.

Should there be some slip in the carriage of the Scopes case into the supreme court after the trial, the second petition filed in behalf of a citizen will, pursuing the steps of the Oregon case, give them a clear route into the higher courts, he indicated.

In Dayton everything dates from next Friday.

Tourists arriving, newspaper correspondents streaming into town on every incoming train, merchants, hotel keepers, garage men, venders and plain citizens point forward to Friday as the beginning of things.

With the removal last night of every trace of fear that the Scopes evolution trial might be removed through intervention of the federal courts through an injunction to prevent further prosecution of the case by state authorities, the town settled down today in earnest to the work of completing preparations.

Concessions Spring Up.

A mushroom growth of concession stands sprang up during the night, lining the sidewalk along Market street, in front of the court house. Furniture trucks sped through the streets with furnishings for homes that long had been vacant to supply the needs of the expected new arrivals.

Here as well as in the stores and shops the period of prosperity will begin Friday. Persons storing automobiles in garages are warned that the price for storage will be raised Friday. At hotels and private homes, incoming guests are informed that "after Friday" the rates will be higher, or that it will be a certain price "until Friday."

Steps have been taken wherever possible, however, by city authorities to prevent any profiteering.

**

Orders "Red" Soda

Dayton, Tenn., July 7 (U.N.)—After lunch, William Jennings Bryan, in his shirt sleeves, went over to Robinson drug store, sat down at the table where the evolution argument started and ordered a strawberry ice cream soda.

The flavor was chosen in tribute to the great strawberry industry of the Dayton district.

**

INTELLECTUAL BRAKES

Just what has evolution to do with mathematics? That is the question raised by the Paducah, Ky., board of education in refusing to re-engage the sister of John T. Scopes. The young woman refused to deny a belief in evolution and thereby made herself undesirable as a teacher of mathematics. One can hardly imagine two fields of learning more unrelated.

Of course there is heterodoxy in mathematics. Miss Scopes might tell her pupils of the question involved in the parallel postulate of Euclid and of the contrary system of geometry worked out by Lobatchewsky. She might inform them that in some systems of mathematics a straight line is not the shortest distance between points. But what if she did? Her pupils will not be educated in mathematics if they are unaware of the existence of non-Euclidean geometry.

There is no law in the case, and there will be no demand for one. It is recognized that mathematical truth is not a subject for legislation. Imagine a legislature feeling impelled to decree against the teaching of mathematics in terms of anything except orthodox lines and planes! Imagine a law excluding from the textbooks mention of Einstein's fourth dimensional concept! It isn't done; it is impossible to determine truth by legislation and an effort to protect by law any concept implies lack of confidence in the strength of that concept to withstand attack.

There is nothing to indicate that Miss Scopes has been teaching mathematical heterodoxy or that this would make her objectionable. The Paducah board merely goes one step farther than did the Tennessee legislators. In Tennessee the legislature said, "You shall not teach the theory of evolution." In Paducah the board says, "If you believe in evolution you shall not teach anything." And yet there are those who try to argue that freedom of thought and freedom of learning are not involved in the Dayton case.

Thursday, July 9, 1925
The Des Moines Register

CHARGE BRYAN SEEKS U.S. LAW ON EVOLUTION

Defense Sees in His Speech Move for New Federal Amendment.

Dayton, Tenn., July 8 (A.P.)—A move for a new constitutional amendment was seen today by defense counsel as the outstanding inference to be drawn from the address last night of William Jennings Bryan before the Progressive Dayton club.

In a statement issued today by Dr. John R. Neal, chief defense counsel, in which he summed up the inferences drawn by the defense attorneys from the address of Mr. Bryan last night, he declared:

"He forecast that he will move rapidly from the lower court to the supreme court of Tennessee, then to the supreme court of the United States, and having lost his fight on account of the existing constitutional guarantee of religious and educational liberties, he intends immediately to wipe out these constitutional immunities by a new constitutional amendment."

The statement follows:

"We regard Mr. Bryan's speech last night as the most remarkable utterance ever made by a lawyer just before his entrance into a trial of a criminal case.

Holds Speech As Challenge.

"His speech comes as a challenge to the defense not to confine the test of the anti-evolution law to the existing limitation of the constitution of Tennessee or even the United States, but instead to put on trial the truth or the lack of truth of the theory of evolution, the conflict or lack of conflict between science and religion.

"Having demonstrated as he apparently expects to do at least to his own satisfaction that evolution is untrue and it is destructive to Christianity, he forecast that he will move rapidly from the lower court to the supreme court of Tennessee; then to the supreme court of the United States, and having lost the fight on account of the existing constitutional guarantees of religious and educational liberties, he intends immediately to wipe out these constitutional immunities by a new constitutional amendment, a very ambitious program, I should say—even for Mr. Bryan.

State Law Major Issue.

"We have no objection to his undertaking it but, however, we shall insist as we did at the very inception of the case, that the great issue in this case is not whether evolution is true or untrue, or even whether it conflicts with religion, but whether the Tennessee legislature has not transcended the limits set upon its powers by the constitution of Tennessee and the constitution of the United States in passing the anti-evolution law, and thus attempt to control the mind in its struggles after the truth."

The statement was issued after a conference between Dr. Neal, John Thomas Scopes, John L. Godsey, local defense counsel, and Dr. George W. Rappleyea, as one which summed up their reaction to the address of Mr. Bryan last night.

Presiding Judge Arrives.

Judge John T. Raulston arrived late today to preside at the trial which opens Friday. Other principal figures are en route.

Thomas Scopes, father of the defendant, came from Paducah, Ky., to attend his son's trial, announcing soon he had warned him to "fight shy of reporters."

Judge Raulston soon after arrival announced he was prepared to preside at the "evolution case" if the task required "all summer." Judge Raulston said he had received many letters offering him free advice in the conduct of the case.

Takes Slap at Jurist.

One letter, he said, spoke of the writer having read the judge's "erroneous charge" to the grand jury and assuring him that he was satisfied that his ancestors enriched themselves by depriving the Tennessee Indians of their property through illegal measures.

William Jennings Bryan of the prosecution admitted today he has a list of witnesses.

"I have a list of witnesses," he replied, "but not to give out," adding that the prosecution did not yet know how many witnesses would be necessary.

Walter White, officially named as the prosecutor in the case, called on Mr. Bryan today.

Dr. Neal, when shown by The Associated Press a copy of a telegram sent from New York by Bainbridge Colby today, expressing his regret that Mr. Colby would be unable to come to Dayton for the trial, expressed pleasure over the inference that Mr. Colby would remain in the case.

Bryan's Son in Case

William Jennings Bryan announced the addition of another lawyer to his side. The latest lawyer in the much discussed case is William Jennings Bryan, jr., now living in Los Angeles, Cal., but formerly assistant United States attorney in Arizona.

Mr. Bryan said that his son is now on the way to Dayton and should arrive tomorrow. He also expressed regret when informed that Bainbridge Colby would not attend the Scopes trial.

"I am sorry to hear it," said Mr. Bryan, "Colby is a fine fellow and I had looked forward with pleasure to having him on the other side."

Show Little Surprise.

Defense attorneys in Dayton expressed little surprise at its report from Chicago that Colby would be unable to appear in Dayton for the trial. They declined to say just what significance would be attached to the report. Dr. John R. Neal said that from the first it had not been expected that all attorneys aiding in the presentation and preparation of the case would be able to attend the trial.

"There are several attorneys," he said, "who have been following various lines in preparing the case who, from the first, we knew would not be able to come to Dayton.

"The defense attorneys have never said that Mr. Colby would or would not appear in Dayton for the trial," said Dr. Neal. "I am certain that he is remaining in the case and will participate in its further developments in the supreme court."

Mr. Bryan went the shirt-sleeved contingent one better today by appearing in a shirt without a collar.

Posing for photographers he read a book while being photographed. He offered to write this as the caption for the picture: "It was a warm day and Mr. Bryan was reading a book on 'Ice'."

**

Darrow Leaves for Dayton

Chicago, July 8 (A.P.)—Clarence Darrow, Chicago lawyer and associate counsel for John T. Scopes, Tennessee schoolteacher charged with violating the state's anti-evolution teaching law, left tonight for Dayton, Tenn., to participate in the trial opening Friday.

"I wish we might have been successful with our petition for a federal injunction," he said as he boarded the train, "but maybe the trial will serve an educational purpose anyhow."

Civilization and not a school teacher is going on trial, he said adding:

"If William Jennings Bryan thinks a Tennessee court or jury is going to have any influence on thought and investigations of the world, he's a very gullibel man."

**

Rum Sleuths Busy

Dayton, Tenn., July 8 (A.P.)—A warm reception is being prepared for violations of the laws who may come here during the Scopes' evolution trial.

Dayton police officers today were installing a special detail of local men to "look after" violators of the ordinance against liquor buying and selling and the ordinary troublemakers of a non-professionsal type.

The town marshal has arranged for a squad of trained experts from Chattanooga and Knoxville police departments to aid them in crime detection. This detail will be assigned to check the activities of swindlers and "city slickers" who are regarded as too smart for small town officers, the marshal said.

Federal prohibition authorities have already set up machinery by which they expect to defeat efforts of bootleggers to trade in illicit wares. A special examination of the mountainous, wooded slopes around Dayton will be made for stills, they say. Their usual monthly seizure of stills in this territory is four or five which are brought into Dayton.

Dayton itself is without a prison, but Rhea county has offered the use a commodious jail in which offenders against federal state and local regulations will alike be housed.

**

Signs Everywhere

Dayton, Tenn., July 8 (A.P.)— A gallery for display of the sign painter's art is Dayton, where the legal battle over the Tennessee law against teaching of evolution in public schools begins Friday.

Placards, lettered banners, posters and window inscriptions shout the many phases of the John T. Scopes case and call attention to features of the legal controversy which might be lost sight of in the confusion of new developments.

First to strike the newcomer's eyes are the banners of a devout religious nature, which suspend from telegraph poles, hang from trees, or cling to walls of barns and business houses. Of widest distribution is the invitation:

"Read your bible."

Placards also inquire:

"Shall we pay our money to damn our children?"

The visitor is surprised to learn that many of these religious signs have been posted here for a year or more and are not the outgrowth of the occasion. "A man passing through" they tell the inquirer, put the signs up and went his way.

A brightly colored banner strung across Main street calls attention to a significant place in the history of the case. Here, the world is told, is "Robinson's Drug Store—Where it Started." Inside, seated around an ice cream table, F. E. Robinson, proprietor, the young high school instructor, his friend, George W. Rappleyea, and other local residents, began the argument for the new state law which resulted in filing charges against Scopes. An inlaid inscription now marks the table as the birthplace of the litigation over which the whole country has become aroused.

Friday, July 10,1925
The Des Moines Register

Darrow and Malone on Scene of Evolution Battle

FINISH PLANS FOR START OF TRIAL TODAY

Believe Defense Will Ask for Dismissal; Judge Creates Sensation.

BY RAYMOND CLAPPER.
(Copyright, 1925.)

Dayton, Tenn., July 9.—All principals are here for the opening of the Scopes evolution trial at 10 o'clock tomorrow morning, primed for the greatest battle of the mind since Galileo was imprisoned by the inquisition for teaching that the earth was round.

Clarence Darrow and Dudley Field Malone, of the defense counsel were the last two principals to appear on the night before the trial.

Pending their arrival, the court house janitor, assisted by the county jury, arranged the jury chairs and tidied up the great barn-like trial chamber.

William Jennings Bryan, moving about coatless, in a trick low-necked, short sleeved shirt, made a talk on education to the Rhea county school board, warned school teachers that they had much at stake in the trial and conferred with his associate attorneys.

Judge Springs Surprise.

Judge John T. Raulston, who will preside at the trial, created a sensation by issuing a short statement which was construed on the curbstones as revealing definite sympathies for Bryan and the fundamentalists.

"I approach my duties in the trial of the Scopes case with a deep consciousness that the issues are profound," Judge Raulston said. "I am concerned that those connected with this investigation shall divest themselves of all ambition to establish any particular theory for personal gratification and that we all constantly inquire for the eternal truth.

"If man, without inspiration attempts to delve in the mysterious workings of God he finds himself overwhelmed in perplexities. Therefore, I am much interested that the unerring hand of him who is the author of all truth and justice shall direct every official act of mine."

Select Jury Monday.

While the program for the opening day of the trial is in some doubt it is expected the defense will enter a motion to dismiss and that following arguments on this the court will adjourn until Monday when selection of the jury will begin. This program is subject to change in final arrangements of defense attorneys.

Darrow and Malone arrived on a late train. Earlier, Tom Scopes of Paducah arrived for his son's trial.

W. J. Bryan, jr., appeared at headquarters of the prosecution counsel, and John Washington Butler, author of the anti-evolution law, came in to watch the effects of his handiwork.

Everybody had a last word to say. Bryan made his third speech in three days before the board of education. He told the board it was no credit to him that he was an educated man, but said it was a gift of his parents. He said he had nine college degrees.

"But the moment you put education above religion, you put the machine above the master who controls it," he said.

Warns School Teachers.

Returning to his office Bryan issued a statement warning school teachers, declaring that Mr. Scopes is doing more harm to the teachers of the country than to any other class, and that the harm would be infinitely increased if his views as to the independence of the teacher were established by law.

He said the Tennessee law leaves the teacher free in his personal views with control of what was taught left in the hands of the employers—the taxpayers and parents.

Tom Scopes pattered around town meeting his son's friends.

"We're both bull-headed," he remarked. "Always trying to find out the truth. I've been teaching evolution all of my life and the only reason I haven't been arrested is because I live in Kentucky, which doesn't have an anti-evolution law.

"No, I'm not a school teacher. I'm a machinist but I do a bit of talking on the subject—all in favor of evolution. You can't stop the truth. I used to be a Cumberland Presbyterian but now my only religion is that of Jesus Christ."

Started the Battle.

Then there was Representative Butler, who started it all.

"I've got a son, 14," he said. "He's in the high school and I want him to read about evolution—but he can read it at home. I want him to know for himself how true it is. I have read Darwin's 'Origin of the Species' and 'Descent of Man' but they didn't harm me."

And so it went all day long, everybody giving out his last word before the trial begins. Each tries to define the issue from his own point of view.

The process of popular education—one of the great goods to result from the trial, has already begun. Even the most rusty brain in the remote districts is limbering up.

**

Patrons Are Slow in Arriving for Dayton's Big Free Show

Would Assist Bryan.

Chattanooga, Tenn., July 9 (A.P.)—Patrick Henry Callahan, Louisville, Ky., prominently connected with the Knights of Columbus and Benedict Elder, of the same city, secretary of the Catholic Press association of the United States arrived here today, en route to Dayton to offer their assistance to William Jennings Bryan, prosecution counsel in the Scopes evolution trial.

Both Mr. Callahan and Mr. Elder went to Dayton from here.

"I would look upon the education of the child as a matter in which the most scrupulous care should be taken, and the greatest degree of prudence exercised," said Mr. Callahan. "The attacks upon Tennessee from the outside for seeking to exercise such prudent care seems to me to be injudicious. Whether or not the act of the legislature was necessary and expedient, may possibly be a question, but it was a question for the legislature and the people of Tennessee.

"At all events, however one may differ from him, the efforts of the great commoner deserve the Christian faith of the young of Tennessee and he is entitled to respect."

Saturday, July 11, 1925
The Des Moines Register

COMPLETE JURY TO TRY SCOPES

STATE TO FIGHT THE ADMISSION OF SCIENTISTS

Legal Battle on Evolution Will Start Monday Morning.

Dayton, Tenn., July 10 (A.P.)—The twelve men who will try John Thomas Scopes on a charge of violating the Tennessee law prohibiting the teaching of theories of evolution in the public schools of the state were chosen today.

The first day of the trial moved swiftly, bringing into the open the first legal battle to be fought Monday, the question of admission of scientific testimony in regard to evolution.

Twelve of the twenty prospective jurors examined were accepted with but few questions from the state.

The defense propounded a number of questions to each man, but used only two of its three peremptory challenges. One objection was made by the state, the court ruled four possible jurors incompetent, and one was excused on account of his age.

The jurors are:

W. F. Robinson, farmer.
J. W. Bagley, farmer
Jim Riley, farmer.
W.B. Taylor, farmer
R. L. Gentry, farmer and school teacher
J. A. Thompson, fruit grower and former United States marshal.
Jesse Goodrich, shipping clerk.
J. H. Bowman, farmer.
R. W. Day, farmer.
R. L. West, farmer.
J. S. Wright, farmer.
W. D. Smith, farmer.

No Session Tomorrow.

No session will be held tomorrow, the defense requesting a day to confer on the points it desires to stress in the contention that scientific testimony to show that the theory on evolution and the story of divine creation as told in the Bible are not in conflict. The question will be argued before Judge John T. Raulston Monday.

Judge Raulston announced today court would open at 9 o'clock, continue to a recess at 11:30 o'clock, reconvening again at 1:30, to close at 4:30 o'clock.

The first move today was to swear a grand jury and present a new bill against Scopes, the present indictment being considered of doubtful legality on account of an oversight in elapsed time before the summons to the grand jury and the actual meeting of that body.

Atty. Gen. A. T. Stewart presented a new bill and the defendant was reindicted in almost the identical language used in the first document.

Clarence Darrow, of counsel for the defense, showed the first issue at hand, when he said that the defense considered scientists competent witnesses in the case to explain what evolution is.

State Plans Battle.

Attorney General Stewart disagreed, asserting that should the defense insist on introducing scientists and Bible students as witnesses, the state would take the position that it was not competent to have scientists testify on the definition of evolution or interpret the Bible.

The jury included nine farmers, one school teacher, and farmer combined, one fruit grower and one shipping clerk. Only one was not a church member. Three denominations are represented on the jury—Baptist, Methodist and Christian.

Defense counsel was augmented today by William O. Thompson of New York, Frank McElwee of Rockwood, Tenn., and G. C. Harris, a Spring City lawyer.

Visiting attorneys participating in the trial were welcomed by Judge Raulston. These included on the defense side in addition to Mr. Thompson, Clarence Darrow, Dudley Field Malone and Arthur Garfield Hays. The prosecution, including William Jennings Bryan and his son, William Jennings Bryan, jr., were introduced.

The defense, in adding two lawyers, increased the total only one, as John L. Godsey, Dayton attorney, has withdrawn, after representing Scopes since his preliminary hearing.

Allege Violation of Law

The indictment under which Scopes is being tried charges that he did "unlawfully and wilfully teach in the public schools of Rhea county, Tenn.., certain theory and theories that deny the story of the divine creation of man as taught in the Bible, and did teach instead thereof that man has descended from a lower order of animals, against the peace and dignity of the state."

In charging the grand jury today, Judge Raulston departed only slightly from the charge he delivered to the grand jury May 25. He first read the law and then the story of the creation in Genesis.

He repeated his former statement that he would regard violation of the statute as a high misdemeanor. The judge said he made reference to the evil example of the teacher disregarding constituted authority in the very presence of the undeveloped mind, whose thought and morals he directs and guides.

"If a teacher openly and flagrantly violates the laws of the land in the air of his profession, regardless of the policy of the law, his example cannot be wholesome to the undeveloped mind and would tend to create and breed a spirit of disregard for good order and the want of respect for the necessary discipline and restraint in our body politic."

With defense attorneys, however, this feeling was mingled with one of surprise at the attitude of the prosecution toward the introduction of expert scientific testimony , brought from Dr. John R. Neal, chief defense counsel, and Dudley Field Malone charges of a "change in front."

"We have moved faster than I expected," Darrow said, "and obtained the kind of a jury I expected—pure fundamentalists."

William Jennings Bryan said:"Whenever a jury is satisfactory to the attorneys on both sides and to the judge, the public ought not to complain."

"One of the outstanding developments of the day to my mind was the evident change in the prosecution attitude," Mr. Malone said. "They appear to be afraid to face the testimony we wish to produce from scientific experts of national and international renown."

As soon as court convened for the afternoon session, names of prospective jurymen were ordered placed in a hat. The first name drawn by the sheriff was W. F. Robinson. He said he had formed an opinion to some extent of the guilt or innocence of the defendant but under questioning from the judge he said he could disregard this opinion and bring in a verdict from the evidence. He was accepted by both sides and took the first seat in the jury box.

"Had Heard Rumors."

J. W. Bagley was the second called, and said he had heard rumors of the guilt or innocence of the defendant but could disregard these rumors. He was accepted by the state. Clarence Darrow questioned the prospective juryman about his knowledge of evolution. Bagley replying that he had "no ideas about evolution." After saying that he could be perfectly fair, he was accepted.

Jim Riley pushed his way through the crowd to be questioned. He said he had not formed a definite opinion and knew nothing of the facts in the case. Darrow asked him if he was a member of the church, the reply being in the affirmative, a Baptist. He was accepted, after saying that he had not read of evolution, had not heard a sermon on it, and had not heard Mr. Bryan speak on the subject.

After J. T. Massengale, a Baptist minister, was called for questioning, Mr. Riley was asked if his inability to read was caused by poor eyesight. His reply was that he was uneducated.

Mr. Massengale, when he said he was a minister with four charges, was asked by Darrow if he had ever preached on evolution. He said he had. "On which side? asked the lawyer. "I'm strictly with the Bible," was the reply.

This caused an outburst of applause and drew a sharp reprimand from the judge and a threat to exclude everyone guilty of making a demonstration.

Admits His Opinion.

Under further questioning from the court and Darrow, the Baptist minister said he thought Scopes taught a theory of evolution in conflict with the divine story of creation. Judge Raulston finally excused him with the statement: "I want every juror to start with an open mind, so I will excuse you, Brother Massengale."

W. G. Taylor said he had formed or expressed "to a certain extent" an opinion about this case. he said he could give a fair verdict on the evidence. Replying to a question from Mr. Darrow he said he was a Methodist. He was accepted.

Tom Jackson "expected he had formed an opinion" as to the case. Pressed for the extent of his opinion he said it was not fixed.

The Defense challenged him.

R. L. Gentry had read of the case in the "papers" but agreed, when asked by the judge, that he did not know if everything he saw in the papers was true. He had belonged to the Baptist church for twenty-five years. He told of having read books that taught evolution and had heard speeches for and against it, naming several books he had read.

Mr. Gentry said he had been reading evolution for thirty or thirty-five years and had been studying the Bible that length of time. He was accepted as a juror.

W. A. Ault, a merchant, gave his church membership as Methodist Episcopal, South. He told Darrow that he had a positive opinion on whether man had evolved from a lower organism. He heard Mr. Bryan deliver an address and "say something about evolution." The defense challenged him.

J. R. Thompson said he thought he could try the case wholly on the law and evidence. He said he owned a farm but was not a farmer. Asked if he could pick out the defendant, he said he could not, and Darrow pointed Scopes out to him.

"Glad to know you," was a greeting from the prospective juror. He said he was a church member, a Methodist, "but not a good member." He had never given any thought to evolution but could not say that he had no opinion. He said he had made no study of the question. He said he would pay attention to the evidence in the case but might not pay much attention to the lawyers.

"Well, you might be right about that," was Darrow's comment.

Will Weir, a school teacher was called. He admitted a definite opinion about guilt or innocence of Scopes and was excused by the court.

W. D. Smith told Darrow that he didn't know anything about evolution and was not anxious to find out about it. He said he had heard preachers preach on evolution but he didn't know whether they were for it or not. He gave his church as Methodist and attendance as "about once a month." He had read the bible but not all through. He said that he neither knew nor cared what his neighbors thought about evolution. He was accepted.

Excluded by State.

J. B. Leuty, farmer, said that he was not a member of the church. He had heard of evolution since this case came up. He had not made up his mind about the case. He was excluded by the state.

Jess Goodrich had been a member of the Christian church for eight years. He had heard a good deal about evolution but had not paid much attention to this discussion. He was accepted.

J. H. Bowman, farmer and cabinetmaker, gave his church membership as Methodist. He has not made a study of evolution. He said that he had read the bible through. He was asked if he had any opinion on the question of whether the bible and evolution are in conflict and replied that he had not. He became a member of the jury.

Bill Day, a farmer and a member of the Baptist church, said at his home at Yellow Creek, fifteen miles from Dayton, there had been little excitement over evolution. He had not read a book on the subject nor paid a great deal of attention to it. He was accepted.

R. L. West said he was a member of the Baptist church. Questioning developed that he had not heard much about evolution until this case came to the front. He did not pretend to know much about the subject, he said. He said that he had a "slight opinion" as to the possibility of conflict between evolution theories and the bible. He was accepted.

J. S. Wright was called next. He is a farmer and member of the Baptist church. He did not know much about evolution, he said. He said he read the bible but had not tried to figure out if evolution and the bible conflicted. He made the twelfth juror.

Court then adjourned until Monday morning at 9 o'clock.

Sunday, July 12, 1925
The Des Moines Sunday Register

DAYTON TURNS FROM BIBLE TO POLITICAL BEES

Hears Colby Will Run for Presidency.

BY ROBERT T. SMALL.
(Copyright, 1925. by The C. P. A.)

Dayton, Tenn., July 11.—It may be a far cry from the bible to politics, but nevertheless political gossip of real national interest has invaded this little evolution struck town of the Tennessee mountain country.

It would be impossible for Mr. W. J. Bryan to be so long in one place without engendering some sort of political talk, despite his deep devotion to religion at the moment. But the gossip does not primarily concern Mr. Bryan. It is about Bainbridge Colby of New York and New Jersey, who was to have been one of the counsel for the evolutionists in this Dayton trial, but who asked to be excused at the last moment because of unexpected legal developments in New York City, where the home rule law of the state was declared unconstitutional.

The gossip is to the effect that Mr. Colby is being groomed, or is grooming himself, for the democratic nomination in 1928. Of course, the mention of Mr. Colby to Mr. Bryan in this connection is like waving a red flag at a bull.

Bryan Disappointed.

Despite the fact that both gentlemen held the portfolio of secretary of state under President Woodrow Wilson, they are as far apart as the poles. They look at nothing in common. The former commoner is bitterly disappointed not to have had a shot at Mr. Colby in the "monkey trial," but will be prepared to oppose any movement which may be started in his behalf for the presidency.

Some of Mr. Colby's friends seriously have broached the subject to him, and according to the reports here, found the one time head of the Wilson cabinet in a highly receptive mood. These friends told Mr. Colby that he easily might claim at least a part of the Woodrow Wilson mantle, for he was about the closest man to the war president during the closing days of his administration. It is pointed out that Mr. Colby was the man whom Woodrow Wilson selected as his law partner when he hoped to be able to practice again. As a matter of fact the law firm formally was organized and existed for some time. Mr. Wilson was able to go over some briefs with his partner from time to time, but his illness never permitted a full fruition of his plans.

Partnership Wilson's Idea.

The law partnership was wholly the idea of Mr. Wilson and is cited by the Colby friends at this time to emphasize the confidence and respect of the president. Just how far the Colby "boom" will go, it is impossible to say at this time. It is a rather early start, to say the least. Mr. Colby, in any event, would not be a complacent aspirant. He has a provocative disposition and very decided views upon many subjects. If he actually goes out for the nomination, his campaign is likely to be a colorful one.

Mr. Bryan has been drawn informally into the field of political discussion since coming here—far enough, at least, to say again that he is positive the next democratic candidate must come from the south or the west. This is a perfectly natural feeling for Mr. Bryan to have, for he comes from the west and is of the south, although he seems to resent the suggestion that he might consider himself again as a candidate.

Some of the "master minds" here at the trial have sensed that Mr. Bryan is going to try for the presidency once again on a platform of religious fundamentalism. There is no question that this fight between fundamentalism and evolution is regarded by the commoner as transcending every other issue before the people today—even the great Coolidge issue of reduction in taxes and the material well being of the people and the country.

Can't Tell About Bryan.

Of course, one can never tell exactly what is in Mr. Bryan's mind with regard to the presidency, but he doesn't seem to be thinking along that line at all. He is going to devote the remainder of his days to religious work, with various and sundry excursions into politics in his peculiar effort to save the democratic party. He will certainly do all he can to save it from Mr. Colby or any other easterner or man of that type. Mr. Bryan feels the democrats can disregard the east. They must win, if at all, with the conservative bond south and the radical west.

Mr. William Gibbs McAdoo, once a Tennesseean, has scores of friends in this section and Mr. Bryan's description of the next possible candidate is interpreted by them to fit the former secretary of the treasury. Mr. McAdoo was born in the south and is of the west. The commoner refuses to "specify," as the southern colored folk say. Last year he produced an obscure candidate from Florida. Maybe he has another such surprise up his sleeve.

**

TIGHTEN LINES OF BATTLE IN SCOPES TRIAL

Lawyers Search for New Ammunition for Opening Fight.

Dayton, Tenn., July 11 (A.P.)—Spokesmen for each side in the Scopes evolution trial tonight gave out lengthy statements on the results of their legal conferences today in preparation for the forensic battle over admissibility of scientific testimony next week.

Court was adjourned last night until Monday at the request of defense counsel, while the lawyers searched for ammunition in their law books and the jurors scattered to their homes.

Presiding Judge Raulston watched with interest the preparations in the courtroom for broadcasting the trial starting next Monday.

The prosecution, prepared to resist vigorously an announced effort by the defense to introduce testimony that the theories of evolution and the teachings of the bible are not in conflict, spent much of the day in the study of law.

State Will Protest.

It was no secret that the state will submit to the court that scientific testimony in the case would be irrelevant and inadmissible.

It was learned tonight that the clash on the competency of scientific testimony may not be heard Monday. The state has served notice that the prosecution will insist that the regular order be followed in the trial.

This would result in the debate on admission of scientists' testimony coming when the defense offered their witnesses, after the state's case is closed.

The defense through Clarence Darrow, announced yesterday that it was the firm conviction of that side of the case that such testimony would be entirely competent and every effort made to get it into the record.

Bonafide State Law.

In a statement this afternoon, William Jennings Bryan suggested that if a law like that which furnishes the issue in this case were passed in New York and witnesses from Tennessee proposed to offer testimony, their presence on the witness stand would arouse objection.

The statement given out yesterday by Attorney General Stewart represents the views of the counsel for the state, said Mr. Bryan: "the trial is a bonafide case in which the state is enforcing a law serious in its purpose and passed deliberately.

"The case will be tried according to the rules of evidence with the possibility of appeal to higher courts. If improper evidence is offered by the defense objection will be added to it and I doubt not that the defense will object to any testimony offered by the prosecution if it thinks that testimony improper.

"Attorney General Stewart has pointed out that the statute which is being enforced is perfectly clear and free from ambiguity. It forbids the teaching of doctrine that denies the truth of the bible record of man's creation, and, that there may be no misunderstanding of the law, it interprets the language used by specifying that the objectionable thing in the doctrine is that man is a descendant of some lower form of life. There is no doubt that evolution asserts man's descent from some lower form of life and no scientific specialist could change the law or its meaning, no matter who these specialists might be or how many there might be.

People Know Best.

"If the people of Tennessee have a right to pass laws for the protection of the religion of their children, then they have a right to determine for themselves what they consider injurious and dangerous to their children. No specialists from the outside are required to inform the parents of Tennessee as to what is harmful. The testimony of such experts therefore is not only incompetent but would be offensive.

"If a law like this were passed in New York and witnesses were called from Tennessee to assure the people of New York that they were unduly alarmed and that there was nothing to fear their testimony would be objected to as offensive as well as improper. It would be absurd for Tennessee experts to advise the people of New York and Illinois as to what is helpful or harmful, why is it not absurd to call experts from New York and Illinois to challenge the right of the people of Tennessee to legislate as they please and according to their own sense of responsibility and their own judgment as to what is harmful and what is objectionable from a bible standpoint?

"The people of Tennessee have a right to protect the bible as they understand it. They are not compelled to consider the interpretations placed upon it by people of other states, whether Christian or scientists or both."

Go on River Picnic.

After a day in which attorneys, as Dr. Neal described them were "lawyers, with a possibility of being orators, Monday," the array of representatives of Scopes' legal interests picnicked with newspaper men in the afternoon, joining a boat ride down the Tennessee river in which the Chattanooga News was host to visiting reporters.

Members of prosecution counsel motored to a mountain resort near Dayton in the late afternoon. Mr. Bryan has two engagements tomorrow, the first to teach a bible class at Sunday school exercises of the Methodist Episcopal church, south. In the afternoon he will conduct a union service, in which all the Dayton churches are joining, speaking from the bandstand in the yard of the courthouse.

Members of the jury evidently faithfully observed Judge Raulston's instructions to avoid assemblies, meetings or services where any discussion of the case might take place. Ten of the twelve who will decide the case live in the country, far removed from Dayton and they were at home. The two town representatives were following their daily pursuits as if they were not to become famous Monday.

**

Darrow Accuses Bryan of Seeking to Evade Major Issues

SAYS SCIENCE FAILS TO BACK STATE'S VIEW

Law Would Bar Geology and Astronomy

Dayton, Tenn., July 11 (A.P.)—Clarence Darrow of counsel for John T. Scopes in a statement today accused the state's legal representatives in the prosecution of the Tennessee evolution case of making an effort to "run away from the facts" in their fight to prevent the introduction of expert testimony on science and religion.

He charged that this "effort" is "doubtless on account of their inability to get any scientific man in the world to deny the facts that prove the correctness of evolution."

The Chicago lawyer, associated with local attorneys who are defending the young Dayton biology teacher, directed his attack particularly against William Jennings Bryan, assisting the state in the prosecution, who has held that evolution and Christianity are irreconcilable.

"...Millions of the ablest men in the world, including a large proportion of students of religion, are both Christians and evolutionists," Darrow asserted. "and among these are the ablest scientists of the world."

Would Bar Astronomy.

Mr. Darrow declared that the fact that any theory of scientific view may be contrary to any religious idea furnished no right for a state to prohibit it.

"If this were true, he said, "then most of astronomy and geology would fall under the ban."

Darrow's statement follows:

"There are two things necessary to crime under the Tennessee statute.

"One, teaching the theory of creation contrary to the divine account as recorded in Genesis; two, teaching that man was evolved from the lower form of animal life. These are purely questions of fact.

"With one or two exceptions, every juror in this case has stated he knows little or nothing about evolution. The same thing could be said about almost any jury that would be assembled in any state in the union. As there are some thousand different religions and some five hundred sects of Christians, naturally there is some difference of opinion as to the divine account as taught in the bible.

"More than one account is given of the creation of man in the bible and these do not agree. Men have debated a long time as to the meaning of much in the bible and especially of the account of creation, and yet a Tennessee jury that has given no attention to evolution is supposed to know, first, what evolution is, and second, what the bible teaches with reference to the creation of man, and third, whether these theories and the account in the bible are in conflict.

"And Mr. Bryan says they should decide all this without evidence. It is obvious that no jury can accomplish any such thing.

"The effort to keep the defense from offering evidence in this case is a plain effort to run away from the facts and is doubtless on account of their inability to get any scientific man in the world to deny the facts that prove the correctness of evolution.

This is further shown by the fact that Mr. Bryan delivered a public talk here and said the facts of religion and evolution will at last be brought to light. This Tennessee jury is expected by the state without any evidence to find that no man can be a Christian and an evolutionist and this despite the fact that millions of the ablest men in the world, including a large proportion of students of religion are both Christians and evolutionists. And among these are the ablest scientists of the world.

"Mr. Bryan's statement about the rights of Tennessee to protect its religion is ambiguous if he means that any state has the right to pass a law which prohibits the teaching of a theory that is contrary to any religion, and he is flying in the face of every state constitution. The fact that any theory or any scientific view may be contrary to any religious idea furnishes no right for a state to prohibit it. If this were true, then most of astronomy and geology would fall under the ban.

"State Constitution O.K."

"The constitution of Tennessee contains one of the strongest guarantees of religious liberty amongst all the states of the union and no law that would undertake to establish religion or measure conduct would have any validity in the state or any other state without first getting rid of the constitution.

"Whether the scientists come from Tennessee or outside to tell the meaning of evolution cannot matter. Science is the same everywhere."

**

DOCTORS POINT OUT EVOLUTION TEST IN BABIES

Gill Cleft and Blood Reactions Are Cited.

With the opening of the Scopes trial at Dayton, Tenn., evolutionists and anti-evolutionists the world over began marshalling facts and arguments on the evolution issue.

Dr. Walter C. Alvares, biologist of the University of California, made a statement in San Francisco that a baby with a tail was born there recently. Such a phenomenon, he declared, is reported in this country on an average of every two years.

"In the clinics we find, occasionally, a child with an abscess, or hole, in the side of the neck," Dr. Alvarez said. "It is a gill cleft, exactly like a shark's, kept from the embryonic stage—one of the few which do not disappear."

When questioned concerning Dr. Alveraz' statement, Dr. Julius S. Weingart of Des Moines said that while the abscess or hole on the neck is a common thing, that he had never heard of a child born with a tail. After describing embryonic-phenomena of a similar nature, however, Dr.

Weingart continued:

Gill Cleft Is Common.

"The gill cleft is a common occurrence, a small hole or abscess appearing in the neck of the child. This hole is directly related to the gills of a fish. The ear is a part of the gill cleft, traces of which can be found in all mammals."

"There are a great many other things which indicate a relationship between the mammals," Dr. Weingart said. "During the early stages of embryonic development it is extremely hard to distinguish between the pig and the human or the human and any other mammal. As the period of development progresses, however, it becomes easier to see the difference between the less closely related mammals.

"It has been said that the embryonic development of the human reproduces the history of its species in evolution. This is true, in a very general way.

Cites the Blood Test.

"Another interesting thing which shows a relation between man and the higher apes is the precipitin blood test. This test is used extensively in medical-legal cases. With it bloodstains that are very old can be used in determining from what animal the stain originates."

The test to which Dr. Weingart refers here is made by use of blood serums. These are taken from living animals and are predetermined to be anti-human or anti-pig, as the case may be. The serum, when mixed with the blood of an animal produces a reaction. It is from this reaction that the species of the animal from which the blood was taken is determined.

For instance, when an anti-pig serum is mixed with pig blood a positive reaction will occur. If the same serum is mixed with the blood of a wild boar, a positive action, but less definite, will occur. If the serum were mixed with the blood of a chicken, however, a negative reaction would result.

In proving the relationship of man and the higher ape by this test, scientists have taken an anti-human serum, which reacts positively to the blood of humans and negatively to the blood of pigs and other mammals, and mixed it with the blood of apes and chimpanzies. In every case the result has been a positive reaction, practically equal to the reaction produced by human blood.

On Science and Religion.

In concluding his statement on evolution, Dr. Weingart said:

"I am not interested in the trial at Dayton since it seems so inutterably silly. It is true that the evolutionary hypothesis is only a hypothesis, but so is religion.

"Religion is the reaction of the human mind to the wonder of existence and represents in a symbolic way its longings and aspirations. Science results from the play of intelligence upon the data of consciousness, and represents men's efforts to explain these in a way that will satisfy his reason.

"It is beyond the province of religion to explain historical or scientific data. In music we have laws governing the relation of tones, and yet the love of music rests deep in man's emotions. No music lover would resent or lose his appreciation of its beauty if the physicists were to promulgate a new theory of sound."

"The test of what we call truth is in whether or not it works, and in whether or not it relates the facts of experience to each other in a way which satisfies our reason.

"If we could find a better theory of the relation of living forms on this earth to each other, and one which would be more productive in discovery than the present theory of evolution, we would be obliged to discard the latter in favor of the former."

**

TEACHERS BACK SCOPES IN FIGHT FOR "FREEDOM"

Letter Says Hypocrisy Must Be Defeated.

Chicago, July 11 (A.P.)—The American Federation of Teachers, in a letter to John T. Scopes, defendant in the Tennessee anti-evolution trial, made public today, asserts the public school is on trial at Dayton and that the "danger can only be removed by the final if not the immediate success" of the defense contentions "in behalf of freedom of education." A recent convention of the organization, which is affiliated with the American Federation of Labor, resolved to support Mr. Scopes and all others who may oppose legislation similar to the Tennessee law, prohibiting instruction in the theory of evolution in the public schools.

The letter, mailed yesterday, expresses the view that the establishment of the principles embodied in the Tennessee law would replace the professional spirit of scholars with hypocrisy and cant.

The text follows:

"Mr. John T. Scopes:

"Dayton, Tenn.

"Dear sir:

"On the opening day of your trial I wish to extend, in the name of the American Federation of Teachers, a message of confidence in the issues on which you stand.

Free Schools at Stake.

"Out of the mass of uncertainty which attends the present efforts to restrict and deprive education through legislation, the question of the continuance of the American free public school system is emerging.

"Mr. Bryan is quoted as expressing the belief that the taxpayers have the right to determine what the schools shall be and do, and in the broadest sense he is correct. But if, as he seems to advocate, each loyal community, regardless of preparation for its task, can prescribe the exact content of the subject matter taught in the schools, confusion and chaos must follow. If teachers and school administrators must look to the spokesmen of local sentiment and be governed thereby in their educational activities, or if they must submit a thorough searching as to their views of all controversial matters whenever the occasion suggests, professional spirit, all too meager at best, must give way to hypocrisy and cant.

Usurp Teachers' Functions.

"Under the proposed plan, state legislatures are to usurp the functions of educators and scholars. Local boards of education are to be the final word, giving the reactionary groups who would gladly see the end of the free public school system and its training for citizenship, their opportunity.

"Once settled that teachers must hold the views on all controversial matters, that suit the particular community, what persons of independent thought and action will become and remain teachers? Must the ranks be filled by those who are less than the best?

"From the viewpoint of the American Federation of Teachers it is neither science nor religion that is on trial, but the public school. It stands as the emancipator from ignorance, prejudice and intolerance. It is in danger. That danger can only be removed by the final if not the immediate success of your contentions in behalf of freedom and education."

**

WILBUR WOULD BAR TEACHING OF EVOLUTION

Sees Darwinism As Menace to Religion.

San Francisco, July 11 (I.N.S.)—Curtis D. Wilbur, secretary of the navy, has taken sides in the sensational Tennessee evolution controversy. He is firmly against teaching Darwinism to children.

He will say so himself in an address scheduled at the First Congregational church here tomorrow on "Evolution and the Bible." Excerpts from the speech follow:

"Let the scientific teachers beware of dissipating God into a vacuum and of trying to teach pupils that man, as it were, has lifted himself by his own bootstraps from the protoplasmic state into his present condition.

"The question of the relationship of evolution and the Bible is one of the most vital questions in the realm of religion.

"That all form of life now upon the earth are developed from cell life, we all know.

" The real question which is unanswered by the theory of evolution is: How did the fertilized cell get the power to multiply and differentiate so as to become what it has become, as distinguished from what other fertilized cells become—a man in one case, a whale or a snake in another?

"The Bible story of creation as we have taught it for several hundred years does conflict with the evolutionist theory of creation.

"Consequently, those who see in the teaching of evolution in the public school a menace to religion are correct insofar as they see a menace to the Bible story of creation as we have taught it.

"Man is the capstone of creation and represents the triumph of all the agencies for his uplift.

"The Bible story presents man as created in the image of God, in the stage of perfection.

"Evolution presents man as always developing upward. It presents the thought of possibilities yet undreamed of. This seems to be in line with the thought of Christ that men would constantly get better and that men would outdo the miracles he performed, and accomplish more by their teaching and preaching than he was able to accomplish."

**

Mr. Bryan has been photographed so much that he no longer blinks or starts when a cameraman touches off a flashlight powder unexpectedly.

**

No matter how that trial turns out, somebody will always laugh when Dayton, Tenn., is mentioned.

**

One lawyer who withdrew from the Scopes case said he didn't care for the publicity. Now he is getting some anyhow.

**

The thunders of applause greeting Mr. Bryan at Dayton, Tenn., probably remind him of the happy days when he thought he would be elected president of the United States.

**

Apparently Bryan and Darrow are to be the stars of the Scopes trial, with the professor merely in the role of a spear bearer.

**

Looking for the Absolute.

Madison Lake, Minn.—To the Editor: There is one point on which I heartily disagree with your paper, and that is on the evolution question. From time to time you have printed—almost featured—articles that have had the most fantastic designations for certain scientific discoveries. As far as I know, you have not given the other side any serious attention. I think you will find some mighty fine material on the other side of this question in Prof. O. A. Tinglestad's (of Luther college, Decorah, Ia.,) article on the "Proof of Evolution." He proves that the geologists look to biology for ultimate proof and that biology, if cornered, circles back to geology. Can you find clearer case of begging the question? Your paper tries to be fair: why not take up this side of it also? When the others say evolution is a fact, a thinking person must revolt. To prove that I am no street corner demagog I merely incidentally mention that I hold the highest degree (Th.D.) that Harvard university offers. J. Magnus Rohne.

**

Religion and Science.

Clio, Ia.—To the Editor: Luther and his various followers were not ready to carry out the very principles he contended for. His words spoke greater than the brain prompting them. To him and his followers for generations to come his "right to private opinion: meant that he had a right to private opinion. Those who differed from him in opinion deserved nothing but eternal damnation or burning at the stake as his follower, John Calvin, was instrumental in torturing Servetus to death for his opinion. Scientists were persecuted by his followers as by the mother church. It was not until the backbone of fundamentalism was broken that the churches came to acknowledge any mental freedom to others than themselves.

Mr. Smay would desire to see the creation theory and evolution theory presented side by side in the schools. In reply would say all truths that have been demonstrated as such should be taught as truths. Theories should be presented as theories, not as facts, when there are any reasonable chances of them being solved by reason or observation. In presenting theories the doubts should have as prominent a place as the affirmative features. But the fundamentalists will not hear to having any doubts entertained in the schools regarding religion. The only remedy then is to keep any such theories out of the schools. A.A.Snow

**

Monday, July 13, 1925
The Des Moines Register

DAYTON PASTER QUITS AS CHURCH BARS MODERNIST

Say Members Threatened to Wreck Church

Congregation Promised Violence If Services Were Held.

Dayton, Tenn., July 12 (A.P.)— Rev. Howard Gale Byrd withdrew from his pastorate of the Methodist Episcopal church, (northern), here today when a large part of his congregation protested against Rev. Charles Francis Potter, modernist minister of New York, taking the church pulpit. Dr. Potter purposed to preach a sermon on evolution.

Rev. Mr. Byrd called off the three regular Sunday preaching services and announced to newspapermen at the parsonage:

"I have quit. I have not resigned—I have quit."

Dr. Byrd, who invited Dr. Potter to occupy his pulpit, is pointed to as the original inspiration for the filing of charges against John T. Scopes, whose trial on an indictment alleging violation of the state law against teaching evolution in public schools began here Friday.

Mr. Byrd explained that he "quit" because he had invited Potter and intended to stand by him.

Learning of the protests, Dr. Potter told Mr. Byrd that he would "under the circumstances" withdraw his acceptance of the invitation.

Threatened by Congregation.

The New York minister then posted this notice on the window of Robinson's drug store, where the local controversy over the Tennessee anti-evolution statute started:

"Dr. Potter has cancelled his evolution sermon this morning at the Methodist-Episcopal church owing to the threat of congregation."

Questioned as to the significance of the expression, "threat of congregation," Dr. Potter declared:

"More than half of Mr. Byrd's congregation called on him last night in a body and told him that if I were permitted to speak in the church today, they would wreck the church."

George W. Rappleyea, original prosecutor of the evolution charges against John T. Scopes, agreed to Potter's explanation. Rappleyea is a Sunday school teacher in Byrd's church and an ardent admirer of the local minister.

"Yes, they threatened they would break up the church," he said.

Pastor for Three Years.

Rev. Mr. Byrd is 31 years old and has been pastor of the local church for three years. Members of his congregation declared that the church had grown more in the three years of Byrd's ministration and had done more religious service than in all its history of many decades.

Mr. Byrd said he was at a loss to know now what he would do, having withdrawn from his pastorate. No provision exists, under the polity of the Northern Methodist church for him to resign. The bishop in charge of this episcopal area is now in Europe. The local congregation was without autonomy as the congress of the church assigned Mr. Byrd here and was the sole authority competent to act on his withdrawal.

Member Expresses Regret.

S. C. Patton, chairman of the church's board of stewards, and postmaster here, expressed keen regret at Mr. Byrd's action.

"The church is strong for Brother Byrd," Mr. Patton said. "He has done more good here than any other preacher in town. We consider him to be soundly orthodox.

"The congregation to its pastor. If he goes we will all be mighty sorry."

Dr. Potter called reporters together and discussed the case in the lobby of the Hotel Aqua. He distributed copies of an abstract of the sermon he had prepared for delivery.

The New York advocate of religious modernism lamented what he said were conditions prevailing in the south.

"People in the south don't know that evolution is.

"The best thing to do is to establish a new system of education here and all over the south."

Opponents Meet on Street.

Dr. Potter was met on the street by Rev. T. T. Martin, fundamentalist champion and field secretary of the Anti-Evolution league.

Martin and the Unitarian minister had arranged to divide time in a discussion tonight on the courthouse lawn. Mr. Martin, Baptist evangelist of Blue Mountain, Miss., told Dr. Potter he regretted to learn of the cancellation of his speaking engagement.

"I am going to give you the whole time at the courthouse. I want to see you get a square deal," Mr. Martin told Dr. Potter.

Dr. Potter seemed at a loss to reply to Mr. Martin's offer. At length he thanked him and patting the white haired fundamentalist on the shoulder, exclaimed:

"You're a good sport."

Dr. Rappelyea also thanked Mr. Martin and complimented him on his "fine spirit."

Byrd Loathe to Talk.

Mr. Byrd was found at his residence, next door to the church. He was playing with two of his three small children and seemed loathe to discuss his withdrawal.

"Potter is an evolutionist," he said in explanation of the congregation's protest. "Here, you know, an evolutionist is an infidel."

He was asked about his own views on evolution. He believed God could create man and other creatures as well by evolution as by any other method.

"First the blade, then the ear, and after that the full corn in the ear'" he quoted. That sounds like evolution to me. "Christ had nothing to say about evolution. Why can't we follow the example of the Master?"

He was asked if he had ever preached on evolution.

"I preached on evolution last Sunday. But I didn't use the word 'evolution.' I used the words 'progress' and 'development' speaking on the subject 'what it has cost the fathers.'

"The congregation regarded it as orthodox."

Would Escape Publicity.

The young minister protested that he wished to escape "any big notice in the newspaper," he would be glad to have no publicity in the matter.

"I just want to slip out quietly," he sighed.

The minister led his visitors through the simple auditorium of the small church. This had been entirely renovated since he came to Dayton, all carpentry, painting, paper hanging and fine woodwork having been done by the pastor's own hands, his members said.

Mr. Byrd's ancestors for generations have been cabinet makers.

The church now includes ninety-four members.

When Mr. Byrd became pastor he cut out half the membership because "some of them were dead, others had moved away and others had gone over to Satan and sin."

Explains Spelling of Name.

The preacher explained the spelling of his name. It is 'B-y'-Byrd," he said, "I have evoluted from Bird, which has feathers, you know."

Dr. Potter's abstract of the sermon he had prepared said the modernist preacher's concern of the church was to point out "the difference between 'liberal religion and fundamentalism.'"

"We find the fundamentalists asserting as one of their primary doctrines, 'the literal accuracy of the Bible,' the sermon abstract said in part.

"Every word is perfect, it needs no change, not a jot, not a tittle can be changed.

"On the other hand you will find that liberal religion teaches not merely that the Bible is not a complete book, not merely that God spoke outside the Bible, but goes into the heart of the matter. When a fundamentalist asserts the belief in the Bible precludes belief in evolution, a real liberal replies that religion itself is an excellent example of evolution.

Evolution of Religion.

"You will find 'an eye for an eye' in the old testament and then when you turn to the new testament you find instead 'love your enemies, do good to them that persecute you and pray for those who spitefully use you.'

"The evolution of religion itself. . . .

"The second difference between fundamentalists and liberal religion is that fundamentalists are mostly concerned with other worldliness. It is the next world they are thinking about. They are not concerned with the world around them. They are not trying to better conditions here.

"Liberal religion has been concerned with this world. The fundamentalists have called us worldly. We are glad to be worldly. . .

"We are more concerned for the salvation of men's minds, than for the salvation of their souls. Take the world as you find it and try to make it better—that is the message of liberal religion.

"Character counts, not creed. Just because a man did not happen to be born in an old fashioned church and does not believe in some of these old ideas of the first century, B.C., we cannot believe that he is forever damned. Besides, we do not believe in hell, anyway.

"Another point of difference between fundamentalists and the modern religion, the big point of difference, is that, after all, it is the difference between ignorance and education."

**

Dayton Throng Hears Sermons for and Against Evolution

BRYAN ASSAILS WHILE POTTER DEFENDS CREEDS

Sweltering Sunday Crowd Cheers Both Speakers.

Dayton, Tenn., July 12 (A.P.)—William Jennings Bryan preached an old fashioned sermon to a sweltering crowd of believers in an old fashioned God on the courthouse lawn here this afternoon and tonight at the same place the Rev. Charles Francis Potter, pastor of the West Side Unitarian church of New York City told of the creed of the modernists.

"He Calleth Thee" was the topic of Mr. Bryan's sermon and through it he depicted a Christ who alone can save the world from future wars.

The crowd, which began to assemble more than two hours before time for the sermon, applauded now and then, and shouted fervent "amens." Overhead an airplane droned. In the distance a train whistled, drew into the city limits and whistled again, so loudly that the man who was introduced to the audience as the representative of the "lowly Nazarene" was forced to interrupt his sermon while he remarked that the trains seemed to blow more loudly on Sunday than on other days.

Gestures with Palmetto Fan.

Mr. Bryan made his gestures with a palmetto leaf fan and delivered his sermon in coatless summer attire. In simple, homely terms he told of the blind man who called to the saviour as he passed outside the city of Jericho and of the shout "he calleth thee" echoed back to him by the crowd.

The sermon was interspersed with an intermittent clicking of cameras, as news reel photographers ground out pictures of the crowd, the speaker and the courthouse about which they were grouped.

So free from controversial statements was Mr. Bryan's sermon that Dr. Potter, who had planned to answer him tonight, took exception to only one remark.

"The doctrines of Christ have lived for 1900 years," Bryan said, "and they have furnished so complete a moral code that no scholar has dared to add a word to it. Religion was here before education.

When the schools get through with our children they still must have something else. The only advantage of an education is to increase their capacity for service. The dull man with a passion for service will render more service than the man with a keen brain and no passion for service."

Potter Cites Fallacy.

In his talk Mr. Potter said:

"Mr. Bryan said 'you can give a man a dull brain and a passion for service and he will render more service than the man with simply a brain.'

"The fallacy of that is that you do not find a passion for service among people of dull brain. That's a sociological fact. The great services have been given by men of intellect. While he was speaking, over his head was whirring an airplane which was invented by a man of keen intellect and developed by others. There is no record in history of any man of dull brain ever having rendered great service to mankind."

In introducing Mr. Bryan, the Rev. W. A. Moffatt, pastor of the Baptist church, termed him a man who throughout his life had stood for his convictions and fought for what he felt was the right on both political and moral questions.

"And he has been right on moral questions." The words brought a volley of handclapping. "Today I introduce him to you by a title due him as a representative of the lowly Nazarene." He then presented the speaker as "Brother Bryan."

The fundamentalist leader spoke briefly of his activities in the religious world.

Shame Them to Conceit.

"I was drawn into activity again by liberal young men who thought it was too narrow to be Christians. They thought it smart to be skeptical. I visited colleges and universities over the land in an effort to shame these young men out of the conceit.

"In my religious addresses I have followed the same style as in my political ones. I have taken up each point and answered it, trying at the same time to present other arguments that could not be answered.

"Intellectual blindness is a greater affliction than blindness of the eyes. And spiritual blindness is worse than intellectual blindness. It is not hard for me to believe in the trinity because I see in every man the physical, the spiritual and the mental man.

"It is possible to carry education so far that a person will look down upon religion as a superstition."

Tonight Dr. Potter expressed pleasure at "this privilege of preaching here in God's great out-of-doors."

Doesn't Hate Opponents.

"When I was excluded from one of the churches of this town this morning and not permitted to preach because of the prejudice of the congregation against my kind of religion, I was not left without a place to preach. I do not feel badly about it and certainly do not hate my orthodox opponents.

"You see the trouble with certain religious people is that they condemn other religions without knowing anything about them. Consequently I am going to give those who have not heard what liberals and progressives in religion really believe a chance to hear it tonight.

"You have heard what we do not believe, for some of us talk too much about that side of it. But it is the constructive side that is important after all, so I ask your unprejudiced attention while I tell you some beliefs which are very dear to my heart.

Four Points of Belief.

"The four points of my belief are: I believe in Jesus, in the Bible, in God, and in man.

"I believe in Jesus because he was himself a progressive.

"I believe in the Bible because it is a record of the progress of a great race in the search for God.

"I believe in God because he is the great force and power behind all progress.

"Finally, I believe in man because of his internal urge toward progress and growth. Some one has said that human nature never changes, but a wiser man has said that it is human nature to change.

"If we have faith in man and believe in him, if we have hope of his growth upward and onward forever, and above all, if we act in the spirit of love toward him all our troubles will gradually be solved by Paul's formula, faith, hope and love."

**

Evolution talk raises a question in one's mind. If we sprang from monkeys, how far back in the dark ages were we emancipated from fleas?

**

Whatever the court and the jury may do at Dayton, Tenn., Bryan certainly has the gallery with him.

**

Incidentally, that man Scopes has put the state of Tennessee to a lot of expense and the telegraph editors of the country to a lot of trouble.

**

Is Any Honest Belief a Sin?

To the Editor: The scientist as a rule has gone quietly, unostentatiously, studiously and reverently about his business of collecting, classifying, and arranging facts and formulating theories therefrom. I think it may be admitted that the evolution idea as a whole may be still classed as a theory for in the vast field of facts it may be possible that additional facts may be brought into court that will overthrow it in whole or in part but at least it, like many others, is a good working formula and whether true or not the scientist has never held over the head of mankind the threat of damnation for failure to believe what he claims.

Not so the theologians and other soul specialists.

The whole storm centers around the theory of Bible infallibility. That it is a theory is amply proven by the innumerable, conflicting, divergent, often ridiculous and impossible interpretations placed upon the Bible by those who profess to accept it as authority.

To forestall analysis or discussion of this theory they have taught for centuries and are now teaching that there is a virtue in believing it, that it is a sin not to believe, that punishment will surely follow for failure to believe. It is the fear instilled by this vicious teaching that is back of all this controversy.

So long as a little group of men can get by with the teaching that it is a virtue to believe a theological dogma that falls out of the scope of human experience and over which there is no possibility of human control, that it is a sin not to believe these things that have no bearing on the building of human character, there will never be a very profound intelligence or a very high standard of morality.— I. Sylvester.

**

Rippling Rymes

Ancestry.

If I'm descended from an ape, I am not much depressed by that; I shed no tears, I pin no crepe upon by coat sleeve or my hat. If some gorilla was the sire of my proud race, I do not care; I'm nobly toiling at my lyre to settle for the bill of fare. I herd my hens and plow and sow and do not care a tinker's oath what chanced a million years ago to either apes, or men, or both. I do my work in proper shape, I milk the cow and spray the tree, and if my grandsire was an ape it surely cuts no grass with me. I worry over many things connected with the present day; my flivver has two broken springs, I've found some mildew in my hay. The hair is falling from my dome, which makes me murmur and repine; my aunt is coming to my home to visit for six weeks or nine. The chair I sit on falls apart, and lets me down and makes me swear; the cost of living fills my heart with indignation and despair. When I have concrete griefs like these, why should I fill the air with wails because my forebears sat in trees or swung from branches by their tails? I strive to dodge the bogie debt, when buying things I pay the dough, and let the four-eyed savants sweat o'er problems of the long ago. It may be they are talking bunk, it may be what they say is true, but there's no prehistoric monk can stop me when I've work to do. (Copyright 1925 Geo. Matthew Adams.)

Tuesday, July 14, 1925
The Des Moines Register

DARROW TURNS HIS SATIRE ON EVOLUTION ACT

Attempt to Quash Scopes Indictment Up to Judge.

Dayton, Tenn., July 13 (By The Associated Press)—Judge John T. Raulston, presiding at the trial of John Thomas Scopes on a charge of violating the law of the state of Tennessee making it a misdemeanor to teach theories of evolution in the public schools, retired to his chambers tonight to study the question of whether the indictment against the 24-year-old school teacher shall be summarily quashed.

The judge carried with him briefs of the half score points stressed by the contending sides in the case, which ringing in his ears were words from half a dozen oral arguments presented to the court during the day.

It was the first of perhaps other days to be devoted entirely to oratory. The jury's service was brief . Soon after court opened and the state had interrogated one juror, R. L. Gentry, as to whether he had expressed an opinion as to the guilt or innocence of the defendant, the jury was sent from the room, that argument might be made on the motion to quash.

Argument Grows Heated.

Mr. Gentry went with his fellow jurymen after declaring that he could not recall having said that Scopes ought not to be convicted.

"There is no reflection on him," the attorney general explained.

Starting the morning session with a carefully prepared reading of the formal motion to quash and a calm argument by John R. Neal for the defense, the heat of the argument gained intensity as the day wore on. B. G. McKenzie, former attorney general, and Dudly Field Malone, of counsel for the defense, engaged in a clash, ending in smiles, but for the moment giving indications of developing into a spirited exchange.

During Attorney General Stewart's argument for the state in the afternoon he was questioned by defense attorneys on several points.

Mr. Stewart suggested with a smile, "Perhaps you would like to put me on the witness stand."

"We would," was the chorus from the defense table.

The day of speechmaking was brought to a close by the two most extended arguments of the trial, Atty. Gen. A. T. Stewart and Clarence Darrow taking up the entire afternoon session with their discussions of the soundness of the indictment and the constitutionality, wisdom and fairness of the Tennessee law placing evolution theories under the ban in so far as public schools are concerned.

Defends Tennessee Law.

The attorney general vigorously defended the law, declaring that the legislature was well within its rights in passing the statute and that the state should be praised for enforcing it, instead of criticized.

The young prosecuting officer was emphatic in declaring that warrant of law may be abundantly cited to support the contention of the prosecution.

Clarence Darrow, after opening with a pleasant appreciation of the action of the court in bestowing the title of "colonel" upon him, declared in his opening words that the anti-evolution law "was wicked and mischievous." He replaced his smile with almost a scowl as he said he would attempt to place himself in the sixteenth century that he might treat the law seriously.

The exchange of counsel, furnishing the first real battle of words in the trial, was started by John Randolph Neal, who fired the first gun but took no later part.

Mr. McKenzie, veteran of many a Tennessee legal battle, was speaking when Dr. Neal inquired:

"Is the general discussing our motion, or the admissibility of evidence?"

The former attorney general said that he was replying to the extensive speech of Arthur G. Hays on evolution and incidentally to the general argument, adding:

"These questions have all been settled in Tennessee and favorably to our contention. If these gentlemen have any laws in the great metropolitan city of New York that conflict with it, or in the great white city of the northwest that will throw any light on it, we will be glad to hear about it. They have many great lawyers and courts up there."

Malone Aroused.

Dudley Malone was on his feet instantly to say:

"We object to this argument. The motion before the court does not involve the discussion of admissibility of evidence. We are discussing the constitutionality of this indictment on a motion to quash. And I would like to say here, although I do not mean to interrupt the gentleman, that I do not consider allusion to geographical parts of the country as particularly necessary, such as references to New Yorkers and to citizens of Illinois. We are here, rightfully , as American citizens in a court of justice."

Before M. McKenzie could reply, Judge Raulston broke in:

"Colonel Malone, you do not know General McKenzie as well as the court does. Everything he says is in good humor. I want you gentlemen from New York or any other foreign state to always remember that you are our guests and that we accord you the same privileges and rights and courtesies that we do any other lawyers."

"We appreciate the hospitality of the court and the people of Tennessee," said Mr. Malone, "but while we are in this court room we are here as lawyers and not as guests."

Mr. McKenzie gained the floor to say, "We have the highest regard for these distinguished lawyers. I admit that I have no respect for their opinions that have been advanced as to the law, and do not believe it to be the law. But I love them—I love them all."

"And I'm strong for you," from Mr. Malone, ended the incident.

Although no formal action was taken in court, it was learned this morning that Mr. Darrow had entered a protest with the judge against the custom of opening the court day with prayer.

Judge Raulston said in regard to Mr. Darrow's protest that he believed in prayer and proposed to have it daily in the court. Judge Raulston said that he told Mr. Darrow "this is a matter for my conscience and it is my responsibility."

Charges in Attack.

At the opening of court today, after the indictment had been read to the defendant, John R. Neal made the formal motion for the defense that the indictment be quashed. The defense launched into a general attack on the indictment and the statute under which it was drawn. It was contended that it violated state constitutional requirements, that but one subject shall contain a clear and definite statement of its intent and purpose, and that education shall be cherished. It was contended that the guaranteed right of free worship was abridged, as was the free communication of thoughts and opinions. The law that general laws only shall be passed was also held to have been violated and a charge that the statute was vague and indefinite was made.

Dr. Neal took up the contentions of the defense in order.

"We think that the act makes a crime of teaching certain doctrine in the bible which, we think the court can take judicial knowledge of," said Mr. Neal. "A doctrine in the bible is so indefinite that every man that reads the bible will have a different interpretation as to exactly what that theory is.

"We have been met constantly by the assertion, 'If you don't like this law, have it repealed.' We grant you that the legislature spoke for the majority of the people of Tennessee, but we represent the minority, the minority that is protected by this great provision of our constitution, that was made to protect one individual, or a dozen, or a thousand."

Discusses Word "Teach."

Arthur G. Hays, who followed Dr. Neal with a second argument for the defense, thought the indictment and the act indefinite and devoted himself to this contention. The word "teach" he thought was not made sufficiently clear.

"It should not be wrong to teach evolution, or certain phases of evolution, but not as a fact," he said. If the law means that we cannot teach certain things, it should be definitely stated. If it means that you cannot explain a certain theory, that should be stated plainly, or whether either or both of them can be expounded."

That the attack on the insufficiency of the indictment has been often passed on by the supreme court of Tennessee was the opening statement of Ben T. McKenzie, making the first argument for the state. He vigorously declared that the legislature had the right to direct the operation of the schools. The charge against the caption of the bill not conforming to the text drew from Mr. McKenzie the comment that it has been held that this must be construed liberally, the intent of the law being to prevent fraud and surprise in the enactment of laws.

Cites Nebraska Act.

Declaring the state legislature has the right to proscribe the curricula of the public schools, Attorney General Stewart took up each point in the motion of the defense to quash the indictment and combatted them vigorously. He maintained that the indictment against Scopes was legal; that the act was not unconstitutional, and as such within the right of the state legislature.

"If the state legislature is not to control the public schools, who shall?" he questioned.

Mr. Stewart quoted the following from the so-called Nebraska case, as found in the United States Supreme court reporter:

"The power of the state to compel attendance at some school and to make reasonable regulations for all schools, including a requirement that they shall give instructions in English is not questioned. Nor has challenge been made of the state's power to prescribe a curriculum for instructions which it supports. Those matters are not within the present controversy."

Mr. Darrow began his argument speaking slowly. He referred briefly to the points of the compass from which the case had drawn counsel.

"Within limitations, the legislature has the right to determine what shall be taught in the public schools," he said.

"Back a number of years ago when people were free, the people of Tennessee wrote a constitution. They made it broad and said that the people should enjoy religious freedom.

"Would Destroy Learning."

"There is not a single line of any constitution that can withstand bigotry. Here we find today as brazen and bold an attempt to destroy learning as was made in the middle ages.

"If these proceedings in form and substance can prevail in this section, then any law, no matter how ignorant or foolish, can be made to prevail. All the guarantees have gone for nothing. It is absolutely absurd to think that this patent indictment or any of the proceedings in this case are legal.

"I think the sooner we get rid of it in Tennessee the better for the state. Let us begin at the beginning. The first point we made in this statute is that it is unconstitutional on account of the difference between the caption and the act.

"All the people don't read the laws. Everything that is in an act should be embodied in the caption. Of course, the caption may be broader than the act, but the substance of the act must be in the caption."

He then read the caption, stressing the portion "an act to prevent the teaching of the evolution theory."

"There isn't a word said in the statute in reference to the evolution theory," he continued. "The caption says nothing about the Bible or the divine account of the creation.

"If a person was interested in the right to worship God as he saw fit, he would find out that chaos and riot would follow in the wake of this bill.

No Actual Conflict.

"The intelligent Christian citizens in this country find no conflict between religion and the theory of evolution.

"Is there anything in this caption about religion, or about science, literature and religion? They went to bed in peace, probably, after reading this caption, and woke up to find this work of bigotry

"This is as plain an instance of religious bigotry as any instance of the Spanish inquisition."

Darrow then took up the act itself, reading it and stressing the words "to teach any theory of the origin of man except that contained in the divine account as taught in the bible."

"That was what was forced upon the people under a caption which never meant it. The state of Tennessee has no more right to assume that the bible account of the creation is correct than it has to assume that of the Koran or Confucianism or any one of a dozen is the correct one.

"If the courts of Tennessee stand behind their own constitution these gentlemen will have to arrange their cohorts and go back.

"Of all the weird, impossible you shall not? No, No. It simply says you shall not teach any theory of the creation that is contrary to the divine theory. No legislature in any state in the union is strong enough to say what is divine.

"What is the bible? In a general way, I know what it is. I know that there are millions of people in the world who look on it as the divine book. God. I would be the last one in the world to take any action to take it away. I feel just exactly the same of any other religious creeds.

"Instead of fighting each other as in the past, the peoples of the different religions should help each other."

He then took up a discussion of the different theories of the origin of man, which he said a man must consider before he would know what he could teach. The bill, he said, does not say what a man cannot teach.

"It only says that he must not teach anything conflicting with the bible."

"Who is the chief mogul," he queried, "who can tell us just what the bible means? He ought to write a book and tell us all about it. Different sects have been disagreeing over it through the ages. If Mr. Scopes is to be indicted because he taught a wrong theory of the origin of life, why not tell him what he must teach?

"Nothing like that was ever known until the fundamentalists made their brave charge upon the intelligence of the people of Tennessee.

"Now, let's look at this indictment, If this is a good one, then I have seen one.

"Scopes is here because the fundamentalists are after everybody who thinks. He is here because ignorance and bigotry have combined. But the state must tell him why he is here by indictment.

"After the shooting is all over here and Scopes has paid his fine, some one may indict him all over again. One thing I have never been able to account for is the hatred and venom of some people of very little religious convictions."

Re-reading the indictment, Darrow declared the place the crime was committed was not defined in the bill or what doctrine he taught that was in conflict with the divine account.

Ridicules Indictment.

The defense attorney then went into detail concerning the technical phrasing of the document, subjecting it to ridicule and speaking with scathing sarcasm.

"You might just as well indict a man for being no good," he said.

"This legislation and all similar legislation that human malice can concoct is void because of sections 13, 12 and 3 (of the constitution).

"Section 12 provides that the state shall protect science, literature and learning. I want to say that the construction the attorney general gave to that section is correct.

"The state by constitution has permitted the doctrine of education. I presume that when it is committed to education, it means the teaching of the truth. That indicates the policy of the state of Tennessee.

"But we insist that this statute is absolutely void because it conflicts with the right to worship freely.

"If this section of the constitution of Tennessee cannot be sustained in the spirit, it cannot be sustained in the letter. Free minds don't think alike. Of course they may be caught in a trap by the fundamentalists. But if they are free, they may go together along some lines, but certainly will conflict along others.

Religion Causes Hatred.

"Nothing else has caused the difference of opinion, the hatred and cruelty that religion has caused. There are more than five hundred sects and creeds of the Christian religion. No act should ever be passed to interfere with complete religious liberty.

"A great per cent of the intelligent people of Tennessee are evolutionists. They had not thought it necessary to give up their church because they believed that things had not been formed in a unit, but that they had evolved through various stages until they had reached their present stage.

"And then this bill is forced upon them by the fundamentalists. It is a travesty upon language and constitution to say that any citizen of Tennessee shall be tied down by this statute.

"Your life and mine and the life of every American citizen depends upon the tolerance of his fellowmen. If men cannot live and let live, no man's life is safe.

"Where is the man wise enough to make people go to heaven if they don't want to do it?"

"The legislature has the right to say what shall be taught in the public schools within limits. But they certainly cannot say that everyone must believe in the Bible account of creation. How is it that the caption of a bill can make it a criminal offense to teach evolution and the body of the act an offense to teach something else? How does this come under the police powers of the state?

"The laws must be uniform, otherwise they would be passing laws against Congregationalists, Unitarians or almost anyone."

S. K. Hicks, speaking for the state, cited the case of Lieper vs. the state and quoted a supreme count decision:

"We are of the opinion that the legislature under the constitutional provision may as well establish a uniform system of criminal laws and courts to execute them."

Two grounds existed, he said, under which the legislature might have passed the act if they thought the teaching of evolution harmful to the children of the state, under the police power vested in the state. Or, he said, the question of harmful influence might not enter and the schools could be regulated under the inherent powers vested in the state aside from its police power.

**

Crowds Jam Courtroom As Scopes Trial Proceeds

WISDOM OF LAW WON'T CONCERN SCOPES' JUDGE

Court Declares for a Non-political Decision.

Dayton, Tenn., July 13 (A.P.)—John T. Raulston, presiding at the Scopes trial here today, gave his conceptions of the necessary qualifications of a judge in an interview granted two newspaper reporters.

"In the maintenance of the republican form of government it is essential that powers be distributed in legislative, judicial and executive departments," he said.

"The judicial department has no concern as to the motives, wisdom or policy of statutes, therefore it should be absolutely nonpolitical. No person should be elevated to judicial office because of his political affiliation or partisan activities.

"Fitness and temperament, legal attainments and character should be paramount in the selection of all judicial officers.

"Speaking more in detail, a judge should be industrious, patient, conscientious, courageous and firm. He should be well grounded in the fundamentals of the law and his character should be absolute and superlative.

"In the very nature of things, there can be no such combination as a dishonest individual and an honest judge in the same personality. The standards of dishonesty and those of integrity are too inconsistent and incompatible to coinhabit the same mind.

"A judge should begin all investigations with an open mind and should never hastily and rashly rush to conclusions.

"So long as there is any question of either law or fact in doubt he should diligently inquire for the truth.

"No judge should use the functions of his office for his individual advantage and to the detriment of the public. He should always remember that he is merely a trustee and that the powers and privileges of the office do not belong to him and are not subject to personal appropriation.

"A judge should divest himself of all prejudice, suppress all passion within and have one purpose and one only, and that is to find the truth and to declare justice."

**

Dayton, Tenn. has put a special ban on bootleggers during the Scopes trial. Probably afraid somebody might be seeing blue and yellow monkeys before the hearing is ended.

**

WHAT IS INVOLVED.

The Tennessee assembly, a body of average citizens, decides that evolution is not to be taught in the state schools; it outlaws evolution; and the point arises at once: if the assembly can outlaw evolution from the curriculum, it can outlaw anything else. And more: if it can outlaw certain specified subjects, it can enforce others. It can throw out a scientific theory, and it can bring in another theory in its place. It can make it a misdemeanor to teach one theory in order that the theory favored by the assembly may hold the field free from competition in the schools. It is therefore plain that the truth or error of the subjects taught is not involved in this trial. What is involved is the question whether the subjects taught have the approval of the state assembly. The legislators have decided evolution shall not be taught: it would be ridiculous to assume any competency in the Tennessee legislators to decide on the scientific merits of evolution: simply, they don't like it, and they won't have it in the schools they pay for, so out it goes, and those who teach it are liable to a fine. Later on the assembly may decide that the Copernican solar theory is subversive of Tennessee morals and forbid it (in) their schools too; they may decide that the law of gravitation is not for Tennessee and expel it from their colleges: and they may decide that the earth is flat, that the moon stands still, that matter is solid and that energy is lost, and insist on all this being taught in the science classes of their public schools. And it is this positive side of the question that is the most interesting. Because if the Tennessee anti-evolution law be sus-

Members of the Jury that were seleceted in the first three hour session of Court.

The Courtroom in which the trial is proceeding. Every seat in the room was filled and Spectators crowded the corridors.

tained by the courts it brings not only education, but knowledge itself right into politics at one step. If the state legislatures can decide what is to be taught, then it is politicians, and not scholars, who will set the course of studies, with ultimate consequences which might be both remarkable and curious. —Editorial in Winnipeg Free Press.

**

THE TENNESSEE LAW

"Section 1. Be it enacted by the general assembly of the state of Tennessee that it shall be unlawful for any teacher, in any of the universities, normals and other public schools of the state, which are supported in whole or in part by the public school funds of the state, to teach any theory that denies 'the story of the divine creation of man as taught in the Bible, and to teach instead that man descended from a lower order of animals.'"

Since that is the actual wording of the Tennessee law that John T. Scopes is accused of violating, and since public interest in the trial is undeniably great, it may as well be got(ten) accurate in mind by those who are following the news developments.

In a long statement issued on his own responsibility by John C. Cantrill, president of the Chattanooga Bar association, the whole trial is deprecated as rather an affront to the dignity of the Tennessee bar. Cantrill emphasizes that the "so-called evolution law" is very "narrow in its scope," says the only teaching it really prohibits is the teaching that man descended from a lower order of animals, insists that practically everything in the theory of evolution can be taught with impunity in the state without crossing this law, and roasts the defense for making a national fuss over it.

One paragraph from Cantrill's statement gives the temper as well as the drift:

"The act was unnecessary, but probably entirely harmless. Any teacher who has the sense of a sapsucker, ought to be able to teach evolution freely without the ancestry of man beyond the missing link and without teaching, as a fact, that man is descended from an ape, monkey, jackass or any other lower animal. The fact of such a descent of man is not an essential part of the great theory or doctrine of evolution, and I can see no reason why all the essentials of biology, geology, botany, nature history and other kindred sciences and theories cannot be taught without assuming and teaching as a fact that man is descended from some prehistoric ape."

If that means anything, it means that teachers who are half way clever can safely teach nearly everything there is in the evolutionary theory and can even circumvent the specific prohibition by letting inference do the work. While the president of the Chattanooga Bar association is quite likely right in his point that, despite its far more general caption, the law as it stands prohibits little and that little not very effectively, his statement seems primarily that of a man who wishes there were no such law on the book and who, since it is there, would put the best face on it.

As a defense of Tennessee, which is the real spirit of his statement, it is weak in that it too much minimizes the major point at issue, which is not whether the evolutionary theory is correct or even whether the theory of man's descent from lower forms is correct, but which is rather whether a state should decide by law what part of current scientific thought shall be permitted to reach the minds of the people.

Wednesday, July 15, 1925
The Des Moines Register

Scopes Judge Threatens Reporter With Contempt

ORDERS PROBE OF NEWS LEAK ON HIS DECISION

Premature Publication of Ruling Delays Swearing in Jury.

Dayton, Tenn., July 14 (By The Associated Press)—The third day of the Scopes evolution trial ended amid stormy scenes late this afternoon without the jury having been sworn in and before Judge John T. Raulston had announced his decision on the defense motion to quash the indictment.

"It was a stormy day," the judge remarked as he left the bench.

A moment earlier, he had warned news reporters of possible contempt of court proceedings because of publication of stories intimating the judge would deny the defense motion to quash. A committee of newspaper men was appointed to investigate the premature publication.

A statement from a correspondent of the International News Service was heard by the committee and it announced it would report to the judge tomorrow.

Storm Breaks.

The storm occurred at the end of a long, hot day of waiting to response to the defense's attempt to end the trial by establishing the unsoundness of the indictment and the unconstitutionality of the Tennessee anti-evolution statute. The law in question says that public school instructors shall teach no theory of evolution which denies the biblical story of man's creation.

When the judge at length entered the courtroom after a recess of hours which he employed in writing his decision, he was met before he could make any announcement by the filing of a defense motion asking that the morning prayer be discontinued.

In addition, the motion asked and supported its request with a signed petition from churchmen outside Rhea county, that if the prayer opening should be continued the court permit some minister of beliefs other than those of fundamentalists to lead the devout appeal.

In filing this motion, Arthur G. Hays, for the defense, was interrupted by the objection of Attorney General Stewart who declared that court at this stage was not an assembly met for the purpose of hearing a motion.

Wordy Battle Ensues.

The prosecution's objection was interrupted by Dudley Field Malone, defense lawyer, and a sharp exchange of words flew between the two.

The court restored order after a period of uproar and announced he would refer the petition to the Dayton Ministerial association with the request that this body choose the clergyman who should lead the daily prayer. The crowd applauded.

At this juncture the court announced he would not publish his decision on the quashing motion until tomorrow, explaining he had been informed that certain news reporters or services had presumed to forecast the tenor of his ruling and had dispatched news reports to this effect. Declaring that if it should be established that the privacy of the court had been violated he would immediately institute contempt of court proceedings against the accused persons. Judge Raulston called for a conference of representatives of the press and dismissed the court session overnight.

Names Probe Committee.

In the conference which followed immediately, Judge Raulston repeated his assertion and appointed a committee of five reporters.

Judge Raulston previous to naming the committee of investigation explained that the delay in making his decision of the motion to quash was due to a report he had received that newspaper reporters had "sought to anticipate" the nature of his ruling.

The committee of five newspaper reporters composed of Richard Beamish, Philadelphia Inquirer; Forest Davis, New York Herald-Tribune; Philip Kinsley, Chicago Tribune; Earl Shaub, Universal Service, and Tony Muto, New York Evening Bulletin, immediately went into conference.

Hear Accused Correspondent.

The correspondent of the International News Service appeared before this committee. The committee heard his statement and announced tonight it would submit its report to Judge Raulston tomorrow morning.

The issue over opening of court with prayer appeared at the beginning of today's sessions when Judge Raulston invited Rev. A. C. Stribling, pastor of the Dayton Cumberland Presbyterian church, to offer prayer from the bench before the gavel announced the beginning of the official session.

Prayer had been offered by a Methodist minister on opening of court Friday, the first day. The jury then had not been selected. Yesterday a Baptist minister led the prayer, the jurors, unsworn, sitting in their courtroom seats. This morning as the invitation was made and the court and spectators were directed to stand, the jurymen had not entered.

As the crowd rose, Clarence Darrow held up an objecting finger and addressed the court. He told Judge Raulston that the defense wished to protest against the public court prayer because it might prejudice the case of John T. Scopes in the minds of the jury and the court.

"I object to turning this court into a meeting house," the Chicago attorney declared.

Attorney General Stewart, speaking for the state, asserted it was the custom of the Rhea county court to open with a prayer; the people around this section were a God-fearing peoples, and insisted that the practice be uninterrupted.

Mr. Malone protested:

"I would have you know that the people of my part of the country are just as God-fearing as any in any part of the country."

After some confusion, Mr. Malone formally supported Mr. Darrow's contention. He expressed deep concern for the "beliefs or disbeliefs" of Mr. Darrow and added:

"As a representative of defense counsel who is not an agnostic I wish to protest against the court opening with prayer. We have talked it over in conference and agree that such a practice is prejudicial to the case of our client. All the ministers who have prayed here have been fundamentalists and much of their prayers have been of an argumentative nature."

Overrules Objection.

Judge Raulston wished to be "reasonable" toward all parties. He believed in prayer and practiced it himself. He overruled the objection of the defense and Mr. Stribling led the prayer.

Mr. Darrow then asked that the court permit the record to show that he entered the same objection daily. The court replied that the record would show the objection daily and show that it had been overruled in each instance.

Mr. Darrow had been expected to continue his address of yesterday in support of the motion of the defense to quash the indictment, on the grounds of vagueness in the indictment and unconstitutionality of the anti-evolution law. He told Judge Raulston he would not continue.

The court announced he wished to deliver his ruling on the motion to quash "after fair consideration of the profound issues involved and without guessing." He had been unable to finish the transcript of his decision and to give him time to complete the document he declared a recess until 1 o'clock.

Shortly after the hour set for reassembling, a court attendant reported that the judge would not return until 2:30. At that time, Judge Raulston appeared and told the packed throngs which kept their places throughout the afternoon that he was not yet ready.

Warns Newspaper Men.

He warned newspaper men that his ruling could not legitimately be published until he himself read it from the judicial eminence. He would institute contempt proceedings against any who announced his ruling before the court should declare it.

Throughout the long period of waiting to know the will of the court on the quash motion a great throng packed the Rhea county courtroom. It was freely predicted on all sides that the judge would return a ruling favorable to the prosecution.

When shortly before 4 o'clock Judge Raulston pushed his way through the masses of humanity at the door, he gained his seat with difficulty.

The excitement, steadily growing through the hot afternoon hours had become acute. Spectators, photographers and reporters filled the railed area around the judicial bench and some minutes elapsed before the uniformed deputies enforced the rule of quiet. Mr. Hays, defense attorney, gained the court's attention.

Presents Prayer Petition.

"Before your honor presents a decision or the proceedings go farther," began Mr. Hays, "may I present a petition to the court?

"'We, the following named representatives of various well known religious organizations, churches, synagogues, do hereby petition your honor that, if you continue your custom of opening the daily sessions of the court with prayer . . ."

Mr. Stewart interrupted, addressing himself to the court, and protested that "this is absolutely out of order." Here the record of the proceedings reads:

"General Stewart: "This is not an assembly met for any purpose of hearing a motion of that sort, or anything of that sort, your honor has passed on the motion.'

"Mr. Hays: 'I am making my exception to the court. Will you please keep your mouth shut.'

"General Stewart: 'I am making my exception to the court.'

"The court: "I will hear it.'

"General Stewart: 'It is entirely out of order. And I except to it with all the vehemence of my natures.'

"The court: 'I will hear it: proceed, Mr. Hays.'"

Mr. Hays then proceeded to continue reading of the petition which asked that if the court continued the custom of opening with prayer that "you select the officiating clergymen from among other than fundamentalist churches in alternation with fundamentalist clergymen."

Defense Files Motion.

With this petition Mr. Hays filed the following motion for the defense:

"While preserving our exception to the opening of court by prayer, and without waiving the same and renewing that objection, we move this court that if prayers are to be made, this petition be granted and that on some occasions the prayers be made by men who think that God has shown his divinity in the wonders of the world, in the book of nature, quite as much as in the book of the revealed word."

The petition of the visiting clergymen was referred by Judge Raulston to the Dayton Ministerial association with this comment:

"I shall ask the pastors' association from now on to name the man who is to conduct prayer. I shall have no voice, make no suggestion as to whom they name, but I will invite the man named by the association to conduct the prayer each morning."

The spectators applauded when Judge Raulston referred the petition to the ministerial association.

Names on the petition included Rabbi Jerome Mark, Temple Bethel, Knoxville; Rev. Daniel Welsh, First Unitarian church, Knoxville.

Asked to Alternate.

The petition presented to the court follows:

"To the Honorable Judge John T. Raulston, presiding judge, Rhea county court, Dayton, Tenn,:

"We, the following named representatives of various well known churches and synagogs, do hereby petition your honor that if you continue your custom of opening the daily sessions of court of Rhea county with prayer, you select the officiating clergymen from among other than fundamentalist churches in alternation with fundamentalist clergymen.

"We beg you to consider the fact that among the persons intimately connected with and actively participating in this trial of Mr. John T. Scopes, there are many to whom the prayers of fundamentalists are not spiritually uplifting and are occasionally offensive. Inasmuch as by your own ruling all the people in the courtroom are required to participate in the prayers by rising, it seems to us only just and right that we should occasionally hear a prayer which requires no mental reservations on our part and in which we can conscientiously participate.

(Signed)

"Rev. Charles Francis Potter, minister West Side Unitarian church, New York.

"Rabbi Jerome Mark, Bethel temple, Knoxville, Tenn.

"Rev. D. M. Welch, Knoxville, Unitarian church.

"Rev. Fred W. Hagen, First Congregational church, Huntington, W. Va."

Famous Chicago lawer, stripped of his coat, as he consults with judge Raulston about the procedure of Tennessee Courts.

Apologized for Sharp Words.

Mr. Stewart met Mr. Hays on the street tonight and apologized to the New York lawyer for his sharp retort in the courtroom.

"I am sorry that I spoke as I did," the attorney general said. "I spoke hastily and I ask your pardon."

Mr. Hays grasped the proffered hand of the state's attorney and readily accepted the apology. Mr. Malone also shook hands with Mr. Stewart and they parted in good humor when Mr. Malone said:

"We consider you an embodiment of courtesy."

Attorneys expected Judge Raulston to announce his ruling on the motion to quash at the court opening tomorrow. The procedure thereafter if the motion is denied, will be to swear in the jury, arraign the defendant and receive his plea, and to call in witnesses to support the contention of the state that Professor Scopes violated the Tennessee statute.

Ten or more high school pupils, members of Mr. Scopes' classes of the recent session of the Dayton school, have been summoned by the state and are expected to give their testimony tomorrow, unless further motions by counsel delay the routine.

**

What do YOU think?

Bible Reporting

Mason City, Ia.—To the Editor: It looks like common folks are going to get some mixed over this evolution talk. The editorial of the Winnipeg Free Press, which you recently reproduced, reads in part: "The anti-evolutionists accept the Bible as the true source of information about the origin of life." I know I am ignorant, but I had an idea that the evolution question was not about how life started, but rather a guess at the origin of many varieties of species into which life has been diversified. Again, the Canuc quotes a passage from the book of Joshua, and cites it in proof of the following statement, "This Bible theory about the solar system is the direct opposite of the Copernican theory that the earth and the planets revolve around the sun." I wonder how he gets that way? The passage is not a statement of doctrine at all, but a reportorial story of a certain event, given in the language of the hoi polloi just exactly what the news reporters of today are doing, using the same language, and the same identical unscientific statements as that old-time war correspondent.

I would wager a little money that in the same edition of the paper that carried the editorial, there was printed in some connection, such definite statements as the "sun rose," or the "sun set." Running such positive assertions, it could not object to a fifty-fifty treatment with its own interpretation of the Bible, which would give anyone the right to say that the Winnipeg Free Press "teaches the direct opposite of the Copernican theory."

I believe the Bible teaches the truth, scientific or otherwise, but is handicapped because it has to use a language a fool like me can savvy.
W. L. Richardson

**

Where the Fundamentalist Fails.

To the Editor: We often hear people say, "I believe everything the bible says." Such persons deceive themselves. Nobody believes—nobody can believe—everything the bible says; to do so would be to believe one thing and the exact opposite of that thing at the same time. You cannot believe that it is, both midday and midnight at the same time in the same place.

To anyone who says he believes all the bible, I would say: Read the twenty-eighth chapter of Matthew, the sixteenth chapter of Mark, the twenty-fourth of Luke, the twentieth of John, all of which contain accounts of the resurrection. Note that all of contradict one another in their statement of facts. It is impossible to believe all of them. Read these four chapters and analyze them, and you will be compelled to admit that you can not believe everything the bible says.

Or read the first chapter of Genesis and the second chapter of Genesis. Compare the two. You will find that they contradict each other—not on a question of doctrine, which might be variously interpreted, but on a question of fact, which can not be misunderstood.

Evolution or no evolution, the fundamentalist is the champion of a lost cause. The bible contains conclusive proof of its own fallibility.
Charles B. Holloway.

**

"Perfect" Man Sinned.

Colfax, Ia.—To the Editor: In Mr. Bryan's third speech on evolution, Washington, D.C., he says: "The moment you put education above religion, you put the machine above the master who controls it." But it seems that Mr. Bryan fails to ask if the machine fails to function who is to blame, the machine or its maker? Mr. Bryan's idea is only a belief for which there can be no positive evidence produced.
L. E. C. Vernocom.

**

An Extreme Evolutionist.

Colfax, Ia.—To the Editor: My critic at Mitchellville, asks the question if man evolved from the monkey—where did the monkey come from or who created the monkey? This is a mystery never to be solved: but is it not as great a mystery as if God created the monkey—who created God? I heard a man deliver what he called a lecture, and his first attempt was to prove that there is a God. He said all things had a designer, and at the conclusion of his disclosures he invited questions. The question was asked if all things had a designer, God being a mighty big thing in the eyes of many people, who designed him? Now if there is a God he must be something. Hence the question is just as good in one case as the other, how did God or the monkey come into existence? Evolution is a known fact: the God idea is just a belief which no man knows with certainty. L. E. C. Vernocom

**

Are the Schools for Learning?

To the Editor: It is a real revelation the attitude folks are taking on the Tennessee school case. That the law will finally be declared unconstitutional is a foregone conclusion. The Tennessee legislature erred in passing the law—they should have passed the buck to the school board or some other "it"—the people erred in not being careful to elect school heads and teachers who would represent them as they wished. The "monkeyologist director" is now filling up faster than it otherwise would.

Evolution is unquestionably correct in other spheres, but, it just won't hold water when it comes to man. Teaching evolution to immature minds is about as inconsistent as teaching trigonometry to early graders, and the way evolution is taught is nothing short of a major offense. W. H. Boesrup.

Thursday, July 16, 1925
The Des Moines Register

State Rests With Brief Evidence in Scopes Trial

BEGIN BATTLE OVER EVIDENCE OF SCIENTISTS

Excuse Jury Until Court Rules Upon Testimony of Defense Experts.

Dayton, Tenn., July 15 (By The Associated Press)—Argument as to the competency of scientific testimony in the case of John T. Scopes, accused of violating the state anti-evolution law, will be made in the courtroom here tomorrow. The state had rested its case and one scientific witness, Dr. Maynard M. Metcalf, former professor of zoology at Oberlin college, O., was on the witness stand for the defense when court adjourned late today.

His testimony, however, has not been made a part of the record, for prosecution attorneys voiced objection when questions concerning evolution were asked him and the jury was retired.

Defense attorneys then were permitted to ask Dr. Metcalf questions concerning the subject he has made his life study.

Judge Keeps Own Counsel.

When his examination has been completed the attorneys will argue the competency of such testimony. Whether the court would give his decision at once or defer it to a later court day was not known. Judge John T. Raulston said tonight he has abandoned his practice of answering questions.

Dr. Metcalf's testimony will be heard in the absence of the jury as test to show the line along which the defense hopes to proceed and to which emphatic objection is made by the state. Every indication pointed to a hard fight before the court on the question.

The defense hopes to prove by Dr. Metcalf and other scientific scholars there is no conflict between evolution theories and Christianity. One of the questions asked the witness this afternoon concerned his church affiliations. He testified he is now a member of the Congregationalist church and formerly was a member of the Presbyterian church. He has taught two bible classes, he said.

Case Moves Rapidly.

SCOPES AND HIS COUNSEL

The case moved rapidly after reaching the stage of actual testimony. The first witness took his place on the stand at the second session of the fourth court day.

The more or less neglected jury was brought into the courtroom after an extended period of exclusion. A plea of "not guilty" was entered for Scopes by one of his attorneys, the jury was sworn and at last was actually a part of the case.

The jurymen heard Walter White, superintendent of schools, and F. E. Robinson, chairman of the board of education, testifying for the state. They saw a "civic biology" by George W. Hunter and a bible introduced in evidence.

The state rested and the defense called Dr. Metcalf as its first witness. No objection came from Atty. Gen. A. T. Stewart as the witness was led through a detailed account of his scientific activities since he was 10 years of age.

Question Admissibility.

At the first mention of "evolution" objection came from the state as to the admissibility of such testimony.

It was finally agreed to exclude the jury, permit the witness to answer questions and then argue the competency of his testimony.

The jury retired, but not until Capt. J. R. Thompson, one of the most striking figures on the jury and a former United States marshal, had taken occasion to defend his fellow jurors against the suspicion that they might loiter about the grounds and hear the argument from amplifiers scattered about the lawn.

The court issued a gentle warning to the jurymen to leave the grounds. Captain Thompson, in emphatic language, declared that a suggestion that any juryman at any time had been a long distance listener to argument or discussion in the courtroom was without foundation in fact. The court took occasion to express its full confidence in the integrity of the jury.

Dr. Metcalf told of his years of study and work as a teacher of zoology. He recounted his degrees and connections in scientific research. After this detail Clarence Darrow asked:

"Are you an evolutionist?"

Admits He's Evolutionist.

"Surely," replied the witness, as the attorney general seemed about to interpose an objection.

"Do you know any scientific men who are not evolutionists?" was Mr. Darrow's next question and Mr. Stewart's objection was in this time before an answer could be made.

The court instructed the witness to whisper his answer to the court stenographer and admonished that court attaché not to permit the press to get it. The answer was whispered and entered in the record.

Then Dr. Metcalf was asked to give his definition of evolution. The witness said that he was opposed to definitions but was willing to give descriptions. The question was finally lost in the shuffle, but after the jury had walked away, Mr. Darrow was ready with another.

"Will you state what evolution is in regard to the origin of man?"

Finally it was agreed that certain questions on evolution might be answered to furnish the basis for the discussion to follow before the court.

"Evolution," said Dr. Metcalf, "and the theories of evolution are fundamentally different things. The facts of evolution are all theory. There are theories of evolutions, some of which are largely mistaken and some almost wholly true.

"We are in possession of scientific knowledge to answer flatly that evolution has occurred. Evolution in its final analysis means change of an organism from one character to a different character. The change of an organism from one set of characteristics to a form having a different set of characteristics may be found, in general, to be evolution.

"Starting with the inorganic world, there has been a tremendous series of changes. The sun is comparatively young. The earth has gone through long courses of change. But in inorganic evolution we have to conceive earliest forms of life subsisting solely on inorganic food. Only plants can do that. No animal has been able to live solely on inorganic food.

"From the first living things developed whole series of forms in plant groups, gradually becoming more complex. These form a beautiful series as we study their bodies in the rocks.

Whole Series Extinct.

"I'm inclined to believe there may have been whole series of animals and plants in the earth completely wiped out. They were succeeded by other series of plants and animals on the earth. The evidence is insufficient to determine when the first life appeared. Geologists measure ages not in years and I am not an expert in that line. I would say 600,000,000 years is amongst ages.

Alongside of plants whole series of animals were developing. Animals hustle to get their food and therefore developed locomotive organs. Plants have not. It is not so easy to tell the order in which the plants evolved as to tell about this change in the higher animals. In plants there is a series of increasing perplexities.

"Animal life and plant life probably began at the border line between the water and the land. A long period in early life all living things were marine. When terrestrial life began conditions were more difficult and needs to meet these difficulties of existence have been the occasion of developing conditions to supply these needs. Considerable portions of life on the land have gone back to the sea."

Describes a Mammal.

Dr. Metcalf in describing a mammal said hair developed or rudimentary is a feature and that mammals also suckle their young. They have a vertebral column and two pairs of limbs which always have a shoulder or hip girdle.

Man was classed among the primates. He was not so highly developed in his body as some other animals. His hand was not so skillful as the claw of a bird. Primates included monkeys, tailed or tailless, man and others of which fossil forms had been found.

Fundamental proofs of evolution were found not in man so much as in lower animals. Various proofs found throughout the universe made a tremendous probability in favor of evolution of man.

"The series of proofs are so convincing that any informed man cannot doubt the probability of man's evolution," Dr. Metcalf concluded for the day.

Before Dr. Metcalf could finish examination Judge Raulston ordered an adjournment until 9 o'clock tomorrow morning when it was expected that the former Oberlin professor would continue his expert testimony, which is not yet admitted. The court is to pass on its competency later.

The witnesses, five school boys, F. E. Robinson and Walter White were sworn in en masse. Scopes was not sworn. The action came after Gen. Ben T. McKenzie had again voiced a protest to Dudley Field Malone's outline.

Mr. White, the prosecutor, was the first witness to take the stand. Walter White is superintendent of Rhea county public schools. He said Scopes had told him he could not teach biology without violating the anti-evolution law and that the law was unconstitutional. This statement was made during a conversation between George W. Rappleyea and White, the witness testified.

"He admitted he had taught the theory of evolution as expounded in the text of Hunter's biology and said that he could not teach the book without violating the law," White said.

Introduce Text Books.

The attorney general then announced his intention of introducing a biological textbook and a bible into the evidence. This brought a vigorous protest from Arthur Garfield Hays of the defense, who declared that the prosecution must prove what was the theory of the creation taught in the bible before they could hope to convince Scopes.

"Where in the law do you find that the prosecution must prove that Scopes violated the law by teaching a theory in conflict with the King James version of the bible?" he asked, declaring there were several different versions of the bible.

"Must they not call some one to the witness stand to prove what the bible is?" he asked. He cited several cases in an effort to prove his contentions.

"I am well aware that in the state of Tennessee as well as in other states of the union," Hays continued, " that the court takes judicial notice of the bible. But he does not take judicial notice of the Bible when it is an issue before the jury."

"This is a criminal statute and must be strictly construed," he argued. "They present a book to your honor with perfect assurance. We object to the admission into the evidence of the bible and are prepared to show that the King James version is only one of a half dozen versions of the bible."

The objections were overruled, exceptions were taken, and Mr. Darrow arose to address the judge.

After a brief argument between the defense attorney and the attorney general, the state resumed its examination of the witness. After one question which brought a reiteration of previous testimony, the witness was turned over to the defense for cross-examination.

Darrow brought out first the fact that the book was the official text book adopted by the Tennessee text book commission and that Scopes taught it because it was the official book at that time.

"You never said anything to him about it or to any other teacher, did you?" asked the attorney.

"No, I had no instructions to do so," the witness replied.

The witness said he was 14 years old and had attended the Rhea county high schools last year receiving instructions in science from the defendant. In April of this year, he said, he was studying the text book in evidence with Scopes as the teacher.

Some times the teacher would ask the students questions and again he would deliver lectures, the witness said.

About the second of April, witness said, he taught that animal life evolved from a one-celled animal which eventually became man.

Life Came From Germ.

This theory, the boy said, the teacher had taught by relating that man in the beginning came from a germ which through the evolutionary process came up on dry land as a living cell. He, as well as the book, classified man in the same category with cats, dogs and other mammals, the boy said. Cross-examined by Clarence Darrow, the youth said he had not been taught what a mammal was. The cross-examination conducted in the slow drawl of Darrow, evoked laughter several times.

"Did he tell you anything else that was wicked?" he asked.

The boy slowly shook his head and answered in the negative.

Shown one of the textbooks, the boy read a list of mammals, including monkey and man. Darrow then read an excerpt from the chapter on mammals, relating the method by which mammals feed their young and some outstanding examples, which ended with the classification, "monkey and man."

Relating to the evolutionary process told of by the students as that taught by Scopes, the attorney spoke of the molten mass which once formed the earth, of how it cooled and how the life first existed in a seed, gradually evolving into a man. He was followed by Harry Shelton, a biology student, who testified that Scopes taught that life first existed in a cell. Few questions were asked by the state before the student went to Darrow for cross-examination.

Shelton said he only remembered that the teacher had said life came from one cell.

"You didn't leave the church when he told you that, did you?" the examiner asked.

"No, sir."

Robinson Testifies.

F. E. Robinson, proprietor of the drug store in which the argument leading to the test case took place, next told of a conversation with Scopes about May 4 or 5 in which the defendant said that any teacher in the state who was teaching Hunter's biology was violating the law, and admitted he was teaching it, and had reviewed the entire book since the passage of the law.

He also said that no teacher could teach science in any of the books published without violating the law.

He identified a page of the book in evidence as one from which Scopes had admitted he taught. Attorney General Stewart brought out the fact that Robinson was chairman of the county school board.

Darrow on cross-examination brought out the testimony that Robinson, chairman of the school board, was selling the text book.

Darrow read the page in the biology detailing the evolutionary theory and defining evolution as "a change."

Darrow next read a chapter entitled "Man's place in nature."

The attorney general, as Darrow seemed about to complete his examination of the witness, read the first two chapters of Genesis into the record. The defense attorney listened with a cynical smile.

When court convened at 9 o'clock this morning, Judge Raulston denied the motion of the defense to quash the indictment against Scopes. The judge's decision upheld the constitutionality of the Tennessee anti-evolution law.

Discusses Discrepancy.

Discussing the alleged discrepancy between the caption of the act and the body of the bill itself Judge Raulston said:

"The general title to the act is broad and comprehensive and covers all legislation germane to the general subject stated. The title may cover more than the body but it must not cover less. It need not index the details of the act, nor give a synopsis thereof."

In this particular case, he said, the caption of the act provided that purpose of the act is to prohibit the teaching of evolutionary subjects in the public schools of the state.

"It is true that this provision is rather general in its nature," he said, "and in my conception or the terms employed in the caption and body, those used in the caption are broader and more ployed in the body of the act, but in my opinion the caption covers all the legislation provided for in the body and is germane thereto, and in no way obscures the legislation provided for."

Rules Caption Comprehensive.

"In my judgment, the caption is sufficient to put any member of the legislature on notice as to what the nature of the proposed legislation is and that the caption is really more comprehensive than the body of the act."

The second point alleging a violation of the constitutional provision of the state, he passed over with a brief statement of the law, since the point had not been pressed by the defense.

The next, a purely technical point, charging the bill had not been read a sufficient number of times in the two houses of the legislature before its enactment also was dismissed with a simple reading of the constitutional provision.

Taking up the next phase, which alleged a violation of the constitutional right to worship God according to the dictates of the individual conscience, he declares he failed to see "how this act in any wise interferes or in the least wise restrains any person from worshipping God in the manner that pleaseth him. It gives no preference to any particular religion or mode of worship. Our public schools are not maintained as places of worship, but on the other hand, were designed, instituted and are maintained for the purpose of mental and moral development and discipline."

He also failed to see how the teachers' rights under the same provision of the state constitution were violated by the act since "there is no law in the state of Tennessee that undertakes to compel this defendant or any other citizen to accept employment in the public schools."

These relations, he said, are purely contractual "and if his conscience constrains him to teach the evolution theory, he can find opportunities elsewhere in other schools of the state. . . and give full expression to his beliefs and convictions upon this and other subjects without any interference from the state of Tennessee or its authorities.

No Restraint in Law.

"Neither do I see how the act lays any restraint on his right to worship according to the dictates of his conscience. Under the provisions of this act this defendant, or any other person can entertain any religious belief which most appeals to their conscience."

The alleged vagueness in the indictment, he held, did not exist, since it "substantially copies the word of the statute and therefore is sufficiently certain."

Weakness charged in the law in that there was an alleged discrimination against teachers as a class, he dismissed with a reading of a ruling by the state supreme court in which it was held that "class legislation which have applied equally to all that are in or that may come into the like situation and circumstances and which makes a reasonable and natural classification, is valid and constitutional."

As to Violation of Amendment.

Discussing the alleged violation of the fourteenth amendment to the constitution of the United States, Judge Raulston read a portion of the decision of the supreme court in the case of Meyer vs. the State of Nebraska, in which it was held that a state prohibiting the teaching of any language other than English to children was not in conflict with the fourteenth amendment.

Concluding he quoted from the ruling of the state supreme court in the Leeper case, generally cited as the outstanding authority in similar cases in the state of Tennessee. In this case it was held that the establishment and control of public schools is a function of the general assembly and that if the legislature deems proper it may abandon one plan and try another.

Uniform System Impossible.

In conclusion, he said: "It is further pertinently said that it is impossible to conceive the existence of an uniform system of public schools without powers lodged somewhere to make them uniform and in the absence of express constitutional provisions the power must necessarily reside in the legislature and hence it has the power to prescribe a course of study as well as the books to be used and how they shall be obtained and distributed.

"We find neither reason nor authority that suggests a doubt to the power of the legislature to require a designated series of books to be used in school.

"The rule prevailing in Tennessee by which the courts are governed in passing upon the constitutionality of statutes is this: The rule of construction that every intendment and presumption is in favor of the constitutionality of the statute and that every doubt must be solved so as to sustain it: and where it is subject to two constructions that which will sustain its constitutionality must be adopted.

"The court having passed on each ground chronologically and given the reasons therefore, is now pleased to overrule the whole motion, and require the defendant to plead further."

At the conclusion of the reading of the decision defense counsel noted an exception to the denial of the quashing motion and then filed a demurrer which embodied the same contention of the late motion to quash.

Potter Offers Prayer.

The Rev. Charles Francis Potter, pastor of the West Side Unitarian church, New York, today opened the John T. Scopes trial with prayer. Dr. Potter was called to the platform by the court after President Stribling of the Dayton Pastors' association had announced the name of the visiting minister as the choice of the association.

S. K. Hicks of state counsel, announced that the state denies that there is a religious controversy in the case and objected in behalf of the prosecution "to this heckling" every morning on the subject of prayer. He asked that the court stop the daily protest and place it in the record.

Judge Raulston said he had had no regard for denominational lines in selecting ministers for the morning prayer. He hoped, he said, that these prayers would "do some good." They will not hurt anyone and "may help."

Clarence Darrow noted an exception to the remarks of the court.

Attorney General Stewart was recognized to say that he had made a remark in court yesterday that he wished to withdraw. He had expressed himself in a discourteous manner to Mr. Hays of defense counsel, he said. "I feel very much ashamed that I have not been courteous to Mr. Hays, and there was nothing back of it but a little ruffled temper," he declared.

Mr. Hays rose to say that he was happy to accept the apology of the attorney general.

Hays asked that the state's attorneys avoid reference to the states from which the defense attorneys come and their religious beliefs.

John R. Neal asked the attorney general to then remove from the record a "sneering remark" alleged to have been made toward defense counsel.

Committee Makes Report.

Richard Beamish, chairman of the reportorial committee appointed to inquire into the premature publication yesterday of what purported to be the judge's decision on the motion to quash, reported that the correspondent did not get the decision from the court's stenographer and believed the information he sent out to be true.

The committee recommended that the correspondent be not removed from the court. Judge Raulston asked the source of the information and was told that it came from the court through deduction.

Judge Raulston asked who the correspondent was and Mr. Beamish reported that it was William K. Hutchinson of the International News Service. Mr. Hutchinson was asked to come before the court and Judge Raulston asked if he had a statement to make, explaining that he need not feel obliged to make a statement. Mr. Hutchinson said that he would prefer to make a statement to the court in chambers.

Mr. Beamish spoke up to say that Mr. Hutchinson was "thoroughly ethical." The court then announced that the newspaperman would be given a private audience.

The committee report was signed by four of the five members, Richard Beamish, Philadelphia Enquirer; Earl Schaub, Universal Service; Forrest Davis, New York Herald-Tribune, and Tony Muto, New York Evening Bulletins.

Philip Kinsley, Chicago Tribune, the fifth member, did not sign the report.

Judge Raulston announced tonight that he would take no further action in the matter. The announcement was made by Judge Raulston after a conference in chambers with the reporter.

Mr. Darrow addressed the court in reference to the attorney general's remarks about religious beliefs of members of defense counsel. He said he had no objection to anyone referring to him as an agnostic "for I'm an agnostic." Mr. Darrow objected, however, to reference to creeds and religious beliefs.

Mr. Stewart responded that he was ready to proceed without further reference to religious beliefs of attorneys.

**

Malone Says the Bible Must Be Kept Out of Scientific Field

DEFENSE VIEWS GOD AS SPIRIT AND IN TRUTH

Holds Divine Creation Matter of Faith

Courtroom, Dayton, Tenn., July 15 (By The Associated Press)—The "broad purpose" of defense counsel for John Thomas Scopes will be to prove that the bible is a work of religion which must be kept in the field of theology and not allowed to obtrude into the scientific field, Dudley Field Malone told the court late today in outlining the course to be pursued in the trial.

"The narrow purpose
of the defense will be to prove Scopes innocent of any violation of the Tennessee anti-evolution teaching statute.

Mr. Malone started speaking immediately after the attorney general had addressed the court for but a moment, telling them that the state simply would contend that the defendant was guilty of violating the Tennessee statute prohibiting the teaching of evolution in the public schools of the state.

Believe God a Spirit.

Mr. Malone, making the opening statement of the defense, opened his remarks with the declaration that "the defense believe that 'God is a spirit and they that worship him must worship him in spirit and in truth.'"

"The defendant, John T. Scopes has been indicted for the alleged violation of an act passed by the Tennessee legislature which prohibits the teaching of the evolution theory in all the universities, normal schools and public schools of Tennessee which may be supported in whole or in part by the public school funds of the state," he said.

Malone then read the first section of the act making it unlawful to teach in state schools "any theory that denies the story of divine creation of man as taught in the bible, and to teach instead that man descended from a lower order of animals."

After reading the second section, providing a penalty of not less than $100., nor more than $500. for each violation of the act, he declared that before the prosecution could convict Scopes of a violation of the act, the prosecution must prove first that Scopes taught a theory that denies the story of the divine creation of man as taught in the bible, and second, "that instead and in the place of this theory he taught that man is descended from a lower order of animals."

"The defense contends that to convict Scopes the prosecution must prove that Scopes not only taught the theory of evolution, but that he also, and at the same time, denied the theory of creation as set forth in the bible," he asserted.

"The defense contends the prosecution must prove that the defendant Scopes did these two things and that what he taught was a violation of the statute.

"Must Define Theory."

"We will prove that whether this statute be constitutional or unconstitutional, the defendant Scopes did not and could not violate it. We maintain that since the defendant Scopes has been indicted under a statute which prohibits the teaching of the evolutionary theory, the prosecution must prove as part of its case what evolution is.

"So that there shall be no misunderstanding and that no one shall be able to misinterpret or misrepresent our position, we wish to state at the beginning of this case that the defense believes there is a direct conflict between the theory of evolution and the theories of creation as set forth in the Book of Genesis.

"Neither do we believe that the stories of creation as set forth in the bible are reconcilable or scientifically correct. The defense will also prove by credible testimony that there is more than one theory of creation set forth in the bible and that they are conflicting.

"But we shall make it perfectly clear that while this is the view of the defense we shall show by the testimony of men learned in science and theology that there are millions of people who believe in evolution and in the stories of creation as set forth in the bible and who find no conflict between the two.

Matter of Faith.

"The defense maintains that this is a matter of faith and interpretation which each individual must determine for himself, and if you men of the jury are able to reconcile the theory of evolution, and the theories of creation as set forth in the bible, you are not only entitled to your own view, but you will be supported in it by millions of your citizens who are of high culture, learning and deep religious faith.

"The defense will prove the facts and you will determine the question yourself.

"There may be a conflict between evolution and the peculiar ideas of Christianity which are held by Mr. Bryan as the evangelical leader of the prosecution, but we deny that the evangelical leader of the prosecution is an authorized spokesman for the Christians of the United States. The defense maintains that there is a clear distinction between God, the church, the bible, Christianity and Mr. Bryan. . .

"We will show that science occupies a field of learning separate and apart from the learning and theology, which the clergy expound. We will show that throughout the ages every scientific discovery or new invention has been met by the opposition of a people like those behind this prosecution who have pretended that man's inventive genius was contrary to Christianity.

Evolution Based on Science.

"We shall prove by experts and scientists in every field of scientific knowledge that there is no branch of science which can be taught without teaching the theory of evolution. . . .

"We will show that it will have been impossible for men like Luther Burbank and others without knowledge and faith in the theory of evolution to produce their invaluable experiments and results.

"The defense denies that it is a part of any movement or conspiracy on the part of scientists to destroy the authority of Christianity or the Bible. The defense denies that any such conspiracy exists except in the mind and purpose of the evangelical leader of the prosecution.

"The defense maintains that the book of Genesis is in part a hymn, in part an allegory and a work of religious interpretation written by men who believed that the earth was flat and whose authority cannot be excepted to control the teaching of schools.

"The narrow purpose of the defense is to establish the innocence of the defendant Scopes. The broad purpose of the defense will be to prove that the Bible is a work of religion's aspiration and rules of conduct which must be kept in the field of theology.

"The defense maintains that there is no more justification for imposing the conflicting views of the Bible on courses of biology than there would be for imposing the views of biologists on courses of comparative religions. We maintain that science and religion embrace two separate and distinct fields of thought and learning."

In asserting that "there is a clear distinction between the church, the Bible, Christianity and Mr. Bryan, the defense quoted from what was purported to be a declaration of Mr. Bryan's delivered twenty years ago "on Thomas Jefferson's statute for establishing religious freedom."

"The defense appeals from the fundamentalist Bryan of today to the modernist Bryan of yesterday." Mr. Malone said, and read what he said was a quotation from the comments of Mr. Bryan on Jefferson's principles:

"Jefferson . . . .said in the first place that to attempt to compel people to accept a religious doctrine by act of law was to make not Christians but hypocrites.". . . He said too, that there was no earthly judge who was competent to sit in a case and try a man for his religious opinions, for the judgment of the court, he said, would not be a judgment of law but would be the personal opinion of the judge. What could be more true. No man who has religious convictions himself bears them so lightly that he can lay them aside and act as a judge when another man's religious convictions are involved. . .

"Jefferson put first that which I want to speak of last. It was that the regulation of the opinions of men on religious question by law is contrary to the laws of God and the plans of God. He pointed out that God had it in his power to control man's mind and body but that he did not see fit to coerce the mind or body in obedience to the divine will. . . . Jefferson realized that our religion was a religion of love and not a religion of force."

That part of the statement referring to Mr. Bryan was excluded from the record by the court. Mr. Malone thereafter referred to Mr. Bryan as "this man."

It is not the view or opinion of evolution held by the defense that man descended from monkeys, Mr. Malone told the court.

"No scientist of any preeminent standing today holds such a view," he said. "The most that science says today is that there is an order of men-like animals which are more capable of walking erect than any other animals and more capable than other animals in the use of their forefeet as hands.

**

THE GRADUATE BAN

A new question inherent, in the Tennessee anti-evolution law has been brought up by Dr. Henry H. Rusby of Columbia university. Dr. Rusby would have Columbia and other universities refuse to accept credits and recognize degrees from colleges in states where scholarship is hampered by such laws.

This stand by the country's great universities would be effective in showing the divergence from educational fundamentals involved in legislative restriction. It would not only affect students and graduates but faculties; teachers will have less standing when connected with institutions not recognized by the graduate schools. The ban suggested by Dr. Rusby would call the educational leaders of Tennessee from timorous evasion of the issue, would challenge them to stand by the colors of scholarship.

J. W. Kruth in the Nation says: "In Dayton no one is afraid to tell me what he thinks. But when I go to Knoxville seat of the state university and one of the three largest cities in Tennessee, I enter a different world." There, he declares, he is talked to in whispers and he is forbidden to quote these whispers. Appropriations are at stake. Surely something is to be said for Dr. Rusby's suggestion; something should be done to bring the Tennessee educators to a sense of their present failure and future responsibility.

But on the other hand there are some obvious objections to this procedure. It smacks somewhat of the very bigotry which is responsible for the Tennessee law. A better attitude is that of Johns Hopkins university, there acting President Moss says the policy is to consider mainly the qualifications of the students who apply for admission and only secondarily the character of the colleges from which they come. "The university is confident of its ability to open their minds to the proper approach of knowledge," says Dr. Moss.

However, Johns Hopkins does not admit students without some regard for their previous training. The great universities as a secondary consideration do rate and classify the smaller institutions. And surely limitations such as the Tennessee legislature has set up will result in a lower standard of work in colleges and universities of the state. But there are other limitations on education, limitations erected by appropriations and political endeavor to secure appropriations and endowments, limitations erected by trustees and regents, by school boards in public schools, and by reactionary administrators.

It would seem to be the better course for the great institutions to make no rule simply covering the proscription of evolution but to adhere to the broad standards which will cover this particular limitation of education and will cover at the same time all the other restrictions on free learning.

**

Anyhow, by virtue of his labors in behalf of the cause of evolution, Clarence Darrow has "evoluted" into a full-fledged Tennessee colonel.

**

That may be a "friendly" lawsuit at Dayton, but they are beginning to use some unfriendly words in the arguments.

**

Ho. hum! We suppose Bryan and Darrow will pose for their pictures again today.

**

Years hence those folks in Dayton may look back on the Scopes trial as the time when they fit and sweat for their religion.

**

It's About Intolerance.

Colfax, Ia.—To the Editor: Can you tell me what all this hubbub and ballyhoo is about in Tennessee? The law has been in operation for some time and nobody has been hurt. Even its constitutionality has not been questioned or tested. Scopes admits breaking the law. The people of Tennessee want the law and are glad they have it. What is this whole business about, anyway? Nothing can or will be decided. Neither Bible nor science will be affected. Neither the truth nor falsity of evolution or the creation story will be established. Even the constitutionality of the Tennessee law will not be decided. Nothing is on trial and nothing can be settled, then what is all this excitement about in this hot weather? Isn't it rather unfair to force the monkey out into the sun this season of the year? F.P. Quick.

**

Enlightenment.

Fairfield, Ia.—To the Editor: I write to most heartily indorse the article of Professor Norton of Cornell college on evolution, which appeared in the Sunday edition of your paper. If people generally had reached that stage of enlightenment there would be no anti-evolution laws, and it would be universally conceded that there is no actual conflict between science and religion. William Louden.

**

Evolution and the Horse.

South English, Ia.—To the Editor: Your evolution bunch are just about riding the poor horse to death during this hot weather in their efforts to save their monkey ancestry theory. As a matter of fact there is nothing but mere assumption in all this talk about proving evolution by the horse.

Such an eminent and fair-minded scientist as Sir J. W. Dawson, says: "In America a series of horse-like animals has been selected, beginning with Eohippus of the Eocene—an animal of the size of a fox, and with four toes in front and three behind—and these have been marshaled as the ancestors of the fossil horses of America. Yet all this is purely arbitrary. In Europe, on the other hand, the ancestry of the horse has been traced back to Palaeotherium, an entirely different form, by just as likely indications. Both genealogies can scarcely be true, and there is no actual proof of either. . . such genealogies are not of the nature of scientific evidence."

This distinguished Canadian geologist and naturalist probably knew just as much about this horse evolution as anybody, and he disposes of the whole matter as being made up of claims "purely arbitrary," and of which there are "no actual proofs." And this horse evolution is the strongest proof they have of the theory. Osborn in "Evolution and Religion: calls it the "edition deluxe" of evolution. Please excuse me. --John M. Vankirk.

Friday, July 17, 1925
The Des Moines Register

BRYAN TURNS GUNS ON SCOPES

ARGUES TO BAR SCIENTISTS IN DAYTON TRIAL

Son Joins Him in Day of Oratory
Judge Delays Ruling

By Raymond Clapper
(Copyright, 1925)

Attorney General Stewart of Tennessee reading charges against John T. Scopes.Stewart is fighting bitterly every move of the defense counsel.

Dayton, Tenn., July 16. (U.N.) – The Goliath of the fundamentalists ventured forth to stop the introduction of scientific testimony in the Scopes evolution trial today, but he was met by a missile of unexpected force from the sling of Dudley Field Malone of New York, who stirred even these loyal partisans of the idol Bryan to applause.

William J. Bryan made his big speech of the trial against admission of expert testimony and Malone followed with a brilliant plea which was the sensation of the day.

"We come here for a duel to the death." Malone declared, snatching up Bryan's own phrase in pleading with the court to admit scientific witnesses.

"But are our weapons to be taken from us? Does the opposition mean that our defendant is to be strapped to the board and only the prosecution to have a sword?

"Truth No Coward."

"The truth is no coward. Truth does not need the protection of the law or the forces of government. Truth does not need the protection even of Mr. Bryan.

"We don't fear the truth. We believe we stand with progress. There is the fear," Malone shouted, pointing at Bryan. "We defy it!"

Bryan and Malone made the two spectacular speeches in a day of argument over the admissibility of expert testimony. Judge Raulston deferred his opinion until tomorrow. This will determine whether the trial comes to a speedy end after closing arguments only or whether it is to drag out while evolution and the meaning of the bible are expounded by the scholars.

There was eager expectancy in the courtroom when it got about that Bryan would make his first argument against admitting expert witnesses. These men and women who have been voting for him off and on all their lives, hung with devout attention on every word.

Bryan Uses All Weapons.

Like the ferocious kings of Israel, the grizzled commoner mounted the fundamentalist battlements to hold off the Philistines. He fought with every weapon. He played on local pride, on the ignorant man's suspicion of the expert, on the uneasiness of the parents over the younger generation.

He burlesqued the views of the scientists, held them up to the scorn of the spectators by skilfull metaphor and shot his bitter, devastating repartee at the defense lawyers when they tried to trip him up. "Experts cannot be permitted to defeat the law by coming in the great state of Tennessee to testify that this is not a bad doctrine," Bryan said, waving a palm leaf fan.

"The place to testify to that was before the legislature. If these people were so anxious to keep Tennessee from disgracing itself, why didn't they come here and speak when the law was being passed?

"The people of this state passed a law and they knew what they were doing when they did it for they knew the danger of this doctrine to their children.

Asks for Book.

"Doesn't the book say the very thing the law forbids? Get that book for me."

"Which book, the bible?" asked the court emerging from peaceful reveries. Bryan referred to Hunt's "Civic Biology" which Scopes used as a text book.

"Has it come to the time," Bryan said, when composure had been restored, "when the minority can take charge of Tennessee and compel the majority to pay teachers to take religion out of the hearts of our children.

"No matter whether the board of education approved the book or not, anything in it contrary to the law is prohibited and nobody knew it better than Scopes himself," Bryan said, shaking his palm leaf fan at young Johnny Scopes.

Uses Chautauqua Lingo.

Bryan, arguing his first case in twenty-eight years, found himself falling into the tricks of the chautauqua circuit and only with some difficulty mustered up the proper respectful salutations to the court.

All through his speech he used the phrase "my friends," once adding that some in the room were not his friends, and again correcting himself and using the usual court salutation of "your honor."

"A Christian believes a man came from above, but an evolutionist believes man came from below," he shouted, holding aloft his fan in one hand and Hunter's "Civic Biology" in the other. He showed the court the diagram of the evolution tree in the biology book from which Scopes taught.

"It says here that there are 518,000 species and it lists them," Bryan said with withering heat of sarcasm in his voice. "I note the figures are in round numbers, so it must be a guess for I don't think nature breeds in round numbers.

"There are, it says, 2,500 species of sponges. I'm satisfied from some I've seen that there are more. This is the book you are teaching your children. It says that men are mammals; how dare these scientists put a man in a ring with lions, tigers and animals that have an odor.

Will Scoff at Religion.

"If the children believe this they will go back home to scoff at the religion of the parents. This is the doctrine that they want to force on the schools when they won't let the bible be read. They would send the children home skeptics, agnostics and infidels."

Bryan remarked with some show of pride that he was a member of the American Society for the Advancement of Science. He showed much familiarity with the theory and data on evolution which he said might turn more poorly informed people into infidels.

"Does any scientist tell you where life began?" he asked. "Science wants to commence with an evolution that begins with nothing and ends nowhere. They don't tell you about God. They shut God out of the world."

Can't Harmonize Theories.

Judge Raulston asked whether the evolutionists would have to admit that God created the cell if they sought to reconcile the bible and evolution.

"Yes," Bryan replied, "and even that doesn't make it harmonize with the bible. They don't tell where in the long time between the lowly little cell in the sea and the flower of man that man became endowed with immortality. More than half of them don't believe in a personal God at all.

"There is no place for a miracle in the doctrine of evolution. If evolution is true, it logically eliminates the virgin birth, the resurrection, the doctrine of atonement, it means that man never fell and never needed a saviour, and that Christ was born of Joseph or some co-respondent unnamed.

"Evolution robs the children of God, of their saviour and of moral principles."

Bryan referred to the Loeb-Leopold case and Clarence Darrow's plea to the court to save the lives of those two youths and to their discipleship of Nietzsche, who he said was the only philosopher who dared carry evolution to its logical conclusion.

"We have it from the chief counsel of the other side that the universities and professors who taught the philosophy of the super-man were more responsible for that dastardly deed than those two boys who committed it," Bryan said.

Darrow Enters Objection.

Darrow rose up with gathering indignation at this thrust.

"That's not true," he roared. "Any way Nietzsche never taught evolution. Those two boys were insane. Within a week a clergyman in Illinois killed his wife to marry someone else. I can find ten clergymen who are criminals to every student of science who is a criminal.

"It's your theories that are responsible for it," Bryan snapped.

"You're making the preachers," Darrow retorted, "and you know I object to having another case dragged in here."

"I see no objection inasmuch as I know it won't prejudice the court," Bryan replied.

"But it doesn't do any good," Darrow observed.

Bryan played on the pride of the mountaineers by declaring that there were eleven church members on the jury and that any one of them was a better expert on the bible than any outside expert who was a Christian.

"Amen," Cry Supporters.

"Amen!" shouted the more fervent brethren in the courtroom.

"I want those amens to go into the record," Darrow told the court.

All of this, of course, was lost on the jury, which was kept out of the courtroom all day. The argument is entirely for the purpose—technically—of advising the judge so that he may rule intelligently as to whether to permit the jury to hear scientific testimony.

"The one beauty of the bible," Bryan resumed, "is that it doesn't take an expert to understand it.

"This case is not going to be decided here anyway. No court, high or low, is going to decide the issue between the unbeliever and revealed religion. The bible is its only authority and the son of God, born of the Holy Ghost and the virgin Mary isn't going to be driven out by experts who trace man back to the jungle. You can't humiliate this great state of Tennessee by allowing people to come in here to overturn this law because they don't agree with it.

"If these gentlemen want to broadcast their theories let them convene a mock court, for it will deserve the title of mock court if its purpose is to mock the bible out of the hearts of men."

Crowd Cheers Commoner.

When the commoner finished there was a burst of applause and friends rushed over to shower congratulations on him. With his mastery of speech and argument, and the tricks which always work on his audiences, he seemed to have made another cross of gold speech.

But across at the defense table a handsome youngish man rose, with an Irish twinkle in his blue eyes, and a soft touch to his voice, all marking him off as the anti-thesis of the plain-spirited commoner. Dudley Field Malone, regarded here as somewhat of a New York dandy, little known except as a Roman Catholic of New York, seemed like a stripling David going out to be eaten up in the great maw of the fundamentalist goliath.

"We have a right," he said, "to show by witnesses that the Bible is not to be taken literally, in a course of science.

Children Growing Wiser.

"The issue is as broad as Mr. Bryan has made it and why fear a meeting of the issue here where truth is scrutinized? What is this psychology of fear, I don't believe the scientists are in a conspiracy to destroy our children. Are the preachers the only ones who are looking out for our youth?

"I am not worried about the children of this generation. They are probably much wiser than many of their elders. Give children all of the light and all of the information there is. We have just had a war with 20,000,000 dead. Civilization need not be so proud of the grownups. For God's sake close no door or knowledge to their youthful minds.

"Mr. Bryan spoke some days ago about the wisdom of the jury system. But who is excluding the jury from this courtroom for fear they will hear something? We came here ready for a duel to the death. But does the opposition mean to strap our defendant to the board and is the opposition alone to have a sword. Are our weapons to be taken from us?

"The truth is no coward. It does not need the protection of the law or the forces of government. It does not need the protection of even Mr. Bryan.

Ready to Tell Truth.

We are ready to tell the truth as we understand it and we don't fear all of the truth that they can tell. We believe we stand with progress.

"Over there is the fear. We defy it!"

Malone's short whirlwind argument was the big surprise of the trial and the lawyers on both forts.

Attorney General Stewart closed the argument for the state.

"I am not an evolutionist," he said. "I don't believe man came from the same cell as a monkey. I believe man has developed from a more primitive stage, but I don't believe he has descended from a lower order of animals.

"It would be a prostitution of the courts of Tennessee to throw the doors of the court open to the scientific witnesses.

As the preceding speakers had made a field day of it, Stewart leaped over the fence and ran at large for a few minutes.

"I regret that the greatest criminal lawyer in the country has gone so far astray," Stewart said of Darrow's agnosticism.

"Great God," exclaimed Stewart, "what could not a mentality like that have done had it aligned itself with the forces of right instead of those which sink their fangs into the bosom of Christianity."

This brought the fireworks to an end far away from the quiet, timid, technical argument which was begun in the morning by William J. Bryan, jr. He clung strictly to the law in the case and was forgotten in the great mob scene that followed.

Judge Raulston hopes to have his opinion ready tomorrow morning.

**

Darrow Outlines Views of Scopes Defense on Creation of Man

SAYS ALL LIFE COMES FROM SINGLE CELL

Holds Bible Definition of Man, Figure of Speech

Dayton, July 16 (A.P.)—Clarence Darrow outlined the views of creation which the defense desires to present through expert testimony during an informal questioning by Judge Raulston in open court today.

This contention would be that the statement in Genesis that God created man out of the dust of the earth not be construed literally, but as a figure of speech.

"The belief is that man was not created by God as a carpenter builds a house," he told the judge, "but gradually through a process called evolution."

"Is this your belief, Colonel Darrow?" asked the court.

"As for myself I don't pretend to know," Darrow responded. "I am an agnostic to that as well as other things about which there is mystery. I don't profess to have any opinion on it, but we wish to show through our witnesses that they hold that belief.

"The theory of evolution which I believe teaches that life originated in the single cell and progressed through various stages to man, branching off in different directions to form the other animals.

"We think the bible story of creation not inconsistent with the evolutionary theory that all life comes from the single protoplasmic cell and progresses through variations of animal structure to man. Many evolutionists believe in immortality. Some do not."

**

What Do YOU Think?

For a Full Hearing.

To the Editor: Really I think you are unfair in your space given to opponents of evolution. Are more letters sent in to you which are favorable to evolution or do you give them the most space and censor or cut down those you do not agree with? Remember your editorials are all one sided on this subject, as well as the head lines you give this "Darrow" of the agnostic side. It certainly was wonderfully planned and the place selected for this great controversy, much better in Tennessee than in Chicago or New York, where that last democratic convention was held. The atmosphere of the liberty loving, quiet, unobtusive jury selected in Tennessee will decide the question right. Already the judge has heard the Darrow storm blow over his head and was unaffected by it, overruling Darrow and having the defendant stand trial, and then came the cutting out of the prayer requested. He was overruled once again and that was two points not headlined in your paper, as it would have been if Darrow had won the points. This second request of Darrow's shows just why he was there to attack religion and nothing else. All we care about is where evolution contradicts the bible, for if the bible is disproven in one part, then it's all wrong. Either God did create man in his own image, as he says, and animals to produce after their own kind or else God is not, there is no bible or any revealed religion.

This thing of saying bible and evolution agree is bosh, and the merest pettifogging of lawyers to talk about flat earth, ends of earth and creation in seven days.

In one place in the bible it says, "The day is with the Lord as a thousand years." Sometimes we speak of man's life as a day. He who created the sun, earth and time could hang the sun in the sky 1,000,000 years and call it a day.

Then you say the legislature has not the right to say what shall be taught in public schools. Whom would you delegate the right to select what should be taught in the schools? Such as Darrow or some scientists who don't agree on any theory? We would soon be where Russia or China are at the present. The school board selects the books taught by the authority of law, so the same law can be invoked to keep out the attack on the bible where the bible has already been kept out and where it has no chance to defend itself from attack.

It is a poor law that will rule out the bible and put in evolution and if that has been done it can be reversed. Darrow may be able to so befuddle a jury to free murderers, but those common folk of the mountains of Tennessee are going to undo him and his army of newspaper pals. J. P. Gilhousen.

**

What Is Learning?

Waukee, Ia.—To the Editor: Your leading editorial in The Register today "What Is Involved," is lifted from the Winnipeg Free Press. You have wasted an unnecessary amount of printer's ink to make it stand out as the darkest feature of the page. I assume you wish to emphasize—that those are you sentiments.

I am not sure that the legislature of a state should not be as competent to say what are proper subjects to be taught in the schools as the various boards of education to fix what should be embodied in courses of study. If the offending solons of Tennessee are less intelligent than their constituents a new set could be chosen.

Perhaps the whole discussion is ridiculous. I am inclined to think so, but it is worth while if it brings this country to its senses enough to realize that we cannot escape the results of what we decide shall be taught the younger generation.

This country has gone pretty strong on law and constitutional guarantees that the bible shall not be taught in public schools. Legislatures everywhere have banned the teaching of German language. The only excuse for school taxes is that we conceive we get our moneys worth for the information, mental and moral development we give the youth.

I think you are childish to be so fussed up for fear some legislature may produce some freak legislation. For my part if we must settle our ancestry doubts by law, I think I would prefer we require the schools to teach that we did not descend from apes rather than that we did. But I do think it is a misuse of public funds to finance schools to do either one. You are denser than darkest Tennessee. N. M. Leonard.

**

In Tennessee the silly season is more virulent than ever this year.

**

That judge at Dayton, Tenn. evidently realizes how necessary prayers are in a courtroom where a lot of lawyers are gathered.

Saturday, July 18, 1925
The Des Moines Register

SPEED SCOPES TO CONVICTION
Judge Bars Testimony of Science on Bible Vs. Evolution

DEFENSE CALLS RULING A BAN ON JURY TRIAL
Predict Verdict of Guilty for Teacher by Next Tuesday.

By Raymond Clapper

Dayton, Tenn., July 17 (U.N.)—Fundamentalist justice has plugged up the ears of the Tennessee mountaineer jury, and all that remains now of the Dayton trial is the quick work of convicting the evolutionist, John T. Scopes, and pronouncing him a criminal in this sovereign state early next week.

Judge Raulston ruled today on admission of expert witnesses and how it may be reconciled to Genesis of the bible as irrelevant. He then adjourned court until Monday. He will hear affidavits Monday on what expert witnesses would testify and decide whether he was correct in excluding them.

The array of lawyers on both sides will make their closing arguments to the jury. The jury will retire and unless some heretic is concealed on it, young Scopes will be adjudged guilty and the court will pronounce sentence.

Trial May End Tuesday

The trial should end Tuesday night or Wednesday barring unexpected delays.

"We won't ask for the death penalty," Attorney General Stewart remarked facetiously. Scopes, if convicted, will be fined somewhere between $100 and $500, as fixed by law.

There was much bitterness toward Judge Raulston on the defense side.

"This is the end of our attempt to have a trial," John R. Neal of the defense legal staff commented.

We began the trial on the theory that it was to be a trial of a criminal case before a judge and jury," Attorney Dudley Field Malone said. "But because of the constant objection of the prosecution to the attempt of the defense to lay any of the facts before the jury, the jury throughout the presentation of the case has been in the courtroom a total of three hours.

Blames Court Procedure.

"The rest of the time the jury was compelled to hear the case through the newspapers, loud speakers and radio. Science has taken an unfair advantage of outworn judicial procedure.

"Nothing has happened and nothing will happen that has been or will be a surprise to us. Our highest anticipations of procedure have been realized."

Bryan, who fought the introduction of expert testimony, said: "Personally, I am anxious to see the fullest discussion of the subject of evolution, but I cannot ignore the laws of the state of Tennessee relative to the introduction of evidence. The decision of the court could hardly have been otherwise under the law in this state.

"It did not indicate a disposition on the part of the judge or counsel for the state to avoid a discussion of evolution, but the court could not act as a mock court or debating society.

"Suits are tried by evidence and the laws of evidence excluded such expert evidence intended to dispute the letter of the statute or prove the law unwise."

Darrow Assails Bryan.

Darrow declared the court never would have ruled out the scientific testimony had not Bryan asked it. In a scathing attack he accused Bryan of running away from the "duel to the death," which he advertised on his arrival here before the trial, and of seeking shelter under the protection of technicalities.

"The attitude of Mr. Bryan and the prosecution throughout the past week has shown the country that Bryan has done everything in his power to prevent any discussion in court of the subject of evolution and the bible." Darrow said. "Bryan knows perfectly well that the court would not have ruled out the scientific testimony if Bryan had not opposed its admission. Bryan is willing to express his opinions on science and religion where his statements will not be questioned.

"But Bryan has not dared to test his views in open court under oath in contest with testimony of great educators and scientists. Bryan made the issue and then when he found that no reputable scientists and no pre-eminent theologian could be found to support his views in a court of justice, Bryan fled from the issue and sought the protection of technicalities: Bryan, who blew loud trumpet calls for 'battle to the death,' has fled from the field, his forces disorganized and his pretentions exposed."

Judge Raulston left Dayton to spend the week end at his home in Winchester, Tenn., a hundred miles away.

Jury Hears One Side.

Whatever the merits of this dispute the fact remains that these jurors, only one of whom admits having read anything about evolution must adjudge Scopes without having heard any testimony except that he taught evolution.

The judge in excluding the experts held that the law is plain and that it leaves no room for quibble as to whether evolution denies the bible story of creation.

Even old Jim Riley, who can neither read or write, must act without any light save that which may have glimmered into his brain through the harangues of itinerant evangelists he may have heard.

The judge held that the jury needed no information as to what evolution was or as to how thousands of ministers believed both in the bible and in evolution. The judge has construed the law and relieved from the jury the necessity of having to perform more than the most rudimentary mental exercise in reaching its verdict.

The jury has been in the court scarcely at all except when the state put on its four witnesses who testified that Scopes taught evolution. The defense put on Dr. Maynard M. Metcalf, zoologist, but the jury was ordered out before he began telling about evolution.

Darrow Criticizes Court.

The defense came here expecting to be beaten, but they did not expect to have their testimony shut out. Shortly after this blow fell Darrow was so incensed that he criticized the court openly and hung in the shadow of contempt for a tense moment.

"I don't understand why every request of the state is granted and our merest suggestion overruled," Darrow protested.

"I hope you don't mean to reflect on the court," the judge said with some surprise.

Darrow drew himself up and folded his arms.

"You have a right to hope," he shot back.

"The court has a right to do something else, too," Judge Raulston warned.

"All right, all right," Darrow replied.

There was a moment of breathless silence and the courtroom fully expected to see Darrow committed to the dingy jail across the road for contempt.

Judge Holds Temper.

But Judge Raulston showed remarkable self-control and instead of making a martyr of Darrow as he might have done by a hasty contempt sentence, he turned to Bryan and asked a question pending procedure.

After the session, Judge Raulston and Bryan mounted the rostrum to have their photgraphs taken. The judge asked Darrow to join the group, but he declined. Then he asked if Malone would "condescend" to with them.

"No thank you, your honor," Malone said. "We have had our pictures taken together enough. You have it taken with Mr. Bryan and the prosecution."

Shutting out of the expert testimony will stop up the ears of the jury but it will not entirely keep the story of evolution from the public. The defense has a right to present the testimony which is excluded so that the higher courts may examine it and determine if it was properly ruled out. The jury may not hear this, but the statements will be inserted in the written record and these will be broadcast through the newspapers. They may be read in open court, but that will depend on the outcome of a wrangle between attorneys Monday.

"Denial of Justice"

Dayton, Tenn., July 17 (By The Associated Press)--In announcing that he had decided to exclude scientific testimony from the trial of John T. Scopes, Judge Raulston immediately drew fire from defense attorneys in filing of their exception.

In presenting the defense exception, Arthur G. Hays, member of the Scopes defense counsel, declared:

"It is a denial of justice to permit the state to make the case on its own evidence."

"It is contrary to every principle of Anglo-Saxon judicial procedure," Mr. Hays said. The defense then announced that it desired to place its proposed testimony into the court for the purpose of placing it before a higher court.

In reply to a question from Judge Raulston, Hays said the defense had about six branches of science represented by witnesses.

"I think you are entitled to have in the record a sufficient amount of your proof to show the appellate court what your proof would have been," the judge.

The defense contended, however, that it also had the right to argue before the court that the law was unreasonable and to put on evidence to "inform the court" in the absence of the jury. If the evidence be permitted, Mr. Hays suggested that the court would be benefited by such evidence.

Would Reverse Opinion.

Should the court be convinced that it is in error, then he will reverse his opinion, Judge Raulston said.

Attorney General Stewart said that the defense wished to conduct a campaign of education for their theories of education and evolution through the medium of this trial.

Dudley Field Malone denied that a campaign of education was being conducted although he said he thought the way in which the defense had conducted the case was educational. He said that the defense was meeting propaganda started by "a distinguished member of prosecution counsel."

Judge Raulston said he was not inclined after having given an opinion to hear testimony to show that the opinion was wrong.

Crushes Defense Hopes.

Refusal of Judge Raulston to admit scientific and religious testimony into the evidence marked the end of defense hopes for the trial, attorneys for the defense said after adjournment of court until Monday, when affidavits containing this evidence will be admitted to the record for transmission to the higher courts.

"This ends our hope for a trial of this case," was the comment of John R. Neal, chief counsel for the defense.

"Since the beginning of this case," Dudley Field Malone said, "there has been scarcely any motion of the defense except the motion to adjourn today that has been granted by the court.

"We began this trial on the theory that it would be the trial of a criminal case before a court and jury, but because of the constant objections of the prosecution to attempts of the defense to lay any of our attack before the jury, the jury throughout the past week has only been in the courtroom about three hours.

"The rest of the time the jury has been compelled to hear the case of the defense through the newspapers and amplifiers. Science has taken an unfair advantage of outworn judicial procedure.

"Nothing has happened, however, throughout the trial, and nothing will happen before the trial is over that will surprise this defense. Our highest anticipations will have been realized."

**

Dayton Judge Holds Theories of Evolution Immaterial

RULES INTENT OF STATE LAW IS ONLY ISSUE

Declares Statute Worded in Plain Language

Dayton, Tenn., July 17 (A.P.)—After Judge John T. Raulston had excluded scientific testimony in the Scopes case, court was adjourned until Monday morning. The intervening time is to be spent by counsel for the defense in preparing statements for the record of what their witnesses would have testified, had they been permitted to take the witness stand.

Although court was in session only thirty minutes, the judge giving his decision at 9:51 o'clock, it was stormy. After defense attorneys had raised their voices in vehement protest to the court's ruling another argument developed on the question of the weekend recess.

State Protests Delay

The defense insisted on this step and while the state protested, the court finally ruled for the halt in the proceedings.

Judge Raulston indicated, however, that on his return to the bench Monday he would insist on the case moving more rapidly. This was taken to mean that the case might end Monday.

"This case is now before the court upon a motion by the attorney general to (ex)clude from the consideration of the jury certain expert testimony offered by the defendant, the import of such testimony being an effort to explain the origin of man and life. The state insists that such evidence is wholly irrelevant, incompetent and unimportant to the issues impending and that it should be excluded.

"Upon the other hand, defendant insists that this evidence is highly competent and relevant to the issues involved and should be admitted."

Reads Section of Statute.

He read the first section of the statute involved in this case and added: "The state says that it is both proven and admitted that this defendant did teach in Rhea county, within the limits of the statute, that man descended from a lower order of animals, and that with these facts ascertained and proven, it has met the requirements of the statute and has absolutely established the defendant's guilt: and with his guilt thus admitted and established, his ultimate conviction is unavoidable and inevitable, and that no amount of expert testimony can aid and enlighten the court and jury upon the real issues or affect the final results.

"In other words, the state insists that by a fair and reasonable construction of the statute the real offense provided against in the act is to teach that man descended from a lower order of animals and that when this is accomplished by a fair interpretation and by legal implication, the whole offense is proven. That is, the state says, that the latter clause interprets and explains what the legislature meant and intended by the use of the clause 'Any theory that denies the story of divine creation as taught in the bible.'

"But the defendant is not content to agree with the state in its theory, but takes issue and says that before there can be any conviction the state must prove two things:

Defense Makes Two Issues

"First, That the defendant taught evolution in the sense used in the statute:

"Second, That this teaching was contrary to the bible.

"That these are questions of fact, that the proof must show what evolution is, so that the jury may determine whether evolution as taught by the defendant conflicts with the bible, that it is not merely what the defendant said or what the book taught, and that they cannot do this without evidence. That is that the defendant must have taught the descent of man from a lower origin of animals and a theory contrary to that of divine creation as taught by the bible. That the teaching of either would not be crime.

"Now upon these issues as brought up it becomes the duty of the court to determine the question of the admissibility of this expert testimony offered by the defendant.

"It is not within the province of the court under these issues to decide and determine which is true, the story of divine creation as taught in the bible or the story of the creation of man as taught by evolution.

Holds Theories Immaterial.

"If the state is correct in its insistence, it is immaterial so far as the results of this case are concerned, as to which theory is true; because it is within the province of the legislative branch, and not the judicial branch of the government, to pass upon the policy of a statute; and the policy of this statute having been passed upon by that department of the government, this court is not further concerned as to its policy, but is interested only in its proper interpretation, and, if valid, its enforcement.

"Let us now inquire what is the true interpretation of this statute. Did the legislature mean that before an accused could be convicted the state must prove two things:

"First, That the accused taught a theory denying the story of divine creation as taught in the bible;

"Second, That man descended from a lower order of animals.

"If the first must be specifically proven, then we must have proof as to what the story of divine creation is, and that a theory was taught denying that story. But if the second clause is explanatory of the first and speaks into the act the intention of the legislature and the meaning of the first clause, it would he otherwise.

Sees No Ambiguity.

"To illustrate, when the legislature had provided that it shall be unlawful to teach a theory that denies the divine story as taught in the bible; and then by the second clause merely clarified their intention, and that the real intention provided by the statute taken as a whole was to make it unlawful to teach that man descended from a lower order of animals, then there would be no such ambiguity and uncertainty as to the meaning of the statute and as to the offense provided against, as to justify the court in calling in expert testimony to explain.

"The court will seek the aid or opinion of expert evidence only when the issues involve facts of such complex nature that a man of ordinary understanding is not competent and qualified to form an opinion.

"In Tennessee an act must be construed so as to make it carry out the purposes for which it was enacted.

"The legislative intent will prevail over the strict letter and, in order to carry into effect its intent, general terms will be limited and those which are narrow expanded.

Text Is Made Plain.

"In construing a statute we must look to the act as a whole, to the object with which it deals and with the reason and spirit of the enactment, and thereby, if possible, discover its real purpose. The meaning must be determined not from the special words in a single sentence or section, but from the act taken as a whole, comparing one section with another, and viewing the legislation in the light of its general purposes.

"In the act involved in the case at bar, if it is found consistent to interpret the latter clause as explanatory of the legislative intent as to the offense provided against, then why call experts? The ordinary, nonexpert mind can comprehend the simple language 'descended from a lower order of animals.'

"These are not ambiguous words or complex terms. In the final analysis, this court, after a most earnest and careful consideration has reached the conclusion that under the provisions of the act involved in this case, it is made unlawful thereby to teach in the public schools of the state of Tennessee, the theory that man descended from a lower order of animals. If the court is correct in this then the evidence of experts would shed no light on the issues.

"Therefore the court is content to sustain the contention of the attorney general to exclude the expert testimony, the purpose of which is to explain the origin of man and the life in this world."

Sunday, July 19, 1925
The Des Moines Sunday Register

DARROW ASSAILS SCOPES' JUDGE

PICTURES BIAS OF COURT AND ATTACKS BRYAN
Declares Defendant Was Condemned From Start of the Trial.

Dayton, Tenn., July 18 (A.P.)—John Thomas Scopes was condemned from the start of the evolution case, Clarence Darrow declared today in a statement in which he outlined his views of the case, evolution and religion.

"We know that in this state, under the surroundings and conditions of the trial, Mr. Scopes was condemned from the start," he said. "We are now interested in two things:

"That a higher court shall pass upon this case, and that, in other states, those who wish to pursue the truth shall be left free to think and investigate and teach and learn.

Boy witnesses in Scopes Trial *(Pacific and Atlantic photo)*
Left to right-- Harry Shelton, Howard Morgan, Morris Stout, Robert Hagler and James Benson. Five boys who have been called to testify in the Scopes anti-evolution trial in Dayton

"We know that the great majority of the intelligent Christians do not accept the literal interpretation for the whole bible. We have learned here, both from laymen and clergymen, that a large part of the fundamentalists do not accept it. This doctrine is a doctrine of the literalists and we are perfectly satisfied that the majority of the Christian church has long since passed beyond that."

Opposes Praying in Court.

Outlining his views on praying in court, Mr. Darrow said:

"I did object to daily praying in court. This prayer is rare in court even in the south. I objected to it because of the peculiar situation wherein Mr. Bryan had sought to make this trial a contest between religion and science.

"I thought, of all cases, this was one where the court should stand perfectly free of all bias. Even the judge who presides has not followed the regular habit of opening court with prayer until this case arose.

"Every attorney on the part of the defense understands the setting and background of the case. We do not blame anyone in Tennessee for it: we know that all men take their views largely from their environment."

Darrow Calls Bryan Sole Judge.

Mr. Darrow, referring to Mr. Bryan, said:

"Before the trial of this case, I had no idea that there was only one interpreter of religion in the world. Christianity has had in its ranks thousands of able and intelligent men in all of the countries of the world, but these were all set aside and Mr. Bryan is to be the one and only judge of what the bible and Christianity mean."

The theory of evolution as a scientific theory was only announced about seventy years ago, Mr. Darrow continued, and since that time it has been accepted by almost every scientist in the world.

"The believers in evolution are by no means confined to heretics, for the realm of religion and science are entirely separate. Amongst the most prominent evolutionists of the world, are multitudes of men in high standing in all the Christian churches. All of these are pronounced heretics by Mr. Bryan.

Admits He Is An Agnostic.

The scientific man is as kind and humane as the fundamentalist," he asserted, and no one ever heard of a scientific man who sought to call the aid of the law to enforce belief in his theories.

"Men's religious views are involved in this prosecution," Mr. Darrow insisted. "It is true that on the subject of God and immortality I am willing to confess that I am an agnostic; I do not know I fancy that this is a much higher position than that of Mr. Bryan, who says that God was made in his image and is sure that this is true.

"It is hard to understand how an intelligent man can believe that a photograph of a human being needs only to be enlarged to give us a picture of God. On this subject I am not agnostic; I do not believe it. As to the first cause, and the power that is at the heart of the universe, it seems to me that most men must confess that they do not know."

Continuing, he said that he had no desire to have the Christian world give up its belief in God or its bible, but at least a very large portion of the Christian world do not regard the bible as a book of science.

"The scientist does not believe that man has ever fallen, but that man has gone steadily forward. It is the fundamentalist only that believes that man was once perfect and that he afterwards fell."

**

Bryan Calls Darrow Foe of Christianity

Dayton, Tenn. July 18 (A.P.)—A note of progress was observed by William J. Bryan today in a statement in which he declared that the Tennessee evolution case has uncovered a conspiracy against bible Christianity. Declaring that multitudes have been deceived by the use of the term "evolution," he added that their eyes are now being opened. Evolution, as taught by scientists, he said, is an imaginary process, wholly unproven, that begins with life but does not attempt to explain life.

"If the evolutionary hypothesis is true," he said, "man has come up through the animals below him by a cruel law under which the strong kill off the weak.

Cites Bloody Purpose

"The evolutionists bring their doctrine before the public in a jeweled case and praise it as if it were a sacred thing. They do not exhibit, as Darwin did, its bloody purpose; they do not boast that barbarism is its only true expression; they do not tell the public that Darwin, who studied for the ministry and in his youth believed in a personal God and in the 'strict and literal truth of every word in the bible' was led away from Christianity by evolution and died an agnostic.

"The evolutionists have not been honest with the public; even ministers who believe in evolution have assured their congregations that there is no inconsistency between Darwinism and Christianity. The ministers should tell their congregations that evolution leads logically to agnosticism.

"But this trial has had another important effect. The presence of Mr. Darrow here, an avowed agnostic both as to God and immortality—he has so stated in court before the judge—represents the most militant anti-Christian sentiment in the country. He protested against the opening of court with prayer and has lost no opportunity to slur the intelligence of those who believe in orthodox Christianity and to hurl the charge of bigotry against anyone who objects to the teaching of evolution in the schools.

"Mr. Darrow, in the celebrated Loeb-Leopold trial, boldly argued that the boys were not responsible for what they did, laying the blame upon their ancestors and their environment and relieving them of all personality or power to decide between good and evil.

Shows Real Animus.

"Mr. Darrow's connection with this case and his conduct during this case ought to inform the Christian world of the real animus that is back of those who are attempting to enforce upon the schools the views of a small minority, regardless of the fact that the philosophy of life based upon evolution robs the individual of a sense of responsibility to God and paralyzes the doctrine of brotherly love.

"Mr.. Darrow's hostility to Christianity, proclaimed for a generation, and his conduct in this case are now known to the world and will arouse the devout Christians of the nation whose prayers ascend in gratitude for the courage of the state of Tennessee and Mr. Darrow's attitude will compel the Christians who take sides with him to explain to their Christian brothers why they defend a doctrine that strikes at the root, not only of Christianity, but of civilization. Do they know what evolution means? If so do they prefer it to the bible?"

**

EXPECT VERDICT OF CONVICTION NEXT TUESDAY
Allot Each Side Four Hours to Argue Case.

Dayton, Tenn., July 18 (By The Associated Press)—The "Scopes case" tonight was hearing its end. Well informed observers suggested that not more than two or more court days would be required to close the "evolution" test with a verdict that would either exonerate the young school teacher on a charge of teaching evolution theories in violation of the state law or send the case on its way to higher courts.

Constant application of scientists, lawyers and stenographers today failed to complete the task of preparing some eight or ten statements they will place in the record to show what experts in fields of science would have testified had they been permitted to take the witness stand. Judge John T. Raulston excluded this class of testimony as irrelevant to the issue.

It was said by defense attorneys that a portion of tomorrow would be needed to get the statements of the scientists in proper form for admission to the record.

Eight Hours of Speeches.

With the submission of statements expected to be the only testimony offered by the defense, disposal of this part of the program Monday morning would leave only the arguments by the attorneys and charge of the judge to be delivered before it enters the last stage by being placed in the hands of the jury.

It was understood that eight hours would be devoted to speech making, four hours for each side.

It was not considered likely that the court day Monday would be extended to a length that would permit all the speeches. However, the opening of court Tuesday was expected to find not more than two addresses to be made, with the judge's charge to follow.

Barring an unexpected jury entanglement and subsequent tie-up, a verdict of the case was considered certain some time Tuesday.

Today brought almost a dead calm to the scene of the "evolution trial."

Writers Tour Mountains.

The persons who came early in the day to attend the trial, unaware that a halt had been declared over the week-end, went home again and the street crowds were made up of the normal Saturday visitors. Many of the several score newspaper men here went on a tour of the Smoky mountains or to Chattanooga.

Both Clarence Darrow and William Jennings Bryan were in Chattanooga tonight. Mr. Darrow will deliver an address there tomorrow. Bryan has cancelled all speaking engagements for the week end.

**

Bryan will Turn From Evolution to Tour of Holy Land

PLANS TO TAKE HIS RELIGIOUS FRIENDS ALONG

Intends to Spend Next Easter in Jerusalem.

BY ROBERT T. SMALL.

(Copyright 1925, by the C.P.A.)

Dayton, Tenn., July 18.—Just as soon as Mr. Bryan finishes up with all this monkey business here in Dayton, he is going to work upon his next great adventure—the leading of a pilgrimage to the holy lands late in the coming winter.

"This is to be a genuine pilgrimage," says a prospectus of the trip. "Other cruises are largely filled with people who went to escape cold weather and be amused meanwhile. Such tours might not ineptly he characterized as glorified bridge-whist parties. Mr. Bryan's purpose is to gather around himself people who are genuinely interested in religion and who, therefore, while enjoying in full the beautiful travel experience involved, would derive a genuine inspiration from a visit to the land of the book and from Mr. Bryan's interpretation of the book while in the land.

Your imagination can readily visualize and your judgement evaluate the experience of listening to Mr. Bryan at the birthplace of the prince of peace, or on Good Friday in the Garden of Gethsemane; at Easter dawn by the garden tomb, and on Easter afternoon as he reviews the great commission on the Mount of Olives.

Will Charter Steamer.

"The plan is to reserve an entire steamer, taking preliminary cruises around the Mediterranean, spend two weeks in Egypt—enough to visit Cairo, Luxor, Valley of the Kings, Aswan and Abeydos—then to devote sixteen days to the holy land, with the climax—Easter in Jerusalem.

"Mr. and Mrs. W. J. Bryan cordially invite their personal friends and all others who are in sympathy with the spirit of a genuine pilgrimage to the holy land to join them in this unique and inspirational experience. The tour will be a two months' visit between Mr. and Mrs. Bryan and genial companions, with many the first and with some perhaps the last opportunity for such a visit.

"It is a fitting climax to the career of Mr. Bryan that after his years of strenuous devotion to his country and to great moral cause he should now lead the hearts of Christian people personally to the holy land and share with them, both on the way and at the sacred sites, his wide experience of life, the ripened maturity of his thoughts, and the inspiration of his religious convictions.

"It is not necessary that the pilgrims who accompany him should think as Mr. Bryan does on either politics or religion, but it is highly desirable that they be sympathetic to a religious view of life, and approach this experience with a sense of the spiritual values involved.

Plenty of Fun.

"It should be understood, however, that this pilgrimage is not a long faced affair. There will be fun and plenty of it wherever Mr. Bryan is. There will be championship, the stimulus of encountering bright minds and generous hearts, of listening to the conversations or the more formal addresses of men and women who have experienced widely, thought deeply and played their part in the affairs of the world."

The elaborateness of the pilgrimage may be judged by the prices of passage, which will range from $1,475 to about $2,500 for each person.

Flay Foreign Lawyers.

One of the greatest squabbles here in Dayton has been as to how the lawyers from "foreign states" got into this evolution case. The prosecutors for the state have not hesitated to play upon the fact that the leading attorneys for the defense have come from far distant cities down here to Tennessee to tell plain folk of the south what they should do and what they should not do. Mr. Bryan, in open court, has been particularly resentful that New Yorkers should be here and has asked what the New Yorkers would have thought if a lot of Tennesseans had gone to Albany a year or two ago and told New York that it could not repeal its prohibition enforcement laws.

Whereupon, the lawyers for the defense have retorted that Mr. Bryan is responsible for the whole situation. They say that it was under his inspiration that the anti-evolution law was passed. Then, as soon as young Scopes was arrested for violating the law, Mr. Bryan, at Miami, telegraphed offering his services to help prosecute the "poor professor." Messrs. Darrow, Malone and Hays, the "evil trinity" of the defense, say it was not until they read of Mr. Bryan's action that they decided to offer their services to the lad who could not afford to hire defenders of his own. The defense lawyers have tried to picture Mr. Bryan as the grim "persecutor" of the luckless Scopes; but, as a matter of fact, the feeling out of the courtroom among the lawyers has been the pleasantest imaginable.

Bryan, Darrow Good Friends.

It has been a rare picture, indeed, to see Mr. Darrow and Mr. Bryan standing with their arms around each other. Darrow may be the arch-agnostic in court and in general, and Mr. Bryan may be the "arch-conspirator," wanting to send all who differ with him to the torture chamber, but when the grease paint and the makeup of court sessions are removed, Bryan and Darrow become good fellow citizens once more and walk humbly side by side. Mr. Bryan says he has bought all of Darrow's books and wouldn't part with his copies "for the world." Mr. Darrow has replied by quoting from Mr. Bryan's works, showing how thoroughly he has read them.

Court Resembles Revival.

Dayton has been a rare and wonderful place this last week. From a courtroom where the most profound discussion of the ages might be heard, it was possible to step right around the corner, where if you could knock one "baby" down you could get one cigar. At times the courtroom has suggested anything but the scene of a great trial. It has been more like a revival. The judge added to that atmosphere by insisting upon an opening prayer each day and by expressing his regret on one occasion that more people could not get in to hear "the speaking." The judge also stopped court one day to thank an anonymous admirer who had placed a bouquet of flowers on his desk.

**

BRYAN'S NOT OLD

Nobody can quite explain why Mr. Bryan is so generally looked upon as an old man.

Perhaps the lines of his face have something to do with it, perhaps his long political career, so much of it before the war, makes him seem like the survival of a past generation.

As a matter of fact Mr. Bryan is only 65 years old. He was born in Salem, Ill., March 30, 1860. He will be but little past his sixty-seventh birthday when the primaries are held for the next presidential nomination.

Not only is Mr. Bryan not an old man as ages run, he is a man of most astonishing physical vitality, inherited from a vigorous ancestry and maintained by abstemious living.

If anybody is picturing Mr. Bryan at Dayton as an old man with no eye for the passing interest of his time, incidentally with no eye on the politics of 1928, they are not estimating him either with an eye on the almanac, or in keeping with his own abounding vitality.

**

What do YOU Think?
An Old Controversy.

To the Editor: The fundamentalist controversy is a struggle between two ideas. The fundamentalist or orthodox accepts a literal interpretation of the Bible. He believes the Bible was written by God and is therefore infallible.

The modernist does not believe these things. He accepts the Bible as a man-made book including many wonderful pieces of literature and including some which are not true. He believes that the creation of the world is a process extending over countless ages; that the creation of man began with the lowest form of life and believes not in the fall of man but in the rise of man or evolution. His religion is based on good works or in other words, service.

This controversy is not new but has been going on for 2,000 years. It is just a question of which group, those holding the theory of a religion by belief or those holding a theory of a religion by service, is to control the machinery of the Protestant Christian church. Those who control are legal, powerful, regular and respectable, but those who lose have no standing and no rights. O. A. Hammand.

**

Straight Line? Read Einstein.

Sioux City, Ia.—To the Editor: Unless the evolutionists are able to show different, I am content with my reasoning: Once a monkey always a monkey. Once an ape, always an ape. Once a man, always a man. Unless the evolutionist is able to show me where the change took place and start from there and develop a man like man, I will hold to this scientific rule: "An object set in motion will forever move in a straight line, unless acted upon by some outside force."-- J. W. Tutt.

**

There is still a chance that Clarence Darrow will be fined or jailed for contempt of court before that Scopes trial ends.

**

Cheering thought for the day: That Scopes trial can't last much longer.

**

A few months after that Dayton trial is ended some folks won't be able to remember whether it was held in Ohio or Tennessee.

**

A FRONT PAGE AMERICAN STAR

By Mark Sullivan

William Jennings Bryan is one of the wonders of the modern world. His vitality, his longevity as an active and important figure in public life is alone enough to make him unique. What other living American has had any such career? The day he came charging up from his Florida home to fight the evolutionists in Tennessee was almost exactly twenty-nine years after the day, in 1896, when he set out from his earlier home in Lincoln, Neb., to fight the goldbugs at Chicago. Bryan's famous speech, ending up, "You shall not press down upon the brow of labor this crown of thorns, you shall not crucify mankind upon a cross of gold"—that speech, with which he first burst upon the nation and which won him his first presidential nomination, was delivered July 10, 1896. Twenty-nine years later he was again on a scene of battle, again stripped for action in a spectacular fight, again working up his fighting spirit by picturing himself, to himself, sincerely, as the champion of righteousness and his opponents in the terms of enemies of Christ.

—

Bryan really believes that about his fights. His capacity to make himself believe always that his position is God's and that his opponents are God's enemies—that capacity for so staging the fight to himself, is one of the greatest sources of Bryan's strength. The most revealing story of the thousands that almost all of us have heard about Bryan was told by the late Governor Folk of Missouri. Governor Folk was a close friend of Bryan and he had this story from Bryan himself:

Bryan's father was a county judge at Salem, Ill., and, in addition, a devout church member. As a judge his decisions suffered the common fate of lower courts; some were upheld, some reversed. The elder Bryan, talking one day about some decisions of his which the higher courts had reversed, laid particular emphasis on one. He said that as to most of the reversals of his decisions by the upper court he did not ordinarily complain. But as to one particular decision, he said: "I know I was right in that decision because I consulted God about it."

William Jennings Bryan inherits that quality. To be able to convince yourself that God is your partner in a fight is a great strengthening to the arm. Among other advantages it enables you also to convince yourself that your opponents are the enemies of God. That quality of Bryan which makes him intolerant, makes it impossible for him to consider compromise, accounts for a good deal of the irritation many persons feel about him; but it counts much also for the remarkable length of time he has been able to stay in the ring.

—

Bryan has another quality that helps him keep on fighting. It is his capacity to ignore logic, to keep himself free of those weakening embarrassments that attend a man able to see all the facts in their proper proportions, and to see his opponent's case as well as his own. To Bryan, all questions are divided into two sides: one side is wholly white, the other wholly black. What is the side Bryan is on? Bryan might have been an ordinary character if he had happened to have a mind functioning chiefly in the world of logic. He was endowed, happily, for the kind of career he has had, with the ability instantly to thrust a question out of the world of logic and into the world of emotion. Issues present themselves to Bryan in terms of the possibility of orating about them. From this flows Bryan's capacity to swing his audience by emotional appeals. Figures of speech, sometimes by devices which the rest of us regard as tricks of speech, but which never appeal to Bryan as such. I have been told a story about a debate Bryan had in New England about a year ago, on evolution, in which his opponent was a professor of geology. According to the story, Bryan won the debate, or at least got the verdict of the crowd, by a peroration which he ended up: "You believe in the age of rocks; I believe in the Rock of Ages."

I do not know if that story is true, but it is characteristic of Bryan. One of his most effective devices—only to Bryan it is not a device at all but a sincere expression of his natures—is to put questions and arguments in terms that recall biblical situations and religious sentiments. The analogies he frequently makes between biblical situations and the questions he is discussing would disappear before logical analysis. But they yield themselves to emotional oratory.

—

Bryan, in a strict and literal sense, is a born orator, an instinctive maker of emotional speeches. His nature functions spontaneously in oratory as naturally as a bird functions in flight. Oratory is Bryan's natural response to conditions with which he comes in contact. A very revealing story about Bryan as a lad was told years ago by the family physician of Bryan's father's family, Dr. William Hill:

"The lad's political career began at Centralia, where his father took him in his twelfth year to a great democratic rally. Among the orators were some of the most distinguished men in the state. He listened to them all with blushed face and blazing eyes. His little body became a perfect volcano of enthusiasm. . .Finally, he mounted the platform and began to talk. Many laughed outright at the idea, and all smiled. He was undaunted, however. He did not appear to see his auditors or to hear their laughing remarks at the start. As he proceeded the laughter ceased. In forcible and eloquent language, with the energy and diction of the born orator, he pursued his argument. . . . .The audience first became quiet and attentive, then wildly enthusiastic. Cheer upon cheer rent the air. . . When he closed there was a tumult of applause and he was carried from the platform and about the town on the shoulders of cheering men."

There is the picture of a child born to be an orator, who could no more escape being an orator, could no more make of himself a logician than a fish could become a pedestrian.

—

Bryan's vitality, aided by abstemious living, has served him well. In vitality he is a superman. Twenty-nine years he has driven himself up and down the land, nearly always in one fight or another, and always making speeches. During these twenty-nine years Bryan has made an average of 250 speeches a year, in all parts of the country. He must have spent nearly a third of his nights in sleeping cars and more than a third in hotels. It is a life that would kill most of us physically, and wear nearly all of out spiritually.

Of course, Bryan has been beaten rather often, but never suppressed. No American of his generation has had such capacity for "comeback." Again and again we have gone sadly to Bryan's funeral and met him at the graveyard gate galloping out on a new horse.

One of the many times at the San Francisco democratic convention in 1920 Bryan was beaten by the convention's refusal to adopt his stand on prohibition, and by the nomination, much to Bryan's distaste, of Gov. James M. Cox. Bryan himself said: "My heart is in the grave." At that apparently authentic announcement there was another funeral, but the ceremony turned out to be inconclusive.

At one time Bryan's local enemies in Nebraska had him pretty well bottled. When he moved out of Nebraska to Florida they thought it was a case of an old man giving up the fight and retiring to end his days in ease among strangers. Bryan astounded everybody by announcing he was going to go to the democratic convention last year as a delegate from his new state. The politicians thought it couldn't be done. Bryan entered his name, campaigned in every county in Florida and got more votes than any other candidate.

When he thrust himself into the Ku-Klux klan fight in the convention Bryan's opponents thought that would surely be the end of him; but he came out of the convention with his brother, Charley, in possession of one of the two prizes. When the democrats lost the election last year there was one more funeral service for both the Bryans. When W. J. identified himself and his oratory with a real estate development it was thought that surely this was the last phase. And here he is again, this week, a central figure in one of the spectacular situations of his time.

—

The best and most explaining account of Bryan's background and early youth was written by his wife. She got it up as part of a campaign document in the 1896 fight. All the following words in quotation marks are Mrs. Bryan's"

Bryan's father was a "devout Baptist" who "prayed at morning, noon and night, and was a firm believer in providential direction in the affairs of life;" "a fluent speaker" whose "mind was philosophical and his speeches argumentative," and who used to say that "the guest chamber of his home was reserved for 'politicians and divines.'"

"William Jennings Bryan was born March 19, 1860. He learned to read quite early; after committing his lessons to memory he stood upon a little table and spoke them to his mother. This was his first recorded effort at speechmaking....His appetite, which has since been a constant companion, developed very early. The pockets of his first trousers were always filled with bread, which he kept for an gmergency...His father's congressional campaign in 1872 was his first political awakening, and from that time on he always cherished the thought of entering public life....A prize contest always fired William's ambition....During his first year at the academy he declaimed Patrick Henry's masterpiece. The second year he entered with 'The Palmetto and the Pine.' Later he declaimed 'Bernardo del Carpio' and gained the second prize." Finally, with an essay on "Labor," he achieved first prize. The following year he won first prize with an oration on "Individual Powers." In an intercollegiate oratorical contest he won second prize of $50 for an oration on "Justice." Gen. John C. Black of Illinois was one of the judges and marked Mr. Bryan 100 in delivery. Upon invitation of Mr. Black the young man called at the hotel and received many valuable suggestions upon the art of speaking. At his graduation he was class orator and delivered the valedictory.

—

Bryan has stayed in the rig a long time; his vitality is extraordinary. And yet he shows the marks of more than a generation of steady fighting. The Bryan of today, the Bryan of the last stage, is an elderly man in baggy trousers and a black alpaca coat, mostly bald except for a few stringy strands of graying hair that han g, a little untidily, over his coat collar; that once superbly clear and musical voice a little marred by a slightly hissing sound that comes of age's imperfect teeth; the eyes, though they still flash, flashing now with rather the cold hardness of an old fighter who has been denied success rather frequently, and, lacking the warmth and depth that once they had, the quick mobility through the widest range of feeling from satirical humor to tense earnestness.

This later Bryan is the only one that is known in 1925 to more than half his fellow citizens, for a generation, as measured in familiarity with public characters, is very short. Commonly we measure a generation as beginning at its birth but as respects reading the newspapers with any real interest in public affairs, we must measure a generation as being at, let us say, the age of 16 to 20. And so, of all the people living in the United States today, probably we should have to say roughly, that only those over 40 can remember the Bryan of his first phase. Only those of middle age or older can have known, as a personal experience, the sensation with which Bryan first burst upon the country.

He was "beautiful as Apollo," Senator Stone of Missouri said; he was young, he was dashing, he was magnetic. There was romance in the mere fact that one so young should win such fame, and in the daring challenge of his ambition for greater things yet, for in the year in which he seized the nomination of one of the two great parties he was only just the age which the constitution fixes as the youngest at which a man may aspire to the presidency, and younger by ten years than any man who had ever reached the office. Most of all, there was romance in the dramatic swiftness and unexpectedness of his leap to power and public eminence.

—

Those who know only the Bryan of today will find it difficult to realize he is the same man of whom the New York Sun wrote on the day of his highest reach, July 10, 1896—a description that has the more force when one recalls that the Sun detested Bryan:

"From all parts of the convention hall a great roar went up for Bryan, Bryan, Bryan. These cheers were continued and rolled on and on, and 'The boy Orator of the Platte' started for the rostrum to make a speech....Mr. Bryan is a smooth-faced man of early, middle life and his dark hair is long and wavy....His rhetoric and English and his oratorical gestures were almost superb...His voice is clear and resonant and his bearing graceful. He is the idol of the silver camp, and if a vote could have been taken immediately after he had finished he would, without the slightest doubt, have been nominated for president by acclamation."

Or the same Bryan of whom, in his prime, John Clark Ridpath, fired by the ecstatic exaltation about Bryan that was common at the time of his 1896 triumph, wrote:

"The simple fact is that the unanswerable oration of William J. Bryan before the Chicago convention was one of the few inspired utterances of the human soul rising to a great occasion and pouring out the vehement river of truth. Bryan was on that day a chosen instrument ...William J. Bryan came upon the stage in answer to such a call and ...became the third conspicuous leader of American democracy...He vaulted like an athlete into the wild arena, drew his sword and stood defiant, blazing with wrath in the very face of an enemy that durst not attack him with anything but contumely and falsehood...We intend that the patriot and statesman, William Jennings Bryan, shall be, as he deserves to be, the president of the United States....and that under his wholesome and patriotic administration a new century of peace shall be ushered in, in the splendor and revival of which the evil powers which have dominated American society for the last quarter of a century shall wither and perish from the earth."

Monday, July 20, 1925
The Des Moines Register

HINT SCOPES JURY WAVERING ON A VERDICT

Darrow-Bryan Debate Plans Go Forward

Dayton, Tenn, July 19 (By The Associated Press)-The Scopes case verdict should be returned some time Tuesday. Although the defense has admitted that it has no hope of a favorable verdict, constant observers in the courtroom were not so sure. Only unanimous agreement of the jury can result in a verdict unless attorneys on both sides should agree to accept a majority verdict.

The charge against Scopes is a misdemeanor and not a felonly. He cannot be placed in prison in the event of conviction, the statute providing for a fine of not less than $100 and not more than $500.

Ready for Debate

By Raymond Clapper.

Dayton, Tenn., July 19 (U.N.)--The Rhea county courthouse and the pine-covered hills beyond the village outskirts will echo for the next two days with the final arguments of the Scopes evolution trial.

Most of the counsel on both sides will make final speeches to the jury. Clarence Darrow will close for the defense and William Jennings Bryan will follow him with the last word of the prosecution.

This debate, which may run over into Tuesday, will be one of the unique ones of modern times and perhaps as significant in the struggle to break the shackles of the mind as the Lincoln-Douglas debates were in breaking those of the body.

Defense Wants Statements Read.

When court opens at 9 a.m. tomorrow, the defense will seek to have read in court the statements of the exdcluded scientific witnesses.

Judge Raulston has ruled these statements may be printed in the record, but the defense desires that they be read aloud so that the radio audience and the spectators may hear them.

If this reading should be permitted the trial probably would be prolonged an extra day. But if they are merely presented without being read the closing arguments will begin at once. As these arguments are expected to consume about eight hours they will run over into Tuesday. The jury's deliberation no doubt will be exceedingly brief.

Fire Furnishes a Thrill

Today was quiet at Dayton. There would have been no excitement whatever had not a freight car caught fire. The fire siren shrieked just as the village was finishing noonday dinner, and everyone ran down the railroad tracks to watch the flames.

Bryan had intended to speak over the radio at the courthouse, but this was cancelled. He motored sixteen miles over Walden's ridge to Pikeville and made a twenty minute address at an open air union church service, attended by 2,500 persons, who sat on rough planks under trees. Bryan scolded the newspapers and said there is a gigantic conspiracy afoot to overthrow revealed religion.

Darrow Lectures on Tolstoi

Clarence Darrow delivered a lecture on Tolstoi at Chattanooga Sunday. His secretarial staff was busy at "the mansion" typing the statements of the scientific witnesses. One of these statements will run about 20,000 words. The stenographers are mimeographing 35,000 sheets in preparing copies for the press.

Judge Raulston returned from his home in Winchester, Tenn., Sunday night. He received hundreds of letters and telegrams over the week end, some denouncing him in rough language. One letter enclosed $5 to be turned over to local charity.

Chattanooga newspapers have been active in denouncing what they term Darrow's "insult" to the court Friday. Whether this will provoke the judge to administer a reprimand or some other form of judicial notice is a subject for much speculation. Some declare the judge should protect his dignity by rebuking the defense attorneys and others say he would make martyrs of them if he did.

Bryan Lauds State

Pikeville, Tenn., July 19 (A.P.)—A brief but vigorous defense of the Tennessee anti-evolution law and the culture of Tennesseeans marked the appearance here today of William J. Bryan.

Speaking to several hundred Sequatchie valley citizens in an open air meeting twenty miles from the scene of the Scopes trial, the fundamentalist chief began his address by expressing indignation "toward those who have maligned you—those who have come from another state to speak of you as bigots."

Criticizes News Writers.

He expressed the same feeling toward some of the newspaper men who "have spoken of you as yokels."

"I wish that I could have dragged them here and placed them face to face with a humanity they cannot imitate," he declared.

"The world is discussing the Scopes case," he said. "It has gone far enough now for us to uncover a gigantic conspiracy among the atheists and agnostics against the Christian religion.

"The brute standards they advocate would rob man of his high standards and drag him down to the brute basis. That is what they wish to teach your children. It would take from them that belief in immortality which you only can have when you believe in God.

Doctrine One of Blood.

"The doctrine of the evolutionists is a blood one. It teaches the survival of the fittest. All the testimony of all the evolutionists who ever lived is outweighed by the consolation of the twenty-third psalm."

He concluded by comparing a stagnant pool, which he said represented evolution. "The center of disease and death," with a flowing spring, "giving forth all the time that which refreshes and invigorates.

"Christ can make of every human being a living spring through which the goodness of good flows out to the world. The stagnant pool represents the life of those who believe they have come up from the brute."

Mr. Bryan was cheered enthusiastically.

**

ASCENT OF MAN

A Register reader of Ames writes his objection to the phrase "descent of man" commonly used in discussion of evolution, particularly as the discussion has centered recently in the Scopes trial at Dayton. The phrase unquestionably causes confusion, and the reader's point is a good one. So fixed has become the usage, however, since Darwin's "Descent of Man," that changing it is probably hopeless.

The Tennessee law involved in the Scopes case prohibits teaching that man has descended from lower animal forms. Descent in its ordinary usage implies going to lower levels. Descent as used by evolutionists simply means progress in point of time, as we speak of being descendants of those who have preceded us.

Confusion would be eliminated if the phrase used, were "ascent of man." That is precisely what is meant when we say "descended from lower orders." Lest we are not likely to begin calling ourselves "ascendants" of our forefathers. It is all a matter of terms, and once the usage is understood the inconsistency ceases to be troublesome. Apparently we shall have to take the usage as it is, so far at least as the present discussion is concerned.

Let us keep in mind, however, that "descent" in evolution does not mean deterioration, but may mean either that or the contrary. The theory is that some species have deteriorated, but that the general movement is up. In the case of man the connotation is the reverse of deterioration.

**

Mr. Bryan at last seems to be in a position where he can count on the votes.

**

TRIAL BY POPULAR APPEAL

Editorial in Boston Transcript: If Mr. Clarence Darrow spoke with bitterness in the motion to quash in the Scopes case yesterday, he had been given more than a good lead by Mr. William Jennings Bryan, whose conduct in the little Tennessee town has been an outrage on all the principles of justice and decency. He has spoken out of court, in public places, to audiences in a manner that must affect local opinion directly and the jury indirectly. He has prejudiced the issues, distorted facts, aroused passions in a fashion that, had he attempted it in other jurisdictions in Tennessee where the questions had been no more than the ordinary questions of law and fact, would have got him well fined for a contempt.

This has nothing to do with evolution, it has nothing to do with the guilt or innocence of young Mr. Scopes, but it has directly to do with those principles of right to which Mr. Bryan is so fond of appealing. Conceive for a moment of any ordinary citizen in Massachusetts who should proceed to do what Mr. Bryan has done unreproved, who should deliberately adopt mass-meeting methods to prejudice the trial of a case, who should impugn the character of a person accused and attack in anticipation his defense, stir up sectional feeling, play on all the smallest and weakest motives of the human heart. His career as such an haranguer would be dramatically short. He would be silenced and fined and what is more, would get no sympathy nor admiration.

But there at Dayton is Mr. Bryan ballyhooing for the angels in quite the same way that he gives his noon real-estate lectures in the land of alligators, and at the same time preparing the Dayton public to decide that Messrs. Darrow, Malone, Scopes, et al., are utterly wrong. Is this right? Ought it to have been permitted? Taking advantage of his public career and of the faith which thousands of honest folk can still give him, this man in the most impudent and sinister way saps the whole foundation of justice and meets apparently with approval from his audience and indulgence from the court. If we appear emphatic in the description of a situation that never ought to have been permitted, conceive that what has happened in Dayton can be repeated elsewhere and on different specific issues, but always with the sacrifice of the rights of those who are innocent until proved guilty.

Ours is a vocal age and one where the methods of publicity have been over-developed, but never has there been such a spectacle as that of this vain and presumptuous man saying what he pleased, where he pleased and as he pleased.

Tuesday, July 21, 1925
The Des Moines Register

DARROW VS. BRYAN ON BIBLE

Scopes' Lawyer Puts Commoner on Stand as Witness

Biggest Day of the Trial at a Glance

The following were the developments in the Scopes case at Dayton, Tenn., yesterday:

Clarence Darrow put William Jennings Bryan on the stand as a witness for the defense. Mr. Bryan testified to a literal belief in the bible.

Mr. Darrow was cited for contempt for a remark about the court, but was freed after he had apologized.

Court was moved into the open air because the throngs flocking into the building aroused fears that it would collapse.

Scientists' statements on creation and evolution were read into the record of the trial, though barred from the jury.

Dr. Shailer Mathews of the University of Chicago divinity school explained in a statement why there is no conflict between the biblical and scientific interpretations of Genesis.

**

DARROW CITED FOR CONTEMPT, BUT GETS OFF

Court is Moved to Open Air to Avoid Peril From Throng.

Dayton, Tenn., July 20 (By The Associated Press)—The first sensation of the seventh court day in the Scopes case came when Judge Raulston, immediately after the opening of court, cited Clarence Darrow for contempt of court as a result of remarks made Friday by the Chicago lawyer. He was ordered to appear before the bar of the court to answer tomorrow morning.

At the opening of the afternoon session, however, Mr. Darrow gained the floor and extended an apology for his remarks. The overture from the visiting attorney was accepted and Judge Raulston and the lawyer shook hands.

Moves Court Outdoors.

Before this outcome of the contempt citation incident could be passed as news through the court room, packed far beyond its capacity, Judge Raulston announced that the crowd was endangering possible break down of the floor, court would be adjourned to an open air platform on the lawn below. There the court sat for the rest of the afternoon.

Statements of eight scientists and two clergymen were placed in the record of the case by the defense during the day. These statements set forth what testimony would be given if scientific and expert testimony had been permitted in the case.

Judge Raulston, Mr. Darrow, William Jennings Bryan, Attorney

General Stewart, Dudley Field Malone and Arthur G. Hays posed for a "good fellowship" photograph as the crowd fought its way out of the courtroom onto the lawn below.

The exchange of kind words between the judge and Mr. Darrow seemed to restore a general spirit of good cheer among counsel on both sides of the case, and the court and attorneys were in rare good humor as the scene was shifted.

Raulston Cites Darrow.

As court opened for the afternoon session Mr. Darrow was recognized by the court to make a statement. He said that he did not know how hard his words of Friday looked until he had seen the minutes. He said that he was sorry. He said that in his stay in Dayton and vicinity he had been treated with great kindness and appreciated this consideration.

"I don't think any such occasion ever arose before in my practice," he said. " So far as intending to insult the court, I never meant anything of the kind. I have been sorry I made the remarks ever since I had a chance to read them.

"Of course, your honor will remember," said Mr. Darrow, "that whatever took place was hurried, one thing following another and the truth is, I did not know just how it looked until I read over the minutes as your honor did and when I read them over I was sorry that I had said it.

"On Friday I determined immediately on reading it over to tell the court just what I thought this morning. In the meantime I had seen one paper which stated that the court thought that I was trying to get in position where I would be held in contempt.

"Now, I want to say that what I say is in good faith, regardless of what your honor may think is right for you to do. I have been practicing law for forty-seven years and I have been pretty busy most of the time in court, and I have had many a case where I have had to do what I have been doing here, fight the public opinion of the people, in the community where I was trying the case—and I never yet have had any criticism by the court for anything I have done in court."

Sorry He Made Statement.

He added that he thought he had gone further than he should have gone and "so far as its having been premeditated or made for the purpose of insult to the court, I had not the slightest thought of that."

He continued that he had never, perhaps, been in a community where his religious ideas differed as widely from the great mass as here, but nevertheless he had never been treated better, kindlier or more hospitably.

"Personally, I don't think it constitutes a contempt, but I am quite certain the remark should not have been made and the court could not help taking notice of it, and I am sorry that I made it, ever since I got time to read it, and I want to apologize to the court for it."

"If this little incident had been personal between Colonel Darrow and myself," said Judge Raulston, "it would have been passed by unnoticed, but I could not pass them by when I represent the great state of Tennessee."

Judge Accepts Apology.

After telling of some of the great men of Tennessee, Judge Raulston said:

"My friends and Colonel Darrow, the man that I believe came into the world to save man and died for him on the cross, taught that it was right to forgive, pleading with God for the men who crucified him. I believe in these principles: I accept Colonel Darrow's apology; I am sure the words were not premeditated. He spoke at the moment when perhaps he had suffered one of the greatest disappointments of his life. I speak for the state of Tennessee when I say we forgive and forget."

Mr. Darrow stepped to the judge's stand and the incident was ended with a handshake.

The order of the court, read by Judge Raulston from the bench at the opening of the session, directed that Mr. Darrow make a bond of $5,000 and "not depart from the court without leave."

Frank Spurlock , Chattanooga lawyer, and George W. Rappleyea, Dayton business man, became sureties for the leader of the defense counsel.

In his order Judge Raulston read excerpts from an exchange

between Mr. Darrow and the court Friday, in which Darrow's reply to a statement from the court, "I hope you do not mean to reflect upon the court," was, "Well, your honor has the right to hope."

Why Darrow Was Cited.

Part of the colloquy read by the judge in citing Mr. Darrow follows:

The court—Colonel, what is the purpose of cross-examination?

Mr. Darrow—The purpose of cross-examination is to be used on the trial.

The court-Well, isn't it an effort to ascertain the truth?"

Mr. Darrow—No, it is an effort to show prejudice. Nothing else. (Laughter.) Has there been any effort to ascertain the truth in this case? Why not bring in the jury and let us prove it?

The court—Courts are a mockery—

Mr. Darrow—They are often that, your honor.

The Court—When they permit cross-examination for the purpose of creating prejudice.

Mr. Darrow—I submit, your honor, there is no sort of question that they are not entitled to cross examine, that all this evidence is to show what we expect to prove and nothing else, and can be nothing else.

The court—I will say this: If the defense wants to put their proof in the record, in the form of affidavits, of course, they can do that. If they put the witness on the stand the state desired to cross- examine them. I shall expect them to do so.

Mr. Darrow—We expected it and take an exception.

The court—Yes, sir, always expect this court to rule correctly.

Mr. Darrow—No, sir, we do not. (Laughter.)

The court—I suppose you anticipated it.

Mr. Darrow—Otherwise we would not be taking our exceptions here, your honor. We expect to protect our rights in some other court. Now, that is plain enough, isn't it? Then, we will make statements of what we expect to prove. Can we have the rest of the day to draft them?

The court—I would not say—

Mr. Darrow—If your honor takes a half a day to write an opinion—

The Court—I have not taken—

Mr. Darrow—We want to make statements here of what we expect to prove. I do not understand why every request of the state and every suggestion of the prosecution should meet with an endless grant of time, and a bare suggestion of anything that is perfectly competent on our part should be immediately overruled.

The court—I hope you do not mean to reflect upon the court.

Mr. Darrow—Well, your honor has the right to hope.

The court—I have a right to do something else, perhaps.

Mr. Darrow—All right, all right.

Textbook Is Admitted.

With the first incident disposed of attorneys for the state and defense became involved in three clashes, resulting in a victory for each side and what might have been called a draw.

The defense failed in an effort to get into the record Governor Peay's message to the Tennessee legislature when the Butler bill, under which Scopes was brought to trial, was approved, but the text book on biology recently accepted by the state was admitted over objection of the state.

When the question of the submission of statements from eight scientists and two clergymen came up, the defense sought the right to read them into the record while the state would have had them placed in the record of the case without comment from attorneys.

The defense desired these statements in the case as showing for the benefit of a higher court, if the case is appealed, what would have been testified if these witnesses had been permitted to testify. The court finally ruled that parts of the statements might be read in the absence of the jury, one hour being devoted to this. The ten statements offered for the record contained more than 60,000 words and Arthur G. Hays, reading for the defense, sketched them rapidly as he read.

**

EXPLAINS BIBLE CREATION STORY

Shailer Mathews says Genesis Accounts Differ.

Dayton, Tenn., July 20 (A.P.)—"A correct understanding of Genesis shows that its account of creation is no more denied by evolution than it is by the laws of light, electricity and gravitation," said a statement of Dr. Shailer Mathews, dean of the divinity school of the University of Chicago, read into the record of the Scopes trial today.

"The bible deals with religion. There are two accounts in Genesis of the creation of man. They are not identical and at points differ widely. It would be difficult to say which is the teaching of the bible. The aim of both, however, is clear and wonderfully inspired.

"Each shows that God created man and how man differs from beasts in resembling God, in that he possesses a moral and spiritual nature.

"In the first account in Genesis it is said that God made beasts, cattle and all creeping things by having the earth bring them forth as living creatures. The Hebrew expression here used, 'Nephesh chayah,' is the same as that used in the second chapter of Genesis to describe man when created.

Man Part Animal.

"The first story then continues with the creation by God of man in the divine image, male and female being created on the sixth day. In the second account God is said to have formed man from the dust of the ground and to have breathed into him the breath of life.

"Man thus became a living soul. In the Hebrew, the same word is used as that previously used to describe the animals, which the earth brought forth.

"This living creature, Adam, is placed by God in a garden which he is to till. He is forbidden to eat of the tree of knowledge of good and evil. He, however, disobeys and eats the fruit. God then declares that man has become 'one of us knowing good and evil.'

"Genesis thus says that an animal life, produced by God from the earth by his spirit, came to be like God through a development born of experience. Thus, so far from opposing the Genesis account of the creation of man, the theory of evolution in some degree resembles it.

Religious Interpretation.

"But the book of Genesis is not intended to teach science, but to teach the activity of God in nature and spiritual value of man. It is a religious interpretation of nature and God's relation thereto, in which the inspired writers use the best of the then current knowledge of the universe to show how God was in the creative process and how that process culminated in man possessed of both animal and divine elements.

"The theory of evolution is an attempt to explain the process in detail. It does not take place in a vacuum, but in an environment in which is God. Genesis and evolution are complementary to each other, Genesis emphasizing the divine cause and science the details of the process through which God works. This view that evolution is not contrary to Genesis is held by many conservative evangelical theologians such as Hall, Strong, Micou, Harris and Johnson. Mullins also holds to a theistic evolution."

**

JOSHUA COULD STOP THE SUN, BRYAN AVERS

He Hotly Calls Questioning a Ridiculing of God.

Dayton, Tenn., July 20 (A.P.)—Admitted agnosticism met fundamentalism here today as Clarence Darrow, counsel for the defense in the Scopes evolution case, drew out William Jennings Bryan, associate counsel for the prosecution, upon the witness stand.

Hundreds of men and women, drawn from the peaceful hills and valleys for miles around, pushed close to the rough wooden platform behind the courthouse as the verbal swords of the two clashed time and again, sending off flashes that drew volleys of handclapping and booming mountain fox calls.

A silence, broken only by the rustling of the maple trees, settled over the crowd as Arthur Garfield Hayes announced the intention of the defense to call Bryan to the witness stand.

The purpose was explained later by Mr. Darrow as an effort to "show the people what fundamentalism is." Bryan arose from the witness stand to tell Darrow, the judge and the assembled, spectators that its purpose was to cast "slurs upon the bible."

The nature of the examination brought Atty. Gen. A. T. Stewart and other members of counsel for the prosecution to their feet time after time to interpose objections. Frequently it even caused Darrow to arise with objections as the witness proceeded to direct the course himself.

Faces grew strained and lips tightened among the spectators at the apparent irreverence of some of the questions and they arose to cheer as the witness waved aside the protection of the judge with the declaration:

"These gentlemen have not had much chance. They did not come here to try this case. They came here to try revealed religion. I am here to defend it and they can ask me any questions they please."

As it proceeded, insinuations ceased to be insinuations and became either unveiled sarcasm or pointed irony, until argument succeeding argument, a fresh one threatened to arouse more controversial remarks than any of the preceding ones, and Judge Raulston adjourned for the day with several members of both the prosecution and the defense counsel on their feet and hot words on their tongues.

The questioning began with the expert witness, and after Bryan had announced his intention of calling to the stand Mr. Darrow, Dudley Field Malone and Mr. Hays.

The witness said that he had made considerable study of the bible, including its interpretation on the particular question involved.

"Do you claim that everything in the bible should be literally interpreted?

Accepts Bible Literally.

"I believe that everything in the bible should be accepted as it is given there. Some of the bible is given illustratively. For instance, 'ye are the salt of the earth.' I would not insist that man was actually salt or that he had flesh of salt, but it is used in the sense of salt as saving God's people."

"But when you read that Jonah swallowed the whale—or that the whale swallowed Jonah—excuse me please, how do you literally interpret that?"

"When I read that a big fish swallowed Jonah—it doesn't say whale."

"Doesn't it? Are you sure?"

"That is my recollection of it. A big fish, and I believe it, and I believe in a God who can make a whale and can make a man and can make both do what he pleases."

Other interrogations along the same line followed until the query:

"You don't know whether it was the ordinary run of fish or made for that purpose?"

"You may guess. You evolutionists guess," responded the witness.

"But when we do guess, we have the sense to guess right."

"But do not do it often."

"You are prepared to say whether that fish was made specially to swallow a man or not?"

"No, the bible doesn't say."

"But you believe he made them, that he made such a fish and that it was big enough to swallow Jonah?"

"Yes, sir. Let me add, one miracle is just as easy to believe as any other."

A suggestion from Mr. Darrow that one was just as hard for him to believe as another brought an immediate response:

"It is hard to believe for you, but easy for me. A miracle is a thing performed beyond what man can perform. When you get beyond what man can do, you get within the realm of miracles; and it is just as easy to believe the miracle of Jonah as any other miracle in the bible."

"Perfectly easy to believe that Jonah swallowed the whale?"

"If the bible said so; the bible doesn't make extreme statements as evolutionists do."

Thence the interrogation turned to the plausibility of Joshua's making the sun stand still, and brought objection from the attorney general who declared the questions had gone beyond the pale "of any issue that could possibly be injected into this law suit except by imagination."

Mr. Bryan, however, asserted "it would be too exacting to confine the defense to the facts. If they are not allowed to get away from the facts what have they to deal with?"

The next query from Mr. Darrow was:

"Have you an opinion as to whether, whoever wrote the book, I believe it was Joshua—the Book of Joshua—thought the sun went around the earth or not?"

"I believe he was inspired."

"Can you answer my question?

"When you let me finish the statement."

"It is a simple question, but finish it."

"You cannot measure the length of my answer by the length of your question."

"No, except that the answer will be longer."

Bryan Says He Thinks the Bible is Inspired

"I believe that the bible is inspired and whether the inspired author, one who wrote as he was directed to write, understood the things he was writing about, I do not know."

"Do you think whoever inspired it believed that the sun went around the earth?"

"I believe it was inspired by the almighty, and he may have used language that could be understood at that time instead of using language that could not be understood until Darrow was born."

"So, it might have been subject to construction, might it not?"

"It might have been used in language that could be understood then."

"That means it is subject to construction?"

"That is your construction. I am answering your question."

"Is it your opinion that passage was subject to construction?"

"Well, I think anybody can put his own construction upon it, but I do not mean necessarily that it is a correct construction."

"Don't you believe that in order to lengthen the day it would have been construed that the earth stood still?"

"I would not attempt to say what would have been necessary, but I know this, that I can take a glass of water that would fall to the ground without the strength of my hand and I can overcome the law of gravitation and lift it up. If my puny hand can overcome the law of gravitation, the most universally understood, to that extent, I would not deny power to the hand of Almighty God that made the universe."

Darrow Demands He Give Direct Answer

"I read that years ago. Can you answer my question directly? If the day was lengthened by stopping either the earth or the sun, it must have been the earth?"

"Well, I should say so."

"Yes?"

"But it was language that was understood at that time, and we now know that the sun stood still as it was the earth."

"We know also the sun does not stand still?"

"Well, it is relatively so, as Mr. Einstein would say."

"I ask you if it does stand still?"

"You know as well as I know."

"Better. You have no doubt about it?"

"No. And the earth moves around."

"Yes?"

"But I think there is nothing improper if you will protect the Lord against your criticism."

"I suppose he needs it?"

"He was using language at that time the people understood."

"Now, Mr. Bryan, have you ever pondered what would have happened to the earth if it had stood still?"

"No."

"You have not?"

"No, the God I believe in could have taken care of that."

"I see. Have you ever pondered what would naturally happen to the earth if it stood still suddenly?"

"No."

"Don't you know it would have been converted into a molten mass of matter?"

Bryan to Get Revenge When His Turn Comes

"You testify to that when you get on the stand. I will give you a chance."

"Don't you believe it?"

"I would want to hear expert testimony on that."

"You have never investigated that subject?"

"I don't think I have ever had the question asked."

"Or ever thought of it?"

"I have been too busy on things that I thought were of more importance than that."

"You believe the story of the flood to be a literal interpretation?"

"Yes, sir."

"When was that flood?"

"I would not attempt to fix the date. The date is fixed, as suggested this morning."

"About 4004 B. C.?"

"That has been the estimate of a man that is accepted today. I would not say it is accurate."

"That estimate is printed in the bible?"

"Everybody knows, at least, I think most of the people know that was the estimate given."

Stewart Objects to Any cross-examination

Other questions followed along the same line until Attorney Stewart objected to the cross-examination by Mr. Darrow of his own witness. Bryan, however, assured the court that he desired the attorney for the defense to be given latitude, "for I'm going to have some latitude when he gets through."

Arising, he addressed both the court and the crowd:

"These gentlemen have not had much chance. They did not come here to try this case. They came here to try revealed religion. I am here to defend it and they can ask me any questions they please."

Applause from the spectators brought an interchange of remarks between the attorney and the witness, which concluded with the declaration of Mr. Darrow that "you insult every man of science and learning in the world because he does not believe in your fool religion."

Another objection came from the attorney general, who asserted that Mr. Darrow was making an effort to insult the witness. Judge

Raulston, however, indicated that he did not wish to be purely technical and allowed the examination to continue.

Bryan Tells His Views on Ark and the Flood

An effort was made to establish the date of the flood. Bryan asserting that the bible gave the date as about 2348 years BC.

"You believe that all the living things that were not contained in the ark were destroyed?"

"I think the fish may have lived."

"I am asking you whether you believe?"

"I do."

"But the bible you have offered in evidence says 2340, something, so that 4,200 years ago there was not a living thing on the earth excepting the people on the ark and the animals on the ark, and the fishes. "Don't you know there are any number of civilizations that are traced back more than 5,000 years?"

"I know we have people who trace things back according to the number of ciphers they have. But I am not satisfied they are accurate."

"You are not satisfied there is any civilization that can be placed back 5,000 years?"

"I would not want to say there is because I have no evidence of it that is satisfactory."

"Would you say there is not?"

"Well, so far as I know, but when the scientists differ from 24,000,000 to 306,000,000 in their opinion as to how long ago life came here. I want them to come nearer together, before they demand of me to give up my belief in the bible."

Rejects Any Science in His Interpretation

"Do you say that you do not believe there were any civilizations on this earth that reach back beyond 5,000 years?"

"I am not satisfied by any evidence that I have seen."

"I didn't ask what you are satisfied with. I asked you if you believe it."

"I am satisfied by no evidence that I have found that would justify me in accepting the opinions of these men against what I believe to be the inspired word of God."

"And you believe every nation, every organization of men, every animal in the world outside of the fishes—"

"The fish, I want you to understand, is merely a matter of humor."

"I believe the bible says so. Take the fishes in?"

"Let us get together and look over this."

"Probably we would better. We will after we get through."

"Don't you know that the ancient civilizations of China are six or seven thousands years old, at the very least?"

"No, but they would not run back beyond the creation, according to the bible, 6,000 years."

"You don't know how old they are, is that right?"

"I don't know how old they are; but probably you do. I think you would give the preference to anybody who opposed the bible, and I give the preference to the bible."

Admits He Is in Dark on Old Civilizations

"I see. Well, you are welcome to your opinion. Have you any idea how old the Egyptian civilization is?" "Do you know of any record in the world, outside of the story of the bible, which conforms to any statement that it is 4,200 years ago or thereabouts, since all life was wiped off the face of the earth?"

"I think they have found records."

"Do you know of any?"

"Records reciting the flood, but I am not an authority on the subject."

"Have you ever heard anything about the origins of religion?"

"Not a great deal."

"And you don't know whether any other religion ever gave a similar account of the destruction of the earth by the flood?"

"The Christian religion has satisfied me and I have never felt it necessary to look up some competing religions."

"Do you consider that every religion on earth competes with the Christian religion?"

"I would not say competitive, but the religious unbelievers."

Darrow Then Calls Him a Hostile Witness

"Unbelievers of what?"

"In the Christian religion."

Another objection from the attorney general as Darrow continued his examination brought the response from the defense attorney that he had a right to cross-examine a hostile witness.

"Is there any way by which a witness can make an affidavit that the attorney is hostile?" asked Mr. Bryan, referring to the procedure in Tennessee by which an attorney is required to make affidavit that he was surprised by the testimony of the witness and with the discovery that he was hostile.

A discussion of Confucianism followed.

"Do you know it is more ancient than the Christian religion?"

"I am not willing to take the opinion of people who are trying to find excuses for rejecting the Christian religion where they attempt to give dates and hours and minutes. They will have to get together and be more exact than they have yet been able, to compel me to accept just exactly what they say as if it were absolutely true."

"I have all the information I want to live by and to die by," the witness said in response to one question.

Questions and answers came fast as the examination continued. Both grew short as the questioner sat hunched forward on the corner of the table, the witness swaying a palmetto leaf fan.

"And that's all that you are interested in?"

"I am not looking for any more religion."

"You don't care how old the earth is and how long the animals have been here?"

"I am not so much interested in that."

Eludes Answering Question by Darrow

The witness here eluded his questioner and explained the differences between Confucianism and Buddhism, comparing each with Christianity. Buddhism he termed an agnostic religion.

The course was then shifted to a questioning of the story of the tower of Babel. Rebuke, not fear, inspired the action of God in causing confusion among the builders, the witness said.

He refused to attempt to tell how old the earth might be, although he said:

"I could possibly come as near as the scientists do."

As both interrogations and replies became faster and shorter, the attorney general was brought forward again to ask the purpose of the examination.

"The purpose is to cast ridicule on everybody who believes in the bible, and I am perfectly willing that the world shall know that these gentlemen have no other purpose than ridiculing every person who believes in the bible," declared Bryan.

Darrow Calls It Fight on Bigotry and Ignorance.

"We have the purpose of preventing bigots and ignoramuses from controlling the education of the United States; and you know it, that is all," Mr. Darrow fired back.

The two faced each other on the platform. The witness asserted:

"I am simply trying to protect the word of God against the greatest atheist, or agnostic, in the United States. I want the papers to know that I am not afraid to get on the stand in front of him and let him do his worst. I want the world to know that agnosticism is trying to force agnosticism on our colleges and on our schools and the people of Tennessee will not permit it to be done."

A general argument seemed imminent.

Sue K. Hicks, Attorney General Stewart, Bryan, Darrow, Hays and Malone were drawn across the platform and heated words were fired back and forth. Judge Raulston allowed the examination to continue.

"The reason I am arguing is not for the benefit of the Supreme Court. It is to keep this gentleman from saying that I was afraid to meet them and let them question me, and I want the Christian world to know that any atheist, agnostic or unbeliever can question me any time as to my belief in God and I will answer him," Mr. Bryan said as he resumed his seat.

Exception was taken by Mr. Darrow to the conduct of the witness and another argument came over the admissibility of the testimony, followed by another declaration by Mr. Bryan that the only reason he had been questioned was "to give this agnostic an opportunity to criticize a believer in the word of God."

Malone Denounces Bryan, Defending Own Beliefs

A stirring address by Mr. Malone was inspired by this remark. He expressed resentment at the reflection upon the belief or unbelief of any member of the counsel for either side in a manner that brought applause from the spectators.

"On this very subject," Mr. Malone declared, "I would like to say that I would have asked Mr. Bryan—and I consider myself as good a Christian as he is—every question that Mr. Darrow has asked him for the purpose of bringing out whether or not there is to be taken in this court only a literal interpretation of the bible, or whether, obviously, as these questions indicate, a general and literal construction cannot be put upon the parts of the bible which have been covered by Mr. Darrow's questions.

"I hope for the last time no further attempt will be made by counsel on the other side of the case, or Mr. Bryan, to say the defense is concerned at all with Mr. Darrow's particular religious views or lack of religious views. We are here as lawyers with the same right to our views. I have the same right to mine as Mr. Bryan has to his, and we do not intend to have this case charged by Mr. Darrow's agnosticism or Mr. Bryan's brand of Christianity."

Bryan Recites Literal Belief in the Flood and the Garden of Eden
How Bryan Looks on Garden of Eden Story

The examination continued with the question:
"Mr. Bryan, do you believe that the first woman was Eve?"
"Yes."
"Do you believe she was literally made out of Adam's rib?"
"I do."

"Did you ever discover where Cain got his wife?"

"No, sir; I leave the agnostics to hunt for her."

"Where she came from you do not know. All right. Does the statement, 'the morning and the evening were the first day,' and 'the morning and the evening were the second day,' mean anything to you?"

"I do not think it necessarily means a twenty-four hour day."

"What do you consider it to be?"

"I have not attempted to explain it—I do not see that there is any necessity for construing words, 'the evening and the morning,' as meaning necessarily a twenty-four hour day, 'in the day when the Lord made the heaven and the earth.'"

Not So Sure Earth Was Made in Six Days

"Then when the bible said, for instance, 'And God called the firmament heaven. And the evening and the morning were the second day,' that does not necessarily mean twenty-four hours? Do you think those were not literal days?"

"No. But I think it would be just as easy for the kind of God we believe in to make the earth in six days as in six years, or in 6,000,000 years or in 600,000,000 years; I do not think it important whether we believe one or the other."

"Do you think those were literal days?"

"My impression is they were periods, but I would not attempt to argue as against anybody who wanted to believe in literal days."

"Mr. Bryan, what I want to know is, do you believe the sun was made on the fourth day?"

"I believe just as it says there."

"Do you believe the story of the temptation of Eve by the serpent?"

"I do."

"And you believe that is the reason that God made the serpent to go on his belly after he tempted Eve?"

Tells What Happened to the Garden Serpent.

"I believe the bible as it is, and I do not permit you to put your language in the place of the language of the almighty. You read the bible and ask me questions and I will answer them. I will not answer your questions in your language."

"I will read it to you from the bible: 'And the Lord God said unto the serpent, because thou hast done this, thou art cursed above all cattle and above every beast of the field, upon thy belly shalt thou go and dust shalt thou eat all the days of thy life.' Do you think that is why the serpent is compelled to crawl upon its belly?"

"I believe that."

"Have you any idea how the snake went before that time?"

"No, sir."

"Now, you refer to the bow that is put in the heaven, after the flood—the rainbow. Do you believe in that?"

"Read it."

The examination concluded a moment later as Mr. Bryan arose and addressed the judge and the audience:

"Your honor, I think I can shorten this testimony. The only purpose Mr. Darrow has is to slur at the bible, but I will answer his question. I will answer it all at once. I want the world to know that this man who does not believe in a God is trying to use a court in Tennessee—"

He was cut short by Darrow's objection.

"I object to your statement. I am examining you on your fool ideas, that no intelligent Christian on earth believes."

As the crowd strained forward and the two faced each other on the platform, the announcement by Judge Raulston that court was adjourned ended the argument.

**

Scientists Deny Conflict With Religion In Scopes Statements

PUT EXPERTS' OPINIONS INTO COURT RECORD
Modern Story of Creation Is Related to Judge

Dayton, Tenn., July 20 (A. P.)—Explanations of the evolutionary theory and the bearing this theory may have on the biblical account of creation, prepared by a group of nationally known scientists, were placed in the records of the Scopes evolution trial here today by defense counsel.

Some salient pronouncements touching on the evolutionary hypothesis and the debated conflict between science and Christianity embraced in the statements, which aggregated upward of 60,000 words, follow:

By Maynard M. Metcalf, zoologist, formerly of Oberlin college, Ohio, and Johns Hopkins university, Baltimore:

"Evolution not only has occurred but evidences of it are visible today in both the plant and animal world.

Denies Any Conflict.

"There is no conflict, no least degree of conflict, between the bible and the fact of evolution. But the literalist interpretation of the bible is not only puerile, it is insulting both to God and to human intelligence."

By Dr. Winnerton C. Curtis, zoologist, University of Missouri:

"The historical fact of evolution seems attested by overwhelming evidence. Science has nothing to conceal; it stands strong in the strength of demonstrable facts and invites you to view the evidence.

"The evidence for man's origin is becoming clearer, year by year. Comparative anatomy, embryology, classification, physiology, geographical distribution, fossils, and the existing races of mankind tell the same story for man as for the rest of the world.

"It is not that men came from monkeys, but that men, monkeys and apes all came from a common mammalian ancestry billions of years in the past."

Not Anti-Christian.

Kirtley F. Mather, chairman of the department of geology at Harvard University, declared:

"None of these facts is really in any way disturbing to the adherents of Christianity.

"Not one of these facts contradicts any teaching of Jesus Christ known to me. None of them could, for his teachings deal with moral law and spiritual realities. Natural science deals with physical laws and material results. When men are offered their choice between science, with its confident and unanimous acceptance of the evolutionary principle on the one hand, and religion, with its necessary appeal to things unseen and unproved on the other, they are more likely to abandon religion than to abandon science.

"If such a choice is forced upon us, the churches will lose many of their best educated young people, the very ones upon whom they must depend for leadership in the coming years. Fortunately, such a choice is absolutely unnecessary. To say that one must choose between evolution and Christianity is exactly like telling a child as he starts for school that he must choose between spelling and arithmetic.

"Thorough knowledge of each is essential to success—both individual and racial—in life."

Philosophy of Change.

Dr. Horatio Hackett Newman, zoologist of the University of Chicago, asserted:

"Evolution is merely the philosophy of change as opposed by the philosophy of fixity and unchangeability. One must choose between these alternate philosophies, for there is no intermediate position; once you admit a changing world and you admit the essence of evolution.

**

WHEN THE TEST COMES

The controversy over evolution in the schools of Tennessee will come to its test when the supreme court of the United States ask themselves whether the Tennessee statute is such a violation of religious liberty as to be against public policy.

The curious fact is brought out that while the first amendment to the national constitution says "congress" shall not make a law respecting religious beliefs, the prohibition is not extended to the state legislatures, and unless the state constitution itself reiterates this prohibition it is claimed that no prohibition is enforceable against the state.

Dean Hall of the Chicago university law school expresses the opinion that, "it is unlikely the Tennessee statute violates the United

States constitution, and there is considerable doubt about its violating any clause of the Tennessee constitution."

In our Iowa constitution the third and fourth articles of the bill of rights read:

"The general assembly shall make no laws respecting the establishment of religion nor prohibiting the free exercise thereof; nor shall any person be compelled to attend any place of worship, pay tithes, taxes, or other rates for building or repairing places of worship, or the maintenance of any minister or ministry.

"No religious test shall be required as a qualification for any office or public trust, and no person shall be deprived of his rights, privileges, or capacities, or disqualified for the performance of any of his public or private duties or rendered incompetent to give evidence in any court of law or equity in consequence of his opinions on the subject of religion."

What is suggested by the wording of our Iowa constitution is the rapidity with which language becomes obsolete and almost meaningless.

How many readers of the Register could promptly say just what the prohibitions of the first of these two paragraphs from our bill of rights specifically refer to?

It is only by the broadest of interpretations that such a constitutional guaranty is construed to meet the situations of a new period, when all the relations are new, and only the principle involved is the same.

Even the prohibition of the national constitution must be interpreted liberally, for all it contains specifically is this: "Congress shall make no law respecting an establishment of religion, or prohibiting the exercise thereof." Literally this covers nothing but creating an established church and interfering with the independent churches.

If the matter is taken to the supreme court of the United States and the court believe a situation has arisen where the freedom the framers sought to secure in the matter of religious beliefs is involved, the court will pay but little attention to the precise words used in the Tennessee constitution or in Article 1 of our national bill of rights.

On the other hand if for any reason the supreme court lean to the notion that a lot of things ought to be left to the local community, and teaching in the public schools is one of them, it will be easy to remand the matter to the people of Tennessee.

The real interest in the Scopes case is going to come when the final decision is rendered defining our constitutional right to freedom of inquiry and belief.

WAY DOWN IN TENNESSEE
BY JOSEPH WOOD KRUTH IN THE NATION.

Even those who do not happen, like the present writer, to have been born and bred in Tennessee should not find it difficult to forgive Dayton. A tiny town set in the midst of fruitful strawberry fields, it had never heard of any Darwin except the one who keeps the local drygoods store until Mr. Bryan enlightened it, and to this day it is ignorant of that famous meeting of the British association when Huxley and Wilberforce thrashed out the question which has now arisen, some sixty years later, to puzzle it. Its faith is no narrower than that of every other community equally remote; its temper is better than was the temper of Oxford half a century ago; and if some of its inhabitants turn to the law to protect their children against the teaching of a dangerous theory, it is with a simplicity of mind which has no conception of the questions of academic freedom involved.

Dayton, moreover, once the law was passed, was ready and anxious to deal as best it could with all the questions, legal and scientific, involved. While the president of the state university sat in his office praying that he might be allowed to violate the law in peace; while he was quietly issuing (as several members of his faculty have assured me he was) unofficial instructions to his teaching staff that they should make no changes in their instruction; and while he was, at the same time, seeking to retain the friendship of both sides and accepting the congratulations of various fundamentalist bodies for his stand against evolution, Dayton was arranging to settle in simple honesty what the representatives of serious education and enlightenment were anxious only to dodge.

And so when I sit at the little table in Robinson's drug store where the argument began and discuss with the county superintendent of schools his attitude as one of the prosecution, I feel that the shame of Tennessee is not in Dayton. There is no state of the union, no country of the world, which does not have communities as simple-minded as this one, and if Tennessee has become the laughing-stock of the world it is not because she has her villages which are intellectually a half century behind the centers of world thought, but rather because among her sons who know better there is scarcely one who has the courage to stand up for what he thinks and knows instead of flying quickly to cover lest he might have to sacrifice to his convictions some political advantage or some material gain.

At Dayton no one is afraid to tell me what he thinks. But when I go to Knoxville, seat of the state university and one of the three largest cities in Tennessee, I enter a different world. One of the most important members of the university board of trustees takes me aside to whisper in my ear; the president of that institution, telling me I am a good fellow, takes me confidentially by the arm; the editor of one of the leading newspapers,distinguished by the safe piety of its editorials upon the subject, closes the door of his office; and the remarks of all might be summarized in what were the actual words of one: "Of course it's a damnfool law—but I won't be quoted." These and other Knoxvillians are defensive and indignant; they resent in various terms the publicity they have attracted and they protest against being judged by the laws their legislature passes, but these Knoxvillians will not admit that, fundamentally, they are to blame. In Tennessee bigotry is militant and sincere; intelligence is timid and hypocritical, and in that fact lies the explanation of the sorry role which she is playing in contemporary history. Dayton's only crime is the naive belief that a law may be intended to be enforced.

Wednesday, July 22, 1925
The Des Moines Register

BRYAN QUIZZES DARROW ON BIBLE

Scopes Guilty, Case Goes to Higher Courts
Fix Fine at $100 and Bail at $500.

BY RAYMOND CLAPPER.

Dayton, Tenn., July 21 (U.N.)—Twelve men of the hills today found John T. Scopes guilty of teaching evolution and the young Tennessee high school teacher is on his way to a place beside Dred Scott on the shelf of lasting fame.

Like the humble Negro slave, who was the instrument through which the chains of human slavery finally were broken, this pleasant young man whose blood comes down from the early Anglo-Saxon lovers of liberty, is the medium through which the supreme court of the United States finally will decide whether a state legislature may chain the mind.

In a swiftly moving three hours' session, Scopes was found guilty, sentenced to a fine of $100, the minimum under the law, and an appeal was taken which started the case on its way to the highest court of the land.

Jury Out Seven Minutes.

Closing arguments were dispensed with to hurry up the case. The jury was out seven minutes. Thompson, the foreman, reported to the court.

The slender freckled faced, good-natured youth, who was compared by one bright newspaper- woman, to Mrs. O'Leary's cow, stepped into the space in front of the judge's rostrum. He stood there coatless, the sleeves of his shirt rolled up, twisting his hands behind him, his head a trifle lowered as a mark of respect for the tribunal before which he was summoned.

The court speaks—"The jury has found you guilty. The court now fixes your fine at $100, and imposes on you—"

"Your Honor, he should be heard before sentence is pronounced," Dr. John R. Neal, one of the defense counsel said.

"Oh, yes," the court apologizes.

Prisoner Makes Statement.

"What have you to say before sentence is pronounced on you?"

The youthful prisoner speaks for the first time in this historic trial:

"I feel that I have been convicted of violating an unjust statute and I shall continue to oppose in every way I can a law which I feel violates the ideals of freedom, the teaching of the truth, and my constitutional and personal freedom."

Bail was fixed at $500, pending the appeal.

Defense lawyers made customary motions designed to start the case toward the higher courts. This ended the technical features of the great evolution trial.

Love Fest Follows.

Then, the law having spoken, came a love fest from participants, a friendly exchange of cordial words which wiped out any stings left from heated clashes of the trial, a scene which could only occur in a hospitable country court where judicial dignity is not toted about after court hours.

Dudley Field Malone of New York was the first to express his thanks.

"I wish to thank the people of Tennessee for their hospitality and the chance to try these great issues," he said.

The court thanked newspaper correspondents for their courteous conduct.

A disheveled, collarless spectator, with a roll of newspapers sticking out of his pocket, climbed upon a chair in the rear and addressed the court.

Hiked to Trial.

"In behalf of the public I want to express my appreciation of the hospitality here and the reasonable expenses." This brought loud cheers. He proved to be Munnell Wilson of Madisonville, Ky., who walked 200 miles to hear the trial.

"I'm an evolutionist and I'm going to start speaking in Kentucky to prevent such a law there," he explained later.

Young Gordon McKenzie of the prosecution staff got the floor next. "On behalf of Rhea county and the prosecution," he said, "I want to say we are delighted to have had you all with us. We have learned to take a broader view of life. You brought your ideas and views and we communicated ours to you as best we could. We do appreciate your views and while much has been said about our narrow minded people, we don't feel hard toward you. We want to be more broadminded than some of you have given us credit for. Should the time ever come when any of you come back to the garden spot of the world we hope you'll stop off so we can talk over the evolution trial again."

Bryan's Parting Words.

Bryan, who sat on the edge of the judge's rostrum during the rendering of the verdict, rose to make his last remarks in the courtroom.

"Dayton is the center of this world famous trial largely by accident," he said. "This cause has stirred the world because it reached into the future beyond the power of man to see. The world cares little about the consequences of this case. But it raised an issue that some day will be settled right. There can be no settlement without discussion.

"The value is not in any incident of the trial. The people will study these questions and they will decide.

"This trial will stimulate investigation. The facts will be known. We should pray that the right should prevail whether it be our will or your will."

As Bryan finished, there were calls from the spectators for Darrow. He worked his way to the judge's rostrum, and folding his arms in his characteristic way across his galluses, he said:

Darrow's Message Brief.

"I appreciate the courtesy of the counsel of the other side—at least the Tennessee counsel. I appreciate the hospitality that has been extended to me and I go away feeling respect and gratitude for your liberal attitude toward me personally. As to my little controversy with the court, I have already made all right with the court. We have done our best to turn back the tide that has sought to test the facts of science by religious dogma."

Then came the final word from the court.

"I recently read that a great man is he who possesses a passion to know the truth and has the courage to declare it in face of all opposition. Sometimes it takes courage to search for facts that may destroy our preconceived notions. A man who is big enough to search for truth and find it and declare it in the face of all opposition is a big man. The greatest man that ever walked the face of the earth, who came down from heaven, was born in a little town. We don't measure greatness by the size of a neighborhood a man may come from. The great Dred Scott decision involved the liberty of just one colored man.

"Truth is indestructible. Another thing that is indestructible is the word of God. It is indestructible by any force. 'My word shall not perish from the earth.' I pray God that I have decided rightly. I'm glad to have had you with us."

Minister Delivers Benediction.

The factory whistle across the railroad yards blew its noontime blast. The court officer rapped the gavel.

"Court's adjourned. Don't crowd as you go out."

Judge Raulston called out for silence again.

"Brother Jones will deliver the benediction," he said.

Brother Jones raised his hand and the crowded courtroom bowed its head. Thus the great trial came to an end, as it had started, with a prayer for the help of the divine hand.

When court was called none of the prosecution counsel was present.

"We opened a little early on account of the judge's watch," the court crier explained after he had called the court to order. "The judge is not fast—it's just his watch."

When Bryan and the other counsel arrived, Judge Raulston announced that he would permit no more testimony such as was extracted from Bryan by Darrow Monday. He also ordered that testimony expunged from the record.

"The issue is simply whether the defendant, Scopes, taught that man descended from a lower order of animals and I feel that the testimony of Bryan can shed no light on any issue that will be pending before the higher courts," the judge held.

Suggests Trial Close.

Darrow, taking exception, then declared that the trial might as well end and suggested the judge order the jury to return a verdict of guilty.

"We have no witnesses to offer any proof that would be admitted as the issue is laid down here. There is nothing to do but bring in the jury and instruct them to find the defendant guilty," Darrow said.

Opposing counsel held a private conference and agreed among themselves to dispense with all closing arguments in the interest of speed.

Bryan, after being refused an opportunity to question Darrow as had been planned Monday, announced he would give to the press the questions he would have asked.

Darrow agreed to answer these questions through the press.

Judge Raulston recessed court for an hour while he prepared his charge to the jury.

At 11 o'clock the jury was brought in. The jurors were in the courtroom about three and a half hours during the whole trial and heard nothing except the reading of the indictment and the brief testimony of the school boys who had studied under Scopes.

Judge Raulston's charge was brief and conformed to the regular legal requirements, including his construction of the law that man descended from a lower order of animals.

Darrow spoke only a few words to the jury. He stepped up close to them, folded his arms and spoke in a low conversational tone.

**

NINE QUESTIONS PUT ON PAPER FOR AGNOSTIC

Expresses His Doubts on Miracles and the Commoner's God.

Dayton, Tenn., July 21 (U.N.)—William Jennings Bryan has had his chance to examine Clarence Darrow, counsel for John T. Scopes, who mercilessly exposed the commoner's ignorance of many facts outside the bible at the open air session of Judge Raulston's court Monday afternoon.

Mr. Bryan put nine questions to Mr. Darrow through the newspapers and in reply, the brilliant Chicago lawyer, confessed agnostic, expressed a disbelief in miracles and doubts as to the nature of God and other fundamentals of religion.

The court had barred further examination of opposing counsel by each other and Bryan had asked permission to put through the newspapers the questions he had intended to ask if he had been permitted to call Darrow to the witness stand. Darrow promptly agreed to answer them in the same way.

Bryan's Nine Questions.

Bryan's nine questions, with Darrow's answers, follow:

First—Do you believe in the existence of God as described in the bible?

Answer—I do not know of any description of God in the bible, although we are informed in one part of it that he is a spirit. If Mr. Bryan would describe what he means by God I could probably tell whether I believe in his God. The question of what was meant by the word was directly put to counsel for the state and one of them answered that God was made in the image of man. I do not believe in that kind of God. As to the origin of the universe, and what is back of it, I do not pretend to know. I haven't the intimate acquaintance with it that Mr. Bryan says he has.

Is the Bible Inspired?

Second—Do you believe that the bible is the revealed will of God, inspired by God.

Answer-- I believe it should be taken as every other book, and that the portions in it that are sublime like such portions of every other great book might by a figure of speech be called inspired. I might even say this of Mr. Bryan's "In His Image," if I could find any such portion in it.

Third—Do you believe in the supernatural Christ, foretold in the old testament and revealed in the new testament?

Answer—I do not believe that any supernatural Christ was foretold in the old testament or revealed in the new. I believe that the Christ that was prophesied in the old testament was a great Jew, who should deliver the Jews from their physical bondage and nothing else.

Do You Believe Miracles?

Fourth—Do you believe in miracles, according to the old and new testament?

Fifth—If you believe in some but not all of them please name a few of those which you accept and those you reject, with the reasons for the same.

Sixth—Do you believe that Christ was conceived of the Holy Ghost and born of the Virgin Mary as recorded in Matthew and Luke?

Seventh—Do you believe that Christ rose from the dead as described in the four gospels?

Answers—As to four, five, six and seven, I do not believe in miracles, and I believe that the universe acts and always has acted in accordance with immutable laws, and that whatever may be back of the universe has never violated these laws.

On An Immortal Soul.

Eight—Do you believe in the immortality of the soul?

Answer—I have been searching for proof of this all my life, with the same desire to find that is incident to every living thing, and I have never found any evidence on the subject.

Ninth—If you believe in evolution, at what point in man's descent from the brute is he endowed with hope and promise of a life beyond the grave?

Answer—I have no knowledge on the question of when man first believed in life beyond the grave. I am not at all sure whether some other animals have not the same hope of future life. The origin may have arisen in vivid dreams, concerning the return of the dead, or from all I know, from actual evidence of the return of the dead.

"I have never tried to impose my views of religion on any human being that ever lived." Darrow added. "I have a right to my own views and would fight as hard to protect every other man's views as I would my own."

**

SHAILER MATTHEWS STATEMENT

Some of the men best informed on evolutionary theory, men of eminence in the sciences who think as dispassionately and clearly and wisely as any of the world, have much difficulty expressing their reasoning to the popular mind. They think and speak in words and phrases that are not readily understandable by the mass—not because the mass is stupid, necessarily, but because the difference in terminology amount almost to another tongue. The scientist is often as helpless to put his ideas in the popular tongue as is the layman to grasp the ideas when put in the terms of science.

If anybody is disposed to infer obscurity of thinking or indecisiveness of argument from this, let him reflect a moment upon medicine and the law. Fill an explanation of a medical view with "posteriors" and "anteriors" and "cerebrums" and "pathologicals," to mention only some of the commonest and simplest and most widely understood terms and what happens to its popular understandability? No matter how clear and logical and accurate every statement may be, it does not get home. As to the law, it is still a mystery and its slowly built up language mostly a lay puzzle, though nobody questions that sound principles lie under law itself.

Partly because of the difficulty of expression and partly because of the fragmentary handling which even the best of newspapers are obliged to give to such things as the long statements by numerous scientists that have been inserted in the Scopes case record, it all does not seem half so conclusive as it would be if any one of the scientists concerned, given the knack of simple language, could make it if he alone to a small audience went in a couple of hours over the whole range of theory and proof.

But some contributions nevertheless have been made which should have growing effect in the clarification of popular thinking on the origin of life. And among these contributions should be listed the statement of Dr. Shailer Mathews, dean of the divinity school of the University of Chicago. What he says is simply that no quarrel really exists between religion and evolution, nor even between genesis and the evolutionary theory. Genesis, he explains, teaches "the activity of God in nature and spiritual value of man"; it is "a religious interpretation of nature and God's relation thereto," which shows "how God was in the creative process and how that process culminated in man, possessed of both animal and divine elements." The theory of evolution, on the other hand, is merely "an attempt to explain the process (of creation) in detail." Evolution "does not take place in a vacuum but in an environment in which is God." And "genesis and evolution are complementary to each other."

Now there is nothing new in this, but it is quite tersely and fairly expressed. And it does get down to the main point in the controversy as between some exponents of religion and science as a whole. The main point is that the explorations of science into the processes of creation do not prove religion, do not disprove religion, have nothing to do with religion. The will, the force, the urge (call it what one will) that is behind creation is for the philosopher, religious or non-religious, to debate about. There is the real debate from the religious standpoint. The scientific theory of evolution, which is a theory not of what is behind creation but of how that force or will expressed itself, has no real part in the debate.

Whether the earth was created "on a certain day 6,000 years ago" or, as every thinking person now knows to be true, many millions of years ago, is a matter of absolute indifference to religionist and non-religionist. The earth, and a great many other bodies, nevertheless were created. It is just as difficult to explain without falling back on a faith as it was a generation ago, or two generations, or ten. The more one learns of creation scientifically—that is to say, of the scope and process of creation, as astronomy and geology and biology bring this out—the more aweinspiring it is. And, far from disposing of the belief that in it all there has been and is one great primary urge, on the contrary every new discovery of science points anew to that urge. And "evolution," from start to finish, simply provides a partial history of the operation of that urge.

Evolution explains more and more the how of creation. It explains or attempts to explain nothing of the why. It is there that religion enters. And there religion is on just as tenable ground as ever it stood on. Thus it is that Dr. Mathews says "genesis and evolution are complementary to each other."

**

During his trial young Mr. Scopes received almost as much attention as a spear bearer in a Shakespearean play.

**

THE MODERNIST VIEW

To the Editor of the New York Times: In the controversy between fundamentalists and evolutionists, the late Henry Drummond, author of the much-loved sermon, "The Greatest Thing in the World," has a very illuminating word to say. I have been surprised to find how much light is thrown upon the turmoil in Tennessee by that great book of forty years ago, Drummond's "Natural Law in the Spiritual World."

For are not the two parties in this case really talking about different things? Science, represented by Mr. Scopes, is standing for the evolution of man with the rest of nature—the man of protoplasm, neurons, glands, etc.—the only man that science pretends to know, and from the human point of view, at least, an enormously important creature. This many people would call the natural man.

Other gentlemen in Tennessee are distressed because they see evolution apparently destroying their belief in man as made in the image of God. Do they believe that God is made of flesh and blood? I doubt it. "God is a spirit, and they that worship him must worship him in spirit and in truth," they would be the first to tell us. They are considering the spiritual man, with which science at present is not concerned.

Natural man, it appears, is the product of evolution: the spiritual man is from God, "a new creature."

The side represented by Mr. Scopes is concerned with the natural; the masses of Tennessee stand for the reality of the spiritual.

Where, then, is the antagonism with this difference of subject matter? Many on the natural side know or care little about the spiritual—but not all, by any means. Of the natural man, those who are spiritually inclined, some fundamentalists especially, know all too little also.

In the present case it seems likely that the jury will be convinced only by men who do recognize a spiritual life in man as well as the "natural" product of evolution, and who can clarify evolution, and who can clarify the issue at that point. As this issue becomes clear, may there not be born a still greater interest in science on the part of religious people, who will recognize that their knowledge is greatly limited unless they understand the creature of evolution, the man of flesh and blood, which, however, from their point of view is incomplete without the greater gift and growth of the spirit?

There are probably many of us who feel that the physical and spiritual are different octaves of the same scale, but who recognize that many miss the highest side –they do not enlarge the bounds of their lives to include the God manifest in his son. Even if they see the creator in nature they may fail to see him in the person of Christ, who stands at the gateway to the life that is most complete. They, therefore, may miss the eternal life, which is the knowing God, the real immortality with which they have established no correspondence. They have only the immortality that is a part of all nature—whatever that be.

It may be the immortality of the germ plasm, life extended in one's descendants alone. It may be an immortality manifest by physical research, which with its "earth bound" spirits and human-like manifestations is, in its lowest stages at least, far removed from the eternal life of the Christian. If the immortality of psychical research be proved, then we may say that the chance for men to attain eternal life—fellowship with God—is extended into the next world; that man can begin there as well as here to grow into the likeness of the God who is spirit; but of that we are not yet sure. Therefore, now is the appointed time to begin the life that is life indeed.

All life is conditioned, and the condition of life eternal seems to be a spiritual life here that can and does know God, the spirit.

Even were the grounds for Professor Drummond's argument from biogenesis to be destroyed, were the gulf between the inorganic and the organic to be completely bridged, were life to spring spontaneously from the nonliving, the spiritual would still be as much a reality as ever in the experience of religious folk.

Why be terrified about the origin of man's body? As long as we are on earth let us study the workings of nature with awe and earnestness; but those who are concerned with the spiritual man have an added task.

If only those who are supposed to have experienced that summum bonum of the spirit would seek as earnestly to reveal that greater life to the materialists, and leave the fightings to the men of mere flesh and blood! Men are never won by contentions and strife, but by the contagion of lives lived in companionship with the one who is the way, the truth and the life. Annette Richards Fallows

**

Rippling Rymes
By Walt Mason

Depravity

Blood flows around like water from voters shot and torn, and grisly tales of slaughter confront us every morn; some pilgrim sliced to ribbons and robbed of his doubloons; what think the stately gibbons, what say the proud baboons? "The human tribes and nations are out with knives and guns; don't say that we're relations of such blood-thirsty ones. We monkeys in the jungle, whom you have doubtless met, may sometimes botch and bungle the rules of etiquette. We have not all the graces that human people know, and on our misfit faces unseemly whiskers grow. But we have rigid morals, though awkward be our port; we don't indulge in quarrels or murder just for sport. We strive to live together as friendly neighbors should, and you may tell us whether this rule of life is good. But oh, these human beings, they're always up in arms! We hear their hully-cheeing, excursions and alarms. They're shot and knifed and wounded for any old excuse; the gangsters' war-cry's sounded, and death has broken loose. The hosts of killers sally from every dark retreat, there's murder in the alley, there's slaughter in the street. They say we are related to raging beasts like these; by savants it's been stated till it's become a wheeze. We patiently meander along our destined way; we stand a lot of slander before we seek a fray. But when the yarn is bruited that we are kin to men, denial must be tooted again and yet again. In highly moral fashion we always have behaved; we are not slaves to passion, and we are not depraved.

Thursday, July 23, 1925
The Des Moines Register

The Other Sciences.

Clio, Ia.—To the Editor: Science must be totally crucified that fundamentalism may live. When evolution was first sounded to the world, that is came in a way to stay, even many scientists hesitated. It seemed too sudden for them. J. W. Dawson, though against it, about fifty years ago in substance made the following concessions: "Evolution, not being true, from revelations made by geology we will have to admit this:—that creation did not take place all at one time, or within six days' time at some so-called beginning., but to the contrary, beginnings have been strung all down the ages, different species first made their appearance on the earth during different ages strung along down the geological periods from the earliest past up to near or about the present. And also, in a general way, the lower forms appeared first and the higher later on up to the present."

"And," he continues further in substance, "judging from past geological history, we may expect that creation is not confined to any period of time of the past, present or future. And that being true we may expect new species to appear at any time, nor can we look for them to appear in their lowest form but, to the contrary, in the highest form or about the highest of any on earth." Mr. Dawson further concluded that there is some law of creation or process not yet discovered but he confidently hoped might be discovered perhaps within a decade or so.

Now in case that fundamentalism does away with evolution to save the old theory it must also do away with geology. If, however, they, in their kindness and toleration allow us to retain geology, then, as their old creation theory is killed by it, it is up to them to give us some other theory or their own house as well as ours will be left without an inhabitant.

But that fundamentalism may live science must be sacrificed at her altar: all must be laid away in one mighty sepulcher. Is it worth the price? Has science been only an obstructer, a pauper? Has it done nothing for the world? Can fundamentalists cast out devils? They have brains enough to blush at the idea. But science has under control the treacherous microbes that take the lives of multitudes. A. A. Snow

**

Clarence Darrow and William J. Bryan do not stage a nice exhibition of temper when they get together and discuss religion or the bible.

Friday, July 24, 1925
The Des Moines Register

Mr. Bryan failed ignominiously in his attempt to make Clarence Darrow less of an atheist.

**

Henceforth, for quite a spell, Dayton, Tenn., will have to be content with the entertainment furnished by an occasional circus or street carnival.

**

The English language is likely to be worn to a frazzle before all the evolution debate is ended.

**

Anyhow, it saves some men a lot of wear and tear on the mind to accept the bible literally.

**

Mr. Darrow comments on the remarkable courtesy with which the Tennesseeans have treated him. Perhaps the folks down there haven't acquired the habit of throwing eggs and pop bottles at the performers.

**

What Do YOU Think?

Bryan's Success and Failure.

Fort Dodge, Ia.—To the Editor: The most thrilling incident in the life of the great commoner was in the democratic convention at Baltimore in 1912. In the voting Clark had a majority of the votes. He was the choice of the Tammany delegation and others of like character. The convention adjourned Saturday night until Monday morning: the Clark forces were in high feather believing they had victory within their grasp.

On the opening of the convention on Monday Mr. Bryan from the platform made a speech in which he repudiated the candidate and the means by which they sought to nominate him.

The first vote taken Clark's majority shrank and soon was gone entirely; the Wilson vote gained steadily until the necessary two-thirds was registered and Woodrow Wilson was declared nominated for president.

That speech of Bryan changed the whole course of history for this generation. Now, if Mr. Bryan would use his great influence and abilities to complete the great unfinished work of Wilson by aiding the of peace and good order to ratify and enforce the league of nations on the part of the United States he would complete the work begun on that fateful day when he made that speech in Baltimore. T. A. Carpenter.

**

Genesis

Waterloo, Ia.—To the Editor: Bryan said he believed everything in the bible literally except certain metaphorically used expression. Now Jesus says, "Fools and slow of heart to believe all that the prophets have spoken."

"Where did Cain get his wife?" He answered that he did not know. This shows the depravity of real vision that Mr. Bryan has. If he had read his bible aright he would have discerned that God created man in his own image and likeness. Now the image and likeness of God is invisible to the naked eye and is that man that permeates and inhabits this physical body. Again the bible says that God made man out of the dust of the earth. Dust being dust of the earth. Dust being visible this man is visible and is the one made through the processes of evolution through the past ages. Through the processes of evolution there were thousands of these beings and Cain took one of these beings to wife.
L. E. Elkelberg.

**

EVOLUTION AND GENESIS, VERSE BY VERSE
By Dr. J. S. Grasty, Geologist, in the Baltimore Sun.

If Mr. Scopes taught scientific facts then he could not have taught in conflict with the Biblical account of the origin of the earth and of life itself, as presented in Genesis, chapter one. That, too, properly interpreted, is a story of evolution. Let us consider the first chapter of Genesis, verse by verse, and then it will be evident that if Scopes knew his science he could not and did not deny that story of divine creation.

Genesis, 1: In the beginning god created the heaven and the earth.

Science—Science admits and must admit the act of creation. No agnostic could profess ignorance of that, and no atheist could deny it. Neither could object to the creator of all things being called God.

Genesis, 2: And the earth was without form and void, and darkness was upon the face of the deep. And the spirit of God moved upon the face of the waters.

Science—According to accepted hypotheses the earth was without form and void. There is no conflict between science and Genesis here.

Evolution From Darkness to Light

Genesis, 3: And God said let there be light, and there was light.

Science—There was evolution from darkness to light, and here again science is in accordance with Genesis.

Genesis, 4: And God saw the light, that it was good, and God divided the light from the darkness.

Science—With consolidation of the earth, the clearing up of its atmosphere and the earth revolving upon its axis—thus was light divided from darkness.

Genesis, 5: And God called the light day, and the darkness he called night. And the evening and the morning were the first day.

Science—These are definitions about which there can be no difference of opinion.

Waters Are Divided.

Genesis, 6: And God said: Let there be a firmament in the midst of the waters, and let it divide the waters from the waters.

Science—Firmament here refers to the solidity and origin of the landmasses, which did "divide the waters" from the waters.

Genesis, 7: And God made the firmament and divided the waters, which were under the firmament from the waters, which were above the firmament, and it was so.

Science—The ground water table, or the matter of subterranean waters, is as widespread today as the firmament—i.e., the lithosphere itself. The oceans also rest upon this very firmament.

Genesis, 8: And God called the firmament heaven, and the evening and the morning were the second day.

Science—This is definition, except that firmament is here used in a different sense and as it is more commonly used today. The word day here must be taken to correspond with a division of geological time.

Formation of Oceans.

Genesis, 9: And God said let the waters under the heaven be gathered together unto one place and let the dry land appear, and it was so.

Science—The integrity and antiquity of the sea, or ocean basins, is not disputed, and taking rank with them in antiquity are the outlines of the continental masses. Hence again science and Genesis are in accord.

Genesis, 10: And God called the dry land earth, and the gathering together of the waters called the seas, and God saw that it was good.

Science—These are definitions in accordance with present usage.

First Act of Creation.

Genesis, 11: And God said, let the earth bring forth grass, the herb yielding seed and the fruit tree yielding fruit after his kind, whose seed is in itself upon the earth; and it was so.

Science—In this verse there is described the first act of creation of life, i.e., plant life; and that plant life was actually the first to appear science itself teaches. Plant life prepared the way to provide sustenance for animal life—which was to come later.

Genesis, 12: And the earth brought forth grass and herb yielding seed after his kind, and the tree yielding fruit after his kind; and God saw that it was good.

Science—The order is in accordance with known facts. Plant life thus continues to develop. The plant life of one of the earlier geological periods is today our main source of fuel—coal.

Genesis, 13: And the evening and the morning were the third day.

Science—We might here attempt correlation with the great divisions of geological time, but that is another story. The biblical day was, obviously, not a day of twenty-four hours.

Sun and Stars Appear.

Genesis, 14: And God said let there be light in the firmament of the heaven to divide the day from the night; and let them be for signs and for seasons, and for days and years.

Science—In the very early period of the earth's history the atmosphere was densely beclouded, but in time it cleared more and more, and at length the stars could be seen. Their relation in the heavens to the seasons is well understood.

Genesis, 15: And let them be for lights in the firmament of the heavens to give light upon the earth; and it was so.

Science—The beauty of the stars, which is here alluded to, cannot be denied.

Genesis, 16: And God made two great lights, the greater light to rule the day and the lesser light to rule the night; He made the stars also.

Science—There has been an evolution of the earth itself, and of our solar system, including the sun. The sun and moon could well have existed long before this, a s previously indicated, but not as well defined lights, from a terrestrial point of view, until they could be seen. A freer and clearer atmosphere had now developed. The evolution of the atmosphere enters into all earth hypotheses.

Dawn of Animal Life.

Genesis, 17: And God set them in the firmament of the heavens to give light upon the earth.

Science—Thus we have more and more light conformable with earth hypotheses, and begin, therefore, to approach the dawn of animal life.

Genesis, 18: And to rule over the day and over the night and to divide the light from the darkness: and God saw that it was good.

Science—The function of the sun and moon as here described is poetically brief. Without light we would be without life.

Genesis, 19: And the evening and the morning were the fourth day.

Science—The earth in its evolutionary creation—for such it was, as it was not accomplished in any one day or any one period of time—was now, as *we* know it today, two-thirds complete. The concordance between the scientific and Biblical account is more remarkable than any difference that may be pointed out. It is doubtful whether any scientific man could convey as much, or in such beautiful language, in a story so briefly told.

Life First in Water.

Genesis, 20: And God said, let the waters bring forth abundantly the moving creature that hath life and fowl that may fly above the earth in the open firmament of heaven.

Science—It must be admitted by science that the Biblical account stated the true origin of life in water, and the order of development, as above stated, long before science, by independent research, came to the same general conclusion.

Genesis, 21: And God blessed them, saying, be fruitful and multiply and fill the waters in the seas and let fowl multiply in the earth.

Science—The great development of life, when animal life appeared, is admitted by science to have been truly "multiplying" in its development. Plant life and the life of the seas were dominant, as science admits, at this stage of the earth's history.

Then Higher Form of Life.

Genesis, 23: And the evening and the morning were the fifth day.

Science—At another time the correlation of fifth Biblical day with the division of geological time may well be presented. Not yet, as will be observed, has the Biblical outline—for, in its brevity, it can be nothing more than an outline—deviated from the general scientific outline.

Genesis, 24: And God said let the earth bring forth the living creature after his kind, cattle and creeping things, and beast of the earth after his kind, and it was so.

Science—Thus the higher forms of life appeared, and science teaches this was so.

Genesis, 25: And God made the beast of the earth after his kind, and cattle after their kind, and everything that creeepeth upon the earth after his kind; and God saw that it was good.

Science—This verse amplifies verse 24 and shows the greater and greater development of the higher forms of life.

Man at Last Appears.

Genesis, 26: And God said, Let us make man in our own image, after our own likeness; and let them have dominion over the fish of the sea, and over the fowl of the air and over the cattle, and over all the earth, and over every creeping thing that creepeth upon the earth.

Science—If science be skeptical as to whether man was made in God's own image—though no such charge is made against science—it is in no position either to deny or affirm it. It is certainly more readily or preferably believed than not. And as to dominion over other animal life, surely man has attained that without doubt.

Genesis, 27: So God created man in his own image, in image of God created he him; male and female created he them.

Science—Science cannot prove that man, as "man," was created in God's image, and it would be truly unscientific to attempt to do so. It is undemonstrable pro or con. It must therefore, be solely a matter of faith and belief. From an evolutionary point of view the question may well be asked. When did man become man? It will be noted that in this twenty-seventh verse it is stated that "male and female created he them." This is in accordance with the origin in general of other species, even though in apparent conflict with Eve being derived from Adam's rib, as described in Chapter II of Genesis, but it must be remarked that Chapter I, here being considered, probably would take precedence.

Injunctions Laid On Man.

Genesis, 28: And God blessed them, and God said unto them, Be fruitful and multiply, and replenish the earth and subdue it, and have dominion over the fish of the sea, and over the fowl of the air, and over every living thing that moveth upon the earth.

Science—This is an injunction to man upon which science need not touch, but, admittedly, man has about done as enjoined.

Genesis, 29 and 30: And God said, Behold I have given you every herb bearing seed, which is upon the face of the earth, and every tree on which is the fruit of a tree yielding seed; to you it shall be for meat.

And to every beast of the earth, and to every fowl of the air, and to everything that creepeth upon the earth, wherein there is life. I have given every green herb for meat; and it was so.

It would appear from these verses that man is admonished to be largely a vegetarian as to his diet. Science certainly knows that that is best for him, and particularly so after he passes middle life.

Genesis, 31: And God saw everything that he made, and, behold, it was *very good. And the evening and the morning were the sixth day.*

Science—Thus ends the biblical account of creation. Considering that it is the shortest account of, potentially, the longest story to be told the outline is in most remarkable accord with scientific facts.

Wherein, then, does the teaching of evolution violate the story of divine creation?

We are not told that God created man in the twinkling of an eye, and if evolution was not pleasing to God, why then did the element of time, which is the essence of evolution, have to enter into the act of creation at all?

Saturday, July 25, 1925
The Des Moines Register

The theory that we are descended from apes is not a new one, but the idea simply has a hard time gaining favor.

**

From Dayton to Knoxville to Washington! The talk about evolution hangs over us all.

**

Evidently Mr. Bryan has as little faith in science as Mr. Darrow has in religion. Which makes it look like a tie.

FOUNDATIONS OF FAITH.

St. Louis Post-Dispatch: Suppose, Mr. Bryan, just suppose that the scientists are right and that Genesis is wrong: suppose it should prove to be true that man is descended from a lower order of life; suppose next year, or thirty years from now, scientists should prove their claims about the descent of man as conclusively as they have proved that the earth is round and that it moves around the sun. Would you then say, Mr. Bryan, that Christianity must be abandoned?

It would be a fair question to ask of Mr. Bryan. For he is arguing now that the Christian religion cannot survive if one of the principal theories of modern science should prove to be true. He is pitting the faith of millions of men against the almost universal opinion of scientific men. Suppose the scientists are right. They may be right. It is possible that Mr. Bryan is wrong. It is possible that the anthropologists know more of the history of man than the theologians. What, on Mr. Bryan's premises, would happen then to the faith of which he proclaims himself the champion?

The campaign, which Mr. Bryan is leading today, is fundamentally an attack on the foundations of the Christian religion. He does not mean it to be, of course, but when he insists that the foundations of religion are in the first two chapters of Genesis he has narrowed the foundations and that the whole structure is imperiled. No wonder the fundamentalists report that their children become unbelievers when they go to college. It is not surprising. They send their children out into the world of knowledge impressed with the belief that if any statement in the Bible is not true then their whole religion is untrue.

Is that the way to defend a faith? Is that the way to make religion secure? It is a strange way indeed, to bring consolation to mankind to tell them they can believe nothing unless they believe also that the Chaldean science of 4,000 years ago is literally true. Mr. Bryan is not protecting the faith of his people. He is saying to them: Your religion is untrue unless science is wrong. He is exposing them to the conclusion that if science is right, then their religion is wrong.

He is repeating once more a mistake that has been made again and again for 2,000 years by well-meaning but unwise champions of religion. In every age there have been men to say that each new advance of science would destroy religion. For this controversy over the evolution of man is merely the latest of a long series of controversies in which, just as in Dayton today, devout men like Mr. Bryan have staked the whole of Christianity against a scientific theory.

The truth of Christianity has been staked on the shape of the earth, on its place in the solar system, on the movement of the plants, on the meaning of comets, on the age of the earth, on a denial that there could be fossil animals, on the flood, on Jonah and the whale, on Joshua and the sun. On each one of these subjects there were theologians who opposed the scientists, as Mr. Bryan opposes them now. In each controversy it was argued that the truth of the scientific view meant the end of Christianity.

If Christianity has no broader foundation than the fundamentalists claim it would not today be the living faith of millions. Christianity, in spite of the fears of the fundamentalists through the ages, is a living faith because it rests on a far solider foundation than the fundamentalists imagine. Mr. Bryan is a man of strong conviction but of little faith. The gospel he brings to the people of Tennessee does not rest, as all sound faith must, on a continuous revelation in human experience. It rests instead on the assertion that Darwin or somebody else was wrong.

What a tiny base on which to erect a religion! What a gamble he makes of Christianity. How little faith he must have at bottom if all his faith depends upon denying something which may be proved conclusively the day after tomorrow! Is it fair, then, to tell the plain people in Tennessee that they must give up their whole religion, their consolation on earth and their hope of salvation hereafter, if the kinship of man with a lower order of animals is indisputably proved?

Who more than Mr. Bryan is threatening to rob devout people of their faith?

**

What Do YOU Think?

Religion and Education.

Chicago-To the Editor: If the eighteenth amendment cannot be violated by the states, why should the first one be made null and void by the state of Tennessee? We must remember that all the opposition to evolution comes from religious sources. The question of its truth or falsity is no longer an open question among scientists. The constitution in article 6 provides for religious liberty, but our fathers thought it did not do so with sufficient definiteness, hence the first amendment to make it irrefragable. After doing this, is it reasonable to suppose they intended that the states should establish religion? The supreme court, in my opinion, would undoubtedly take this view of it. Then the bigotry and malice of the Tennessee law. It provides for fine and imprisonment for any teacher who teaches evolution in any public institution of learning, while it is no crime to teach it elsewhere. Then, while a legislature can make provisions for education and, in a general way, decide what branches shall be taught, no legislature can decide upon the disputed points or a study. This must be done by experts. The only way to handle false teaching is through the fullest and freest liberty of thought and discussion. If the teaching of evolution is false, and that of Genesis is true, are not religious people willing to leave the matter to future investigations? If they have any confidence in their cause, they are. Scientists always have been. Franklin Steiner, Secretary American Rationalist association.

**

Birds of a Feather.

To the Editor: The unconverted church members who believe in the infidel theory of evolution must feel very proud over the kind of company they find themselves associated with in the Dayton trial.

The champion of their cause is Clarence Darrow, an avowed agnostic, who does not believe the bible, who is a free thinker and a free lover, who says marriage is an unnecessary institution, and who for money secures Loeb and Leopold immunity from the death penalty they deserved. He objects to prayer in opening court and ridicules all who believe God's word and seek to obey it.

The old adage "birds of a feather flock together" fits this motley crew of Unitarians, agnostics, and false prophets like Shailer Mathews of the Standard Oil university. John M. Dunkerton

**

EXPECT A CLASH IN CONGRESS ON DARWIN THEORY

Treasury Investigates Status of Wittner.

Washington, July 24 (A.P.)—Whatever may be the outcome of the effort of Loren H. Wittner to throw the evolution question into the federal courts, members of congress now in Washington feel certain that the subject will have full and free discussion in the house and senate at the coming session.

The rider to the District of Columbia appropriation bill, which Wittner seized upon to bring his action in the District of Columbia Supreme court, is certain to be reported in the new supply measure for the Washington government, and so will form the vehicle for congressional debate.

The view of some congressmen is that both the evolutionists and fundamentalists will marshal their forces for the congressional discussion and that each side will find able spokesmen among the membership. Should such be the case the issue would be fairly joined in congress, which would be called upon to determine whether the teaching of the evolution theory is in fact in conflict with the teachings of the bible.

Investigate Wittner.

Hurried conferences were called at the treasury today to determine the status of Mr. Wittner, who precipitated the question of evolution here after treasury officials had been told that, in taking the oath of office as an employee of the internal revenue bureau, Wittner had eliminated the words "so help me God."

Wittner recently said that he holds the views of an atheist. The treasury officials were informed that he had taken the oath of office three times and that on each occasion, the words at the end of the oath were stricken out at his request.

The question was raised as to whether, in these circumstances, Wittner's tenure of office was legal. The department's solicitor was asked for a ruling.

Government officials at first hand were unable to find a direct precedent in the case brought before them, although it was held that the case of Walt Whitman, the poet, might bear on it.

Whitman Ousted.

Whitman was ousted from treasury service soon after the civil war by a secretary who objected to passages in his "Leaves of Grass" but afterwards he rendered government employment in the department of justice. The records in his case have been sent to the library of congress as historical exhibits.

The situation has brought to the treasury the question of whether there is a prescribed oath for government agents, or whether the oath taken by Wittner constituted any oath at all, according to the law. Another angle the officials will seek to thrash out is whether an avowed atheist can take the oath, containing the words "So help me God" without taking a false oath.

A standard oath is furnished each government department by the civil service commission, but officials have been given the liberty of changing it as circumstances warranted.

**

Chattanooga, Tenn., July 24 (A.P.)—The widest discussion of evolution was urged by William J. Bryan in Chattanooga today in a talk with a News representative. He declared that he, in common with his opponents, who aided the defense of John T. Scopes at Dayton, Tenn., urged full discussion of their common belief that the truth was mighty and would prevail. Mr. Bryan, however, hinted that immature minds of boys and girls of fourteen years might not be as much helped by discussion as would adults.

Mr. Bryan was here preparatory to leaving for Winchester where he will speak Saturday. He declared that the Scopes case at Dayton had answered its purpose.

The commoner incidentally made arrangements here for the printing of the address he had intended to make to close the case for the state at Dayton, but had been prevented from making because of the collapse of the trial. It is his intention to release this address in a week or so for newspaper publication.

Sunday, July 26, 1925
The Des Moines Sunday Register

THE CLOSED MIND

The anti-evolution movement has reached Washington. There is the treasury employee who invokes the appropriation rider which forbade the teaching of disrespect for the Bible, and there is promise of several new proposals at the next meeting of congress. Specifically, it is the purpose to bar the Smithsonian Institution from investigating matters concerning the origin of man. The last budget allowed a few thousand dollars for the bureau of American ethnology. All such appropriations will be challenged.

It is in such proposals that the menace of the anti-evolution agitation is manifest. The position is this: Don't ask these questions—don't investigate—don't accept the findings of those who do investigate. We are told that we should not dig into the ruins of ancient cities where we may find records written before that eventful Friday, Oct. 23, 4004 BC, when, at 9 o'clock in the morning we are assured creation occurred. We should not invent microscopes, telescopes, spectroscopes and the like, should refuse to use them once invented. To do so would be to see microorganisms, fossils, and unknown stars, to learn about the structure of matter.

"Don't question, don't look, don't investigate." That leads to the closed mind, stops progress. Everyone knows the danger of trusting to a doctor who believes he has final knowledge in his field, who makes his diagnosis quickly, outlines treatment concisely and admits no possibility of error. All doctors have to do this in particular cases and for brief intervals, but one who doesn't keep abreast of professional literature soon is hopelessly behind the times. Without awareness of progress, without willingness to discard a first practice when a better is offered he can't be trusted in any serious case.

Dr. H. H. Rusby of the Columbia school of pharmacy declares properly that while it is unimportant whether a student believe in evolution it is all-important that he have the intellectual honesty to follow the search for truth wherever it takes him. Surely that is true not only of pharmacy student but students of medicine, zoology, history or anything else. It is true out of school as in school. Yet one of the leading fundamentalists of New York declared not long ago in a public address that they did not demand Dr. Fosdick's belief in their creed, they only asked him to say that he believed it!

There are some who still insist the Tennessee legislature was within its "rights" in enacting the anti-evolution law, that it is an unimportant matter. Yet that same legislature passed a measure providing that any one who had been graduated from high school should be allowed to practice medicine. Only the tact of the president of the state university secured later passage of a substitute measure.

There is a great deal involved in this reactionary movement. It is a movement on behalf of the closed mind, and that is dangerous as well as immoral.

**

When stubborn fundamentalist meets unyielding evolutionist, then comes the tug of jaw.

**

Wonder if Mr. Bryan will be flattered by the knowledge that some flappers are wearing his picture on their painted knees?

**

What Do YOU Think?
Creeds Against Religion.

Red Oak, Ia.—To the Editor: The religion of Jesus has ever been on trial. The doubting of skeptics have lead theologians to fashion his sublime spiritual experiences into creeds. His personality has been lost in the process. Christians thus became defenders of doctrine, more than followers of him.

His tolerance was tempered with a great certainty. He was certain of the love and goodness of God, and of God's presence in the universe to him, nothing was dead, dull, nor grossly material. The essence of things was life—spirituality.

The hope of the world is that more people shall come to accept his position. Many competent observers point out that science is about to swing from a materialistic to a spiritualistic explanation of things. The spirit of liberalism must have sway if this transition is to be accomplished. Let Christians be the first to exemplify it! Ed. L. Peet, jr.

**

The Unity of Truth

To the Editor: Science is classified knowledge. It includes only those facts which have been proved to be true. It therefore follows that there can be no conflict between science and any intelligent religion. If any religion is not intelligent, it is not worth saving and cannot be saved.

Truth is eternal and will prevail. O. A. Hammand.

Monday, July 27, 1925
The Des Moines Register

BRYAN FOUND DEAD AT DAYTON
End Comes During His Afternoon Nap

DEATH CAUSED BY APOPLEXY, DOCTORS SAY
Wife Bears Up Bravely Under Shock; Burial at Arlington

Dayton, Tenn., July 26 (PA)—William Jennings Bryan, three times presidential nominee of the democratic party and known the world over for his eloquence, died here this afternoon.

The end came while the great commoner was asleep and was attributed by physicians to apoplexy. He had retired to his room shortly after eating a large dinner to take a short rest. Mrs. Bryan sent the family chauffeur, Jimmie McCartney, to wake him about 4:30 and it was learned then that he was dead.

Dr. W. F. Thomason and Dr. A. C. Broyles, who examined the body, expressed the opinion Mr. Bryan had been dead between thirty and forty-five minutes before they arrived.

Burial at Arlington.

Funeral arrangements had not been completed late tonight, but would be in Arlington cemetery.

Mr. Bryan, who was a colonel of the Third Nebraska volunteers during the Spanish-American war on several occasions, had expressed a desire to be buried in Arlington.

Mr. Bryan's death came on the eve of another crusade he had planned to carry before the American people—a battle against modernism. He returned to Dayton this morning after having made addresses yesterday at Jasper and Winchester, Tenn., and after having completed arrangements for the early publication of the speech he was to have made in closing the trial of John T. Scopes, who recently was found guilty of violating Tennessee's anti-evolution law.

Despite the strenuous program Mr. Bryan had been following as a member of the prosecution staff in the Scopes case and as a leader of the fundamentalists, he appeared in excellent health.

Shortly before Mr. Bryan entered his room to rest he told his wife he had never felt better in his life and was ready to go before the country to wage his fight in behalf of fundamentalism.

About 4:30 o'clock, Mrs. Bryan said she felt her husband had slept long enough, so she sent the chauffeur, who also was his personal attendant, to wake him. McCartney shook Mr. Bryan twice, before he noticed the latter was not breathing. The physicians and A. B. Andrews, a neighbor, then were summoned hurriedly.

Wife Remains Calm.

Mrs. Bryan accepted the shock bravely and remained calm. "I am happy that my husband died without suffering and in peace," she said. "You know he was a colonel in the Spanish-American war and since it was his wish to rest in Arlington, we probably will place him there," she continued. "But no definite decision will be reported until we hear from William Jennings Bryan, jr."

Sue K. Hicks, who was associated with Mr. Bryan in the recent trial, and Mr. Andrews remarked upon Mrs. Bryan's courage, as she took charge of arrangements.

"During all the excitement Mrs. Bryan was the calmest person in the house," Mr. Andrews said. "She took complete charge of affairs and showed more nerve than I have ever seen in a woman—and she is an invalid, too."

George W. Rappleyea who instituted charges against Scopes in order that the anti-evolution law might be tested, was among those who called to express sympathy to Mrs. Bryan. Hundreds of telegrams and long distance calls of love and sympathy were received at the home.

Attended Church Services.

As for Dayton, the town found it almost impossible to realize that the commoner was dead. During the morning many of the citizens had seen him at the Southern Methodist Episcopal church and had heard him lead in prayer. He appeared in excellent health and his friends expected him to place in his battle against modernism all the vigor and eloquence which marked all his campaigns since the famous "cross of gold" speech.

In his addresses at Jasper and Winchester yesterday, Mr. Bryan spoke with unusual vigor as he was encouraged by the applause of the hundreds who heard him. Last night he returned to Chattanooga and while there completed arrangements for the early publication of the speech which was to have been delivered during the Scopes trial.

Early today he joined A. W. Lessly, Vernon Keith and Miss Bettie Harms at breakfast before leaving Chattanooga for Dayton. Mr. Lessly accompanied him to Dayton and while en route Mr. Bryan talked on various topics of the day and of the appeal made for Scopes.

The death of Mr. Bryan found his family widely separated. William Jennings Bryan, jr., who came here to assist his father in the Scopes case, had returned to Los Angeles, Cal., Mrs. Francis M. Baird, his eldest sister, was at her home at Lincoln, Neb., Mrs. Ruth Bryan Owen, a daughter, was in Mount Vernon, O., to fill a chautauqua engagement. Charles W. Bryan, who was nominated as vice presidential candidate by the democrats in the last general election, was in Colorado and it was several hours before he could be reached.

**

BRYAN LACKED HIS OLD VIGOR DURING TRIAL

The "Silver Tongue" Was Silenced by Malone's Fiery Attacks.

BY FARRIS L. DAVIS.

(Special to The Register.)

New York, July 26. —Those who watched Mr. Bryan direct his last fight in the stuffy courtroom at Dayton must be particularly surprised by his sudden death. There, deriding science, darting indignant glances at the "Agnostic Darrow" alert to every twist of the Scopes trial, he seemed to be at the top of his physical powers.

Mr. Bryan appeared to be in first rate fighting trip from the day he reached the Tennessee village until the final day, when his forces having won, he forecast a continuous struggle between religion and science until victory rested with one or the other. His splendid voice restrained, a look of deep earnestness gripping his features, Mr. Bryan was most impressive in the last moment. He implied that he would lead the crusade for the bible and it was evident he firmly expected to. It was his most dignified moment.

Seemed in Good Health.

Physically, indeed, the commoner radiated vigor. He was only a little overweight, his stern face was a healthy brown, and the famous voice resonant. It was commonly remarked by men who had known the commoner long that he seldom had looked better in late years. One such friend, complimenting the erect warrior upon his "youthfulness," drew from him a characteristic reply.

"I have taken care of myself," said Mr. Bryan, emphatically and with satisfaction, and except for a tendency to overeat, it is doubtful if Mr. Bryan ever indulged any bodily excess.

Yet, those among the commoner's listeners at Dayton, who were inclined to be charitable, asserted his mental powers were failing. They declared he had been outwitted by Clarence Darrow in every brush between the strikingly opposed men. They saw in Dudley Field Malone's besting of the old master on the oratorical field a sign that he had lost effectiveness.

Audience Preferred Malone.

When the courtroom, packed with Tennesseeans from mountain and plain, a people naturally sympathetic with conservative Christianity and acutely responsive to impassioned rhetoric, preferred Malone, it hurt Mr. Bryan.

Whether he himself regarded the defection of his sworn followers to the cosmopolitan young defense lawyer as a signal that his dialectic prowess was diminishing cannot, of course, be determined. What could be seen was that he bent his head for a moment, as if in prayer, while the applause died away, and then redoubled his directive activity.

Even Mr. Bryan's supporters admitted disappointment over his share of the brutal give-and-take between himself and Mr. Darrow under the courtyard trees. Through his career, the commoner had been distinguished by an ability to dismay and confuse those who questioned him in public. But here, sitting uneasily in a swivel chair on a pine plank platform, wielding a palm leaf fan, his features strained by the ordeal, he appeared unhappy to the sympathetic crowd.

Not the "Old Bryan."

"That isn't the old Bryan," observed a veteran political correspondent. Everyone, friend and foe alike, in that harsh atmosphere, hoped Mr. Bryan would regain his mental assurance and agility in the final address to the jury. That address, upon which he had worked steadfastly for two months and which he had expected to match the "cross of gold" speech, was not given because arguments were passed.

But Mr. Bryan looked forward to delivering it in a cross-country tour. He toiled over a revision of the manuscript almost to the end, according to Associated Press reports. Armed with apostolic fervor and this speech, the fundamentalist advocate expected to kindle fires of faith that would sweep evolution from the schools and leave a clear path for a great revival of religion.

It is certain that the fallen leader never committed himself more passionately to any political or economic ideal than he did to the cause of scriptural infallibility. In his twilight at Dayton, he spoke repeatedly with a conviction that approached fanaticism.

Dedicated to the Fight.

In his first talk with reporters—after he had swung energetically down Dayton's main street, coatless and under a pith helmet—Mr. Bryan showed that he regarded himself as a man dedicated to a sacred mission. Although he permitted himself a secular jest, concerning his fathers' baldness and poor handwriting, he took on a tone of severe exaltation whenever the issues were touched upon.

Never in later years a downright genial man, Mr. Bryan moved about Dayton with a fateful bearing. In the courtroom he almost never smiled, and then only in derision. When he whispered advice to his colleagues, he did so with intensity. Seldom, if ever, did Mr. Bryan relax from his urgent attitude.

But it was in his speeches to the Tennesseeans in dining hall and chapel that Mr. Bryan most clearly manifested the burning faith that consumed him. Before the Progressive Dayton club, where he said what was construed by reporters to be the declaration of a fight to put the bible into the constitution, he pledged his best efforts to the war on "scientific speculation."

It was at this dinner that young John Thomas Scopes, sitting opposite and the butt of the commoner's remarks, noted his violation of dietetic rules. Confiding to his fellow diners that he could not eat starch and refusing white bread, Mr. Bryan ate plentifully of potatoes and poured several spoonful of sugar into his iced tea. As was his custom, Mr. Bryan ate largely and with relish.

Spoke on MountainTop.

However, it required the setting of a pitch-black mountaintop, with the rays of a lamp and distant lightning flashes for illumination, to bring out his zeal most dramatically. At Morgan Springs, where he addressed 100 vacationists, Daytonians and mountaineers before the trial opened, he called for a worldwide revival of interest in the old time religion.

This movement, he prophesied, passionately, would sweep out of the fundamentalist south; it would cross the seas until all lands had been subjected to its benevolent purge. One of the fruits would be the expulsion of such science as conflicts with the holy word from education.

In these primitive surroundings, with the lamplight outlining Mr. Bryan's stalwart figure dimly, he appeared the embodiment of an ancient Hebrew prophet condemning the false gods of his people. A bearded father in Zion, carted in his wheel chair miles across the hills by sons, muttered amens. These, and Mr. Bryan's words, were the only sounds, save for an intermittent undertone of thunder. The rumble of the departing storm seemed a faint reminder of the puissance of the God the speaker was invoking.

Audience Magnetized.

The audience, on rude chairs and standing under the boxelders, held its peace. It was inexpressibly moved before the great evangel of the Lord. Those people were magnetized as countless thousands of others had been by the witchery of the Bryan voice, the persuasiveness of the Bryan conviction, and his indomitable spirit.

Perhaps that was Mr. Bryan's last great hour. There on Walden ridge, the southerly spur of the Cumberlands, before a hand full of the simple folk he believed in and fought for, Mr. Bryan triumphed again. Perhaps it was his last great hour.

Whatever else he demonstrated at Dayton, Mr. Bryan showed his fighting heart still potent. Likewise, he remained still the most inspired artist of his day with the spoken words. Some of the finish had worn off the "silver tongue," but it still remained the most charming oratorical instrument in the land.

Nor had he—save for the period when Dudley Malone laid him low in the courtroom—lost the allegiance of the plain people. There was still awe in the glances of the gallused countrymen. Old ladies in bonnets approached him reverently.

Mr. Bryan may have not been at his best in his last fight—but he fought with all the power at his command. He gave no quarter and expected none. It was perhaps fitting that he should die while scarcely cool from a rousing battle.

**

Appeared Unfatigued

Dayton, Tenn., July 26 (By The Associated Press)—Shortly before William Jennings Bryan died today, he remarked that he had never felt better in his life and was ready to go before the country to wage his battle against modernism.

The great commoner had returned to Dayton this morning after completing arrangements for the publication of the address he had prepared to deliver in closing the trial of John T. Scopes, who recently was convicted of violating Tennessee's anti-evolution law.

Publication of this speech at an early date was to mark the opening of the crusade in behalf of fundamentalism, which Mr. Bryan planned to carry before the entire country.

Made Many Addresses.

Despite the fact that Mr. Bryan had spoken yesterday at Jasper and Winchester, Tenn., and had traveled over 200 miles, he appeared in the best of health and unfatigued. He attended services at the Southern Episcopal church and led the congregation in prayer which citizens of Dayton tonight described as one of the most beautiful ever delivered in the church.

Following the services, the commoner was greeted by many members of the congregation. He then returned to his temporary home here, where he ate a large dinner, remarking that his travels of yesterday and the early morning had given him a hearty appetite.

Shortly after 3 o'clock, Mr. Bryan retired to his room to rest and Mrs. Bryan went to the back porch to attend to some correspondence. She was only fifteen feet away from his bed.

"About 4:30 I felt like Mr. Bryan had been asleep long enough, so I sent Mr. McCartney (the chauffeur) to wake him," Mrs. Bryan told friends.

Doctors Summoned.

McCartney entered the room and shook Mr. Bryan.

"He always was a heavy sleeper and was hard to wake," he said, adding that when he shook the body a second time he noticed Mr. Bryan was not breathing.

Dr. W. F. Thomason and Dr. A. C. Broyles were summoned immediately and A. B. Andrews also was called by McCartney. After an examination, the physicians stated Mr. Bryan evidently had been dead between thirty and forty-five minutes and that death had been caused by apoplexy.

"During all the excitement, Mrs. Bryan was the calmest person in the house," Mr. Andrews said. "She took complete charge of affairs and showed more nerve than I have ever seen in a woman—and she is an invalid too.

Several times, Mrs. Bryan said, the Commoner expressed a desire to be buried in Arlington cemetery.

"You know he was a colonel in the Spanish-American war, and

since it was his wish to rest in Arlington, we probably will place him there," she continued.

"But no definite decision will be reached until we hear from William Jennings Bryan, jr."

"I am glad my husband died without suffering and in peace," she said.

Report Spread Rapidly.

Mrs. Bryan was anxious that Mr. Bryan's secretary, W. E. Thompson, be located. She appeared relieved when told that the Associated Press was trying to help find him. Mr. Thompson was believed to be in Matocia, Vir.

The report of Mr. Bryan's death spread rapidly throughout this little town, but people refused to believe it at first. Many rushed to the Bryan home. Among these was George W. Rappleyea, who first brought charges against Scopes in order that the Tennessee anti-evolution law might be tested. Mr. Rappleyea expressed his sympathy and offered his services in any way.

Mrs. Bryan remained in her roller chair receiving only a few of the callers. Sue K. Hicks, one of the attorneys associated with Mr. Bryan in the prosecution of Scopes, was one of these. He remained with her a short while, and on leaving the house remarked on the courage Mrs. Bryan exhibited.

"Nothing definite has been decided yet," he said, "but I expect the body will leave here Tuesday for Arlington."

Hundreds of telegrams and telephone calls came to Mrs. Bryan, expressing love and sympathy. Mrs. Ruth Owen of Mount Vernon, O., one of Mrs. Bryan's daughters, was among those who called over long distance. She wanted to know when and where she could join the funeral party and her mother advised her that she would advise her definitely tomorrow morning.

The crowd in front of the Bryan home appeared unable to realize Mr. Bryan was dead. They stood with bared heads and tears were in the eyes of many.

**

COOLIDGE WARM FRIEND OF BRYAN

Executive Expected to Make Statement Today.

Swampscott, Mass., July 26 (A.P.)—President Coolidge was informed of the death of William Jennings Bryan through The Associated Press. While no statement was forthcoming tonight, it was said Mr. Coolidge probably would pay tribute tomorrow, either in a statement or in a message of condolence to Mrs. Bryan, to the man who was thrice candidate for president.

The president and Mr. Bryan were warm personal friends and just before the executive departed from Washington, Mr. Bryan was a luncheon guest at the white house.

**

DEATH STUNS IOWA FRIENDS

Pay High Tribute to His Service to People.

Des Moines and Iowa citizens, many of them warm personal friends of William Jennings Bryan, were stunned last night by the news of his death.

"The people have lost one of their greatest friends, a man who stood for that which is just, a man who had enduring faith and a crusader whose life work will stand as a monument forever."

This was the statement of Clyde B. Herring, democratic leader and a personal friend of Mr. Bryan.

J. B. Weaver said: "I am profoundly shocked and grieved to learn of the death of Mr. Bryan. For a full generation he has been a great moral force, having a profound influence for the betterment of his party and the life of the nation generally, on all issues making for a finer American citizenship. His most bitter political enemies must everywhere concede his courage, his honesty, his brilliant power as an orator. He was a close friend of my father, General Weaver, and the family of the latter feel an especially poignant regret at his sudden passing."

G. A. Huffman, former postmaster, said: "I have known Mr.

Bryan personally for more than thirty years, since the days that he was in congress, and feel his loss keenly. He has always stood for the good things in life and was a great moral leader. I consider him one of the greatest men that America has produced."

Pastor Praises Him.

Tribute to Mr. Bryan was paid by Rev. N. C. Carpenter, pastor of the Capitol Hill Church of Christ, in his evening sermon yesterday.

"Mr. Bryan's brand of religion has given the world all that is best in literature, music and art," Rev. Mr. Carpenter said. "It has led the way in every worthy cause. The world moves forward only as it receives its inspiration from the Christian religion. Even scientific research goes on just in proportion as Christianity puts up the money to finance its investigations."

His Great Faith

"I have known William Jennings Bryan for twenty years and have believed and admired the things which he stood for since I cast my first vote in 1900 when he was running for president for the second time," Clyde Herring stated last night.

"Bryan had the vision of Andrew Jackson and was a Jackson type of a democrat. He believed in the rights of the people above that of property. Practically every movement, change or reform that he advocated has been adopted by the nation, including woman suffrage, prohibition and the direct election of United States senators.

"These things are all commonplace now, but when Bryan first expounded them he was called a radical. In his field the great commoner was paramount. It is not always the men who gain the seats of the mighty who accomplish things."

Prayed for Invalid Wife.

"No matter what Bryan did he was always sincere. He was a great believer in prayer. Typical of Bryan was a remark which he made during his last visit here when he and myself paid a visit to his old friend, Father J. F. Nugent. One of Father Nugent's first remarks was in regard to the condition of Mrs. Bryan, who had been ill and who for years has been an invalid.

"My wife is in very poor health," Mr. Bryan replied. "It is necessary for me now to carry her up and down the stairs for she is too weak to walk much. I am praying for her and I have faith that my prayers will bring her through."

Mr. Herring declared that he would always remember this statement as typical of the faith of Bryan.

He said that he enjoyed having Bryan for dinner several years ago.

Liked Children

"On this occasion more than any other in our long acquaintanceship I appreciated the plain simplicity of the man," Mr. Herring stated. "He liked children and spent much time entertaining my youngest boy, autographing a picture for him.

"Bryan always liked Des Moines and has appeared here on countless occasions. At one time he came all the way from Kansas to make an address in the auditorium here. He paid his own expenses.

"He always enlivened his talks with sparkles of wit and brought out his points with a humorous story. His life was filled with strenuous effort to put forward his views before the people. When he grew older he continued to make his regular tours about the country even during the hottest weather. Outwardly he appeared to have a wonderful physique, but I sometimes think that it was more his enthusiasm for the subjects on which he talked that carried him through."

"Bryan had the best moral basis of any man I ever knew," H. C. Evans, editor of the Yeoman Shield and a friend of Bryan since 1893, stated last night.

"The scale on which he weighed every question was which was the right or wrong side. He always took the side, which he thought was right, quite often to his own detriment.

"Bryan was a good man and I never knew a better. No one ever made a criticism of his personal life or heard a whisper as to his policies or habits."

Mr. Evans said that he was asked by Bryan to assist in obtaining a fusion between the democrats and the "greenback" party in Nebraska in 1893. A bond of friendship developed, which lasted from that time on, Evans stated.

Claude R. Porter said: "Mr. Bryan was one of the greatest single forces for civic righteousness in the world for many years—his death will be felt keenly by people who believe in the moral side of important questions."

**

Washington, Ia., July 26 (Special)—Senator Brookhart characterized William Jennings Bryan as one of the pioneers of modern statesmanship in America, when informed of his death this afternoon.

"An understudy of General Weaver, Mr. Bryan had probably made as deep a study of the constitution as any statesman in our political history.

"He had been a pioneer in the instigation of statutes written into our constitution, names, the income tax law, the direct election of United States senators, women's suffrage, prohibition and federal regulation of the railroads.

"News of his death comes as a surprise and shock to me. He was a progressive, always he stood for progressive movements."

**

Iowa City, Ia., July 26 (Special)—"The death of William Jennings Bryan means a severe loss to the people of our nation because of the taking away of his religious and educational influence," Federal Judge Wade said tonight. "I care nothing about the party," Judge Wade said, when asked what he thought the effect of the death might be to the democrats.

**

Dubuque, Ia., July 26 (Special)—"The death of William Jennings Bryan removes one of the greatest democratic leaders in the history of the party, but the loss will be felt as keenly by the church as it is in political circles," was the comment of Ann Lawther, former committeewoman of Iowa.

**

Death of Bryan Ends Notable Career As Orator and Statesman.

BRYAN'S LIFE IN BRIEF

William Jennings Bryan's life, in brief, was as follows:

■ Born in Salem, Ill., March 19, 1860. Son of Silas Lillard Bryan and Mariah Elizabeth Jennings Bryan.

■ Received A.B. Degree from Illinois college in 1881 with highest honors.

■ Admitted to Illinois bar in 1883 and practiced at Jacksonville until 1887, when he moved to Lincoln, Neb.

■ Married Miss Mary Elizabeth Baird of Perry, Ill., Oct. 1, 1884.

■ Elected to congress from first Nebraska district in 1891 and served until 1895.

■ Received democratic vote for United States senator in 1893, and was nominated by democratic convention in 1894, but was defeated by John M. Thurston.

■ Editor of the Omaha World-Herald from 1894 until 1896.

■ Delegate to democratic national convention in 1896.

■ Wrote the silver plank and was nominated for the presidency after his famous "Cross of Gold" speech.

■ Made a tour of the country, speaking at hundreds of places, but was defeated by William McKinley.

■ Lectured on bi-metalism during 1897 and 1898.

■ Raised the Third regiment Nebraska volunteer infantry for the Spanish-American war in 1898, and became its colonel.

■ Again nominated for the presidency by democrats in 1900, and again was defeated by William McKinley.

■ Established the Commoner, a weekly political paper, at Lincoln, Neb., after the election, and in 1906 made a tour of the world.

■ Received third nomination for the presidency in 1908 and was defeated by William Howard Taft.

■ Secretary of state in Wilson cabinet from 1913 to 1915, when he resigned because of differences with the president.

■ Delegate to the democratic convention in 1924, after moving his residence to Miami, Fla.

■Aided the prosecution of John Thomas Scopes at Dayton, Tenn., in July 1925.

**

FREE SILVER SPEECH WON NOMINATION

William Jennings Bryan first came into the national political limelight at the democratic convention in Chicago in 1896.

The "free silver" forces gained control of the convention. Mr. Bryan drew up their plank.

The gold-standard bearers sought to have the plank eliminated and a stirring appeal was made by Senator David B. Hill, leader of the gold plank advocates.

It was in defense of his plank that Mr. Bryan made his brilliant speech known as his "Cross of Gold" speech which brought the convention to its feet and swept him into the nomination the following day. He closed his address with his now famous words:

"You shall not press down upon the brow of labor this crown of thorns; you shall not crucify mankind upon a cross of gold."

**

'COMMONER' WORLD FIGURE FOR 30 YEARS

Named Three Times As Presidential Candidate.

(By The Associated Press.)

In all the history of American politics there are few names which carry the brilliant lustre of spectacular effort which has become a part of the memory of William Jennings Bryan.

His life for almost thirty years was a panorama of national sensations, piled one upon the other. At 36 he became almost overnight not only the leader of his party, but the idol of millions. Three times he carried the party standard as its choice for the highest office of the land; in another presidential year – 1912—he reaped much of the credit for placing Woodrow Wilson in the white house; and in almost every other national democratic convention in a generation he was in the very center of every storm that came.

As a recognition, many said, of his long leadership, President Wilson made him secretary of state—a post from which he resigned two years later under the most sensational of circumstances because he felt the nation was verging toward participation in the European war. World peace always had been his passion in his earlier years, just as in his later days he made the espousal of religion his all-absorbing concern, and turned his talents to an attack on evolution.

Brilliance Is Dimmed.

Throughout all his active years, his followers clung to his standard in blind devotion of the man and his ideals, while his enemies reviled and hated him, calling him ignorant and misguided in both his economics and his religion. His great power of eloquence which first brought him to a place of national prominence, remained unimpaired for many years, but toward the last his old time brilliance on the platform and the stump began to dim perceptibly.

Although he found time for many venturesome excursions into other fields, politics was his forte, and the story of his life work is almost a history of the national political campaigns that began when the Chicago democratic convention of 1896 stampeded out of a deadlock by his "cross of gold" speech and made him its candidate for president.

Bryan went to that convention as editor of the Omaha World-Herald and a former member of the house, but entirely unknown to any considerable portion of the rank and file of his party. Nevertheless, he took with him an unfaltering faith in his destiny, and as the leading candidates—now forgotten—began to muster their strength for the fight, he turned to some of his intimate friends in the press stand and remarked that he himself would be the nominee of the convention.

Thought He Was Jesting.

None of them believed him, and very few believed that he was speaking seriously. It was but a few hours later that he set the convention wild with his speech for free silver, and that night a group of delegates hired a band and went to serenade him at the old South State Street hotel where he was staying. He rose from his bed, slipped on a pair of trousers over his nightshirt, and in bare feet received his visitors with a warm handclasp and a smile that soon enough was to become famous the world over.

His first campaign against McKinley was epochal for its fiery earnestness, and not until the votes had been counted did he believe it possible that he could be beaten. In 1900, with McKinley again for his opponent, he adopted "imperialism" for his paramount issue and for a second time stumped the country in a vain effort to reach the great goal of his ambition.

After this second failure, many of the leaders within his party turned away and the nomination four years later of Alton B. Parker was a bitter disappointment to him. In that convention he made a spectacular fight against the forces that he declared were handing over the party to Wall street, delivering a speech which was regarded almost universally as the swan song of his career. Yet in another four years the pendulum had swung back again and he was nominated as the opponent of William Howard Taft.

Denounced Champ Clark.

The part he took in the Baltimore convention of 1912 was a piece of the spectacular strain that ran through and through his whole career. Rising on the convention floor at a time when his long time friend, Champ Clark was within reach of the nomination, he denounced the Clark of Tammany and declared Wall street as trying once again to fasten its talons on the democratic party. The reaction to Wilson, who had been running well behind, was instantaneous and Bryan was one of the first to be named to the Wilson cabinet. The breach between Bryan and Clark never was bridged.

As secretary of state, he came under attack many times, was ridiculed by many both at home (and) abroad for his policies, but always loyally supported by his friends, and finally made his exit from the cabinet rather than sign a note to Germany, prepared by Mr. Wilson himself, on the submarine outrages.

It was after a long talk between the president and the secretary that his resignation was announced. Summoned to the white house on a bright June morning, Mr. Bryan entered the president's private office unruffled, apparently believing that by throwing his powers of persuasion onto the scale he could convince his chief that the note should not be sent. After they had talked alone for an hour, Mr. Wilson pressed a button on his desk and a Negro usher entered to find the president calm and silent, and the secretary nervous and voluble.

Visibly Nervous.

"Mr. Bryan wants a drink of water," said Mr. Wilson.

When it was brought, Bryan's hand was so unsteady that he upset a part of it as he raised it to his lips. He demonstrated later in many ways that he had been cut to the quick by his failure to avoid what he believed was a warlike gesture by his country, and by his parting from the man he had helped lift up into a greater leadership than he himself had been able to attain.

He did not oppose Mr. Wilson's renomination in 1916, but the party candidates of 1920 and 1924 were chosen over his opposition. He went on a vacation trip during most of the campaign of James M. Cox, but he took the stump for John W. Davis in 1924.

At San Francisco in 1920, however, most of his energies were directed toward the writing of a platform rather than the choice of a candidate. His fight this time was for a bone-dry plank, and he took the speaker's stand in its espousal. In old time form, his face shining and his eyes alight, he sent his rounded periods rolling and rollicking through the great convention hall, and when the speech was ended the delegates gave him an ovation that lasted for an hour. His intimates said that until the vote was taken, he firmly believed that once more he had stampeded a national convention; but it was only the tribute of a party for an old and tried friend, for the plank he advocated was lost overwhelmingly.

Led Committee in Prayer.

Even more spectacular was his part in the New York convention of just a year ago. A member of the subcommittee, which drafted the platform, he was in the thick of the fight over the league of nations and the Ku-Klux klan. At the end of one futile all-night session of the sub-committee, when the members had agreed to separate for a few hours' rest, he rose in his place at the committee table and asked his colleagues to remain for a moment while he led in prayer. Then with bowed head he asked providence for guidance in the dark hour of dissension and bitterness.

Later he took the floor before the convention, on one occasion to defend William G. McAdoo, and on another to oppose a plank condemning the Ku-Klux klan by name. But for the first time he had found a democratic convention he could not quietApplause, mingled with hisses and boos, came both from the floor and the gallery. His delivery lacked the fire of other years, and his presence the command that was its wont. Only once or twice was there a flash of the old time brilliance, as when he took up the challenge of a spectator who applauded his remark that this might be the last convention he would attend.

"Don't applaud," he said, "I may change my mind."

Sincere of Purpose.

His career has been likened to that of Henry Clay, who also was three times nominated for the presidency and as many times defeated. Clay, too, became a secretary of state. Friends of Bryan insisted that, like Clay, he was too conscientious, consistent and scrupulous for a politician and that the famous whig's declaration, "I would rather be right than be president," well described the man from Nebraska.

The former secretary of state was born in Salem, Ill., March 19, 1860. His father was Silas Lillard Bryan, a native of Culpepper county, Virginia, a lawyer and judge. The son, after graduating from Illinois college in 1881 and Union College of Law, Chicago, in 1883, entered the law office of Lyman Trumbull, former United States senator. Subsequently he removed to Jacksonville, Ill., where he practiced law until 1887, when he settled in Lincoln, Neb.

During the presidential campaign of 1888, young Bryan's speeches in behalf of the democratic ticket attracted attention and in 1890 he accepted a nomination for congress in the first Nebraska district, a republican stronghold, "because no one else would have it," he said, since it was believed no democrat could win. He was elected and served from 1891 until 1895. He was made a member of the important ways and means committee in his first term.

Gained National Prominence.

Two speeches in this period gave Mr. Bryan nationwide prominence, one against the policy of protection, delivered on March 16, 1892, and the other against the repeal of the silver purchase clause of the Sherman act on Aug. 16, 1893. In the latter he advocated "the free and unlimited coinage of silver, irrespective of international agreement, at a ratio of 16 to 1,"a policy with which his name was afterwards most prominently associated until he entered the cabinet of President Wilson.

The first nomination of Mr. Bryan for the presidency at the democratic national convention in Chicago on July 10, 1896 has since been characterized as one of the "miracles" of American politics. The nominee, after serving in congress, had run for the United States senate and been defeated by Senator John M. Thurston of Nebraska. Abandoning the law, Mr. Bryan became editor of the Omaha World-Herald and championed the cause of bimetallism as vigorously with the pen as he had upon the forum. He had been beaten for a third term in congress on the issue of "sound money" and when the time came for the national convention this question was rending both big political parties. There were free silver republicans as well as democrats, but the nominee of the former, Henry M. Teller of Colorado, threw his support to Bryan when the Nebraskan won the nomination at Chicago.

"Cross of Gold" Speech.

The "cross of gold" speech by Bryan, which has been quoted oftener, perhaps, than any other of his words, and which made him a rival of William McKinley for the presidency, came at the close of a debate on the floor of the convention in advocacy of a free silver plank. Men nationally prominent in the party had preceded him, and opposed the plank unless it should provide for bimetalism by international agreement. The situation was tense when the Nebraskan, then only 36 years old—one year more than the constitutional requirement for a president—

arose to speak. Everybody was tired; everybody seemed ready for compromise. Not so the delegate from Nebraska. There was fire in his eye when he began to speak:

"I would be presumptuous, indeed, to present myself against the distinguished gentlemen to whom you have listened," he said, "if this were a mere measuring of abilities; but this is not a contest between persons. The humblest citizen in all the land, when clad in the armor of a righteous cause, is stronger than all the hosts of error. I come to speak to you in defense of a cause as holy as the cause of liberty – the cause of humanity!"

Then charging the evils of the day—the idle minds, the social unrest and low wages—to the scarcity of money and the "idle holders of idle capital in Wall street," he continued.

Championed Labor.

"The individual is but an atom; he is born, he acts, he dies; but principles are eternal; and this has been a contest over a principle. Having behind us the producing masses of this nation and the world, supported by the commercial interests, the laboring interests and the toilers everywhere we will answer those who demand a single gold standard by saying:

"You shall not press down upon the brow of labor this crown of thorns. You shall not crucify mankind upon this cross of gold."

The convention was stampeded for Bryan, who was nominated over eight other candidates on the fifth ballot, following a speech by a Georgia delegate in which the eloquent young orator was referred to as "a Saul come to lead the Israelites to battle." Subsequently Bryan received the nomination of the people's and the national silver parties.

The nominee broke all speaking records in his first campaign, traveling more than 18,000 miles and making about 600 speeches in twenty-seven states. He polled 6,502,925 votes to McKinley's 7,104,779, and received in the electoral college 176 votes to his opponent's 271. Although defeated, Mr. Bryan remained the leader of his party and, after the Spanish-American war in 1898, in which he commanded the Third Nebraska Volunteer infantry as its colonel, he opposed the permanent retention of the Philippine islands by the United

States.

Defeated Again in 1900

In 1900, when again nominated for the presidency, he made "anti-imperialism" the paramount issue, but refused to omit an explicit party declaration in favor of free coinage of silver in the party platform. This time he was defeated with a popular vote of 6,358,133 as against 7,207,923 for his opponent. He received 155 electoral votes to McKinley's 292.

Mr. Bryan returned to Lincoln and started the publication of a weekly political journal called the Commoner. Four years later, 1904, although not actively a candidate for the nomination, which eventually went to Judge Alton B. Parker, he vigorously opposed democracy's "conservative" attitude.

The interim between this period and the next presidential election of 1908 was occupied by Mr. Bryan, now known by many of his followers as "the peerless leader," in several enterprises that kept him in the public eye. Notable among these was his trip around the world on which he started Sept. 21, 1905. Accompanied by his wife, son and a daughter, Mr. Bryan first went to Japan and China, where he was hospitably entertained, and made numerous addresses, one of which entitled, "The White Man's' Burden," was commended by the Japanese-American society. The Bryans were presented to the emperor of Japan and were everywhere accorded the honor of foremost Americans. Later the party went to the Philippines, where Mr. Bryan's views on Filipino independence were welcomed. During this visit the savage Moros of Mindanao island created the Nebraskan a "datto" or chief of one of their tribes.

Entertained by Royalty.

Leaving the Philippines, the party went to India, the Holy land, Turkey, Austria-Hungary, Germany, Russia, Italy, Norway, Sweden and other European countries, finally arriving in London on July 3, 1906. Meanwhile Mr. Bryan had "interviewed" King Edward VII, the Emperor of Russia, and other potentates, and Count Leo Tolstoi and had made numerous speeches all of which were reported in the American press and which inspired a desire on the part of democrats at home to give him a great reception which was done upon his return to America the following September.

About this time Mr. Bryan came out for world disarmament, an ideal which is said to have prompted his drafting in 1913, when he became secretary of state, of the particular form of peace treaty between the United States and foreign nations "by which all disputes were to be submitted to an impartial investigating commission for a year before hostilities could begin." This has been regarded as Mr. Bryan's greatest achievement, for thirty foreign nations, representing three-fourths of the population of the earth, became signatories to the document. About a year later, the world war broke out in all its fury.

Always "A Good Loser."

In 1908 Mr. Bryan was again named as the democratic standard bearer. The campaign was waged on the principal issue of opposition to "trusts" and for a third time the democratic nominee suffered defeat, polling 6,409,104 votes to Taft's 7,678,908, and receiving 162 electoral votes to his opponent's 321.

Notwithstanding Mr. Bryan's reverses in politics, it is said, he was "a good loser." Of Presbyterian forbears, optimistic and of a religious nature, his setbacks failed to make him lose faith in his future. He refused to become discouraged. For the next four years, or until the campaign of 1912, which resulted in the election of President Wilson, Mr. Bryan continued to edit his newspaper and to attend the councils of his party.

In his first campaign, his home in Lincoln was a mecca for prominent democrats, where Mrs. Bryan, a scholarly woman, formerly Miss Mary E. Baird of Perry, Ill., who had greatly aided her husband in his political career, was a charming hostess. The Bryans had three children, one son and two daughters.

Always in demand as a lecturer, especially at chautauquas, Mr. Bryan's income was augmented by magazines and his authorship of several books. The latter included "The First Battle" (1897); "Under Other Flags" (1904); "The Old World and Its Ways" (1907)' "Heart to

Heart Appeals" (1917). In addition to his Nebraska home, Mr. Bryan, after his final defeat for the presidency, established residences in Asheville, N.C., and Miami, Fla.

Easing up on his political activities with the 1920 national campaign, Mr. Bryan took a greater interest in the affairs of the Presbyterian church and devoted more of his time to lecturing. In 1923 he was defeated for moderator of the general assembly of the Presbyterian church after an exciting contest. He was elected vice moderator at the general assembly of 1924.

Fought Darwin Theory.

An avowed opponent of the Darwin theory of evolution, Mr. Bryan made many addresses on the subject. Speaking in 1923 before the legislature of West Virginia, which was considering a bill to prohibit the teaching of the Darwin theory in the schools of that state, Mr. Bryan said:

"School teachers paid by taxation should not be permitted to teach under the guise of science or philosophy anything that undermines faith in God, impairs belief in the bible or discredits the son of God and the savior of the world. Evolutionists rob the savior of the glory of the virgin birth, the majesty of his deity and the triumph of his resurrection. They weaken faith in the bible by discarding the miracles and the supernatural and by eliminating from the bible all that conflicts with their theories. They render the book a scrap of paper."

Later in an address in New York, Mr. Bryan denounced the Darwin theory as the greatest enemy of religion and declared that in the schools it was undermining Christianity. "I don't object to scientific truth," he said, "for no truth disturbs religion. What we object to is for any scientist to put forth his guess and demand that we substitute it for the word of God. Evolution is an enemy of the bible and furnishes a respectable excuse for men to deny the bible." Among his writings of the subject were "The Menace of Darwinism," and "The Bible and Its Enemies."

It was in this same spirit that Mr. Bryan offered his services as a member of the counsel of Tennessee in the state's trial of John T. Scopes, biology instructor in the Dayton, Tenn., High school. According to the Tennessee law, nothing can be taught in the public schools which upholds the theory that man developed from a lower animal. Scopes admitted his support of the evolution theory in his classroom, and when Mr. Bryan took up the fight against the school teacher Clarence Darrow of Chicago, Dudley Field Malone of New York and other nationally known lawyers came to the support of Scopes.

Mr. Bryan was still at Dayton when found dead today, although the jury found Scopes guilty and the case was appealed to the state supreme court a week ago.

**

CHARLES BRYAN SPEEDS TOWARD NEBRASKA HOME

Tragedy Halts Outing in Colorado

Loveland, Colo., July 26 (A.P.)—Heartbroken at the news of his brother's death, Charles W. Bryan prepared tonight to leave here for Lincoln, Neb. tomorrow morning. The former Nebraska governor was informed of his brother's death as he returned from a day's outing in the mountains.

First news of his brother's death came to Mr. Bryan through his manager, Charles F. Horner, who read Associated Press dispatches that had been relayed here.

Mr. Bryan will leave Loveland via automobile for Denver to catch a Chicago, Burlington & Quincy passenger train that will land him in Lincoln tomorrow afternoon.

He said that he had received a telegram from Mrs. William Jennings Bryan, saying that it was Mr. Bryan's wish that he be buried in Arlington cemetery.

Besides this, the former Nebraska governor had nothing to say regarding funeral arrangements. At Lincoln, he said, he will join his wife and his sisters and proceed eastward, after learning definitely of arrangements for burial.

**

Lincoln, Neb., July 26 (A.P.)—Mrs. Francis M. Baird, eldest sister of William Jennings Bryan, received word of her brother's death at her home at College View, a suburb near here. Mrs. Baird does not plan to leave here tonight for Tennessee, she said this evening. She said she was awaiting definite word from Dayton regarding arrangements being made by relatives.

Mrs. Baird is 67 years old, two years older than William Jennings Bryan.

**

Mount Vernon, O., July 26, (A.P.)—Mrs. Ruth Bryan Owen, daughter of William Jennings Bryan, received the first news of the death of her father from the Associated Press correspondent here when she arrived tonight to fill a Redpath Chautauqua engagement. Mrs. Owen spoke in Columbus in the afternoon, but left that city before the news was received.

Mrs. Owen received the news of her father's death without show of emotion. Her first thought was for her mother. She then called Mrs. Bryan at Dayton and announced that she would remain in Mount Vernon until tomorrow, when she would join her mother.

**

Duluth, Minn., July 26 (A.P.)—Mrs. Thomas S. Allen, sister of William Jennings Bryan, was overcome when she was informed tonight by The Associated Press of the death of the great commoner. Mrs. Allen has been on an outing with Mr. Allen at Birch Plank inn, on Vermillion lake near Tower, Minn.

M. Allen said they would leave immediately for the old Bryan home at Lincoln, Neb. Mrs. Allen said she saw Mr. Bryan last several months ago when he was a guest at the Allen home.

**

Dayton, Tenn., July 26 (A.P.)—Mrs. Ruth Owen, daughter of William Jennings Bryan, in a long distance conversation with her mother here tonight, expressed her love and sympathy and asked when she should leave her home in Mt. Vernon, O., to join the widow and the funeral party.

Mrs. Owen was told by Mrs. Bryan that she did not know tonight where Mr. Bryan would be buried. Mrs. Bryan told her she would telegraph her early tomorrow the time and place of burial.

**

Los Angeles, July 26 (A.P.)—William Jennings Bryan, jr., and his sister, Mrs. Richard L. Hargreaves, will leave here tomorrow for Dayton, Tenn. They made this announcement tonight through Mr. Hargreaves' husband, who explained that the commoner's son and daughter had been deeply shaken by the news of his sudden death and were making preparations to join their mother as soon as possible.

**

HOPED TO MAKE MANY SPEECHES

Spent Weeks Outlining Closing Argument.

(By The Associated Press.)

William Jennings Bryan regarded the contest of issues growing from the "Scopes trial" as the greatest fight of his career—"not without fights"—he said shortly after the trial. Mr. Bryan told an Associated Press representative at Dayton last week that he expected to make many addresses for which he would not permit admission to be charged, emphasizing the issues as he construed them after the first court test of the Tennessee statute prohibiting the teaching of evolution theories.

From the opening of the trial, he was especially in earnest, insisting throughout that a battle was being waged against revealed religion and Christianity. Last Wednesday he showed The Associated Press a sheaf of telegrams from individuals and organizations in many sections of the United States applauding his position in the Scopes case. Then it was that he declared he expected to speak "soon and often" for Christianity.

Prepared Closing Argument.

Mr. Bryan had prepared what was to have been the closing argument before the jury at Dayton. It was no secret that the preparation of this address had been a matter of weeks. Some of his friends thought he expected to make it one of the greatest efforts of his career, suggestion that it would perhaps be his last extended oratorical effort. When arguments were waived and the case sent to the jury without final speechmaking, Mr. Bryan said he would nevertheless deliver his prepared address later, and the first succeeding days in Dayton after the trial were spent in revising his manuscript.

There were no indications of illness in the "great commoner" during the trial. On his arrival at Dayton a few days in advance of the opening of the case, his apparent physical fitness was generally remarked. He spoke only once in court, but delivered several addresses in Rhea county. His public appearances included a speech at a banquet in his honor by the Dayton Progressive club, an informal address to his fellow prosecution lawyers and their guests at Morgan Springs, two religious addresses in Dayton, and one at Pikeville.

Saturday he spoke at Winchester, carrying out a promise made to Atty. Gen. A. T. Stewart, during the trial, that at its close he would deliver an address to the attorney general's fellow townsmen.

Landed at Dayton

As the "leader of the fundamentalists," Mr. Bryan was made to feel very much at home in Dayton and Rhea county. His entrance and departure from the courtroom were marked by a succession of handshakes. Rhea county politically has been found frequently in the republican column and many of opposite political faith were among the most ardent admirers of the former democratic candidate for president and cabinet officer.

"Will you let a lifelong republican shake your hand, Mr. Bryan?" was a question heard more than once in the courtroom. Among his latest discussions with Dayton folk were some concerning the suggestion that a college devoted to fundamentalist doctrine be established there. Approached with the information that sentiment in Dayton favored "Bryan" for its name, should the college be established, his comment was:

"We'll see. There's time enough to discuss the name later."

**

PLAN ELABORATE FUNERAL RITES

Nation and People to Bestow All Honors.

Washington, July 26 (A.P.)—Funeral arrangements here for William Jennings Bryan, if tentative plans for his burial at Arlington national cemetery are carried out, will accord to the wishes of Mrs. Bryan, but they undoubtedly will take on an impressive character.

As a colonel of the Third Nebraska infantry during the war with Spain, the commoner is entitled to a military funeral, and the firing of a salute over his grave, but because of his long advocacy of the cause of peace the military features of the ceremony tonight remained a matter of doubt.

Even without this the funeral services and the interment of the body of the statesman and politician cannot help but be marked here by all honors that the people and the government can bestow. The only advices received here that the burial would be in Arlington was a telegram today to Ben G. Davis, who was Mr. Bryan's secretary at one time and his confidential clerk in the state department. It reported the commoner's death and added that Arlington had been chosen as the interment place.

Should these plans be carried out, his friends undoubtedly will ask that the body be allowed to repose in state, probably in the capital, where many of the leaders of American political life have been placed for a last view by their fellow citizens.

**

Darrow Expresses Deep Sorrow Over Death of His Foeman

TWICE BACKED COMMONER FOR THE PRESIDENCY

Differed With Him, but Respected Him.

Elkmont, Tenn., July 26 (A.P.)—"I am pained to hear of the death of the Honorable William Jennings Bryan," Clarence Darrow Chicago attorney and cross-examiner of the commoner in the recent trial of John T. Scopes at Dayton, Tenn., last Monday, declared this evening when informed of the demise of the notable American by the Knoxville Journal.

"I have known Mr. Bryan since 1896 and supported him twice for the presidency. He was a man of strong convictions and always espoused his cause with ability and courage." Mr. Darrow continued. "I differed with him on many questions but always respected his sincerity and devotion. I am very sorrow for his family and for his friends who loved him."

Mr. Darrow, associated with John R. Neal, Dudley Field Malone and Arthur Garfield Hays in the defense of Mr. Scopes, who was on trial for the violation of the Tennessee anti-evolution act, is spending several days in the great smoky mountains with Mrs. Darrow, his secretary, Dr. Neal and Knoxville citizens, arriving here Friday evening.

Expresses Deep Regrets.

First efforts to communicate with him were fruitless as he was with a party on a tour of Gregory's Bald, one of the mountain peaks of this section. Immediately on return to the Appalachian club tonight he was reached by the Knoxville newspaper, informed of Mr. Bryan's death and expressed his deep regrets.

Dr. Neal, the senior counsel in the defense of Scopes, also expressed sorrow at the death of Mr. Bryan.

"As a citizen of Rhea county, I heartily welcomed Mr. Bryan to Dayton," he said. "I am grieved and shocked that his unexpected death had to come at the end of his stay in my county. My sympathies are extended Mrs. Bryan and members of his family."

Stewart Tells of Sorrow.

Winchester, Tenn., July 26 (A.P.)—Atty. Gen. A. T. Stewart who prosecuted the Scopes case at Dayton tonight expressed great sorrow at the death of Mr. Bryan and felt that the world had lost one of its foremost citizens in his passing. He said:

"I am inexpressibly grieved to learn of the death of Colonel

Bryan. He was one of the greatest men of our time and I feel the world has lost one of its foremost citizens. The cause of fundamentalism to which he has been so devoted for the past several years has lost its greatest exponent, but as he has often said 'the cause will go on'. I feel, too, that the cause will be strengthened by his having been engaged in it up to the time of his death. Colonel Bryan was a staunch, true American citizen and the country's loss is indeed a sad one."

Dawes Bryan's Friend.

Denver, July 26 (A.P.)—Vice President Dawes, on being informed of the death of William Jennings Bryan, issued the following statement to The Associated Press.

"I have been a friend of Mr. Bryan for thirty-eight years, since we started as young lawyers in Lincoln, Neb. Throughout all these years of work and strenuous public service, there shown resplendent a high personal character.

"In all he did Mr. Bryan was in earnest and in it all he tried to do good.

"Those who knew him best respected most his motives and his sincerity. He never did unworthy or mean things. He may have been mistaken at times, as we all are, but he was trying always to do the right as he saw it.

Good and Great Man.

"Of his great influence on the public thought of his day, his public services and his transcendent ability as an orator, I will leave to others to speak, but I want, simply as an old friend and neighbor for many years, to pay my tribute of respect to a good and a great man, whose life has been one of high purpose and helpfulness and whose death brings a sense of personal loss."

Denver was the scene of the democratic nominating convention that in 1908 named William Jennings Bryan as party standard bearer in one of his three attempts to be elected to the white house.

On this occasion he was named the democratic party's choice on the first ballot, taken in the early hours of July 10. Governor J. A.

Johnson of Minnesota and Judge George Gray of Delaware polled 46 and 59 ½ votes, respectively, on this ballot, but the nomination was made unanimous by acclamation after the two candidates assented.

The selection of Bryan was the occasion for a tumultuous demonstration that lasted more than an hour. Ignatius J. Dunn of Omaha, Neb., made the nominating speech.

Undisputed Leader.

"Mr. Bryan has been the undisputed leader in a great cause in politics and in religious movements for more than a generation," Mr. Baker said. "His death will cause widespread grief both among those who followed him and those who admired his firm stand and the greatness of his talents. I have known Mr. Bryan for thirty years and I am greatly grieved to hear of his sudden death."

Atlee Pomerene, former United States senator from Ohio, also a mutual friend of Mr. Bryan, said the Commoner had not been in good health for four or five years, and had been dieting.

"He will be regarded as one of the greatest political orators of this generation," Mr. Pomerene added. "He had a wonderful following, very largely because of his exceptional ability as an orator. His hold upon the public is shown by the fact that three successive times he was nominated by his party for the presidency.

**

Fairmont, W.Va., July 26 (A.P.)—Clem L. Shaver, democratic national chairman, when informed tonight of the death of William Jennings Bryan said:

"In the death of William Jennings Bryan the country has lost a great citizen, the democratic party a commanding figure and the moral forces of America a powerful advocate."

**

BRYAN PLAYED LARGE PART IN LIFE OF MIAMI

Conducted a Huge Outdoor Bible Class

Miami, Fla., July 26 (A.P.)—William Jennings Bryan was an elder in the First Presbyterian church of this city and teacher of its open air bible class, which was conducted in Royal Palm park every Sunday morning. This class has the distinction of being the largest gathering of its kind in the world and is frequently attended by thousands of persons.

Bryan was active and influential in the business, social and religious life at Miami. He frequently filled the pulpit of the First Presbyterian Church and occasionally preached in the other churches here.

Thursday afternoon teas in the Bryan home were probably the most largely attended social functions conducted in or near Miami. His home at Coconut Grove was the mecca of thousands. Recently these teas have been discontinued because of the ill health of Mrs. Bryan.

**

DIED FIGHTING FOR THE WORD OF HIS GOD

Followers See His Passing As Reward.

BY RAYMOND CLAPPER.

Dayton, Tenn., July 26 (U.N.)—William Jennings Bryan is dead, on his chosen field of battle.

He died fighting for the word of God, as he understood it.

His last public pronouncements were declarations of faith, faith in the "revealed word of God," faith in the hereafter; faith in the literal interpretation of the bible, as opposed to such interpretation as is put upon the holy writ by modernists; faith in the teachings of Christ.

He died alone. There was none to see his passing, as his soul was carried away. And to one who saw Mr. Bryan, as I saw him during the stirring days of the recent Scopes evolution trial in Dayton, these things come to mind.

Defender of Faith.

Mr. Bryan saw himself as the defender of the faith. He would have gladly endured torture—even crucifixion—for the victory of his chosen cause.

And for a man of his age, he may be said to have all but endured torture. As the torrid rays of a southern sun beat down he sat day after day in the crowded Dayton courtroom, a silent champion of the "revealed word."

Then came his historic speech. In the closing hours came what proved to be his last real public appearance. For years he had fought in the ranks of a political party. He knew the hardships of the hustlings.

He had dealt with material things. But on his last appearance, he entered the lists as the self-appointed champion of God. He clashed in what was one of the most remarkable court examinations in American jurisprudence with Clarence Darrow.

The noted Chicago attorney, an agnostic, cross-examined Mr. Bryan on his religious beliefs.

Faith Unshaken.

After the cross-examination Bryan was declared to be ignorant by modernists, but the faith of Mr. Bryan remained unshaken.

Some one remarked in Dayton but a few days ago, that the intensely religious people of that section would not have thought it anything unusual had Mr. Bryan been swept away to heaven in a chariot of fire, after his great battle with Darrow.

And now Mr. Bryan has gone. Only the dead ashes of a remarkable man rest tonight in Dayton. And, having sensed the religious fervor of this section of Tennessee, it is not stretching the imagination to picture some of the great commoner's followers visualizing his passing as his reward. In their eyes, God has claimed him as his own.

**

RECEIVED MANY THREATS AGAINST BRYAN AT DAYTON

Commoner Scoffed At Danger From Fanatics.

Chattanooga, Tenn., July 26, (A.P.)—That many threats were

made against William Jennings Bryan's life during the Dayton trial was revealed tonight by Capt. Marion Perkins, who headed the squad of Chattanooga officers who policed the Rhea county town. These threats were ignored by Mr. Bryan, the police captain said. Captain Perkins further stated that he was asked to investigate them, but they were in such numbers that it would have been impractical.

Not only did Mr. Bryan receive threats against life, but others attempted to frighten him away from the trial by saying that they would blow up his home, according to Captain Perkins. Other forms of vengeance were threatened, according to the police captain. Most of the warnings were from northern cities and their authors were thought to have been fanatics.

**

FOUR COMRADES WATCH OVER BODY OF THE COMMONER

Dayton, Tenn., July 26 (A.P.)—Four comrades in his last battle stood watch over the body of William Jennings Bryan tonight.

Sue K. Hicks, Wallace Haggard, Herbert Hicks and Gordon McKenzie, who with Attorney General Stewart were the commoner's associates in the prosecution of John T. Scopes, found guilty of violating Tennessee's anti-evolution law, were selected to watch over the body through the night.

Judge John T. Ralston, who presided at the Scopes trial, has suggested that the body lie in state in the courthouse tomorrow, and will place the matter before Mrs. Bryan early tomorrow.

**

FATHER NUGENT LONG A FRIEND OF COMMONER

Was Fellow Speaker in "Silver Tongue" Days

When told of the death of William Jennings Bryan, Father J. F. Nugent, his life long friend who many times occupied the same speaking platform with Bryan in the days when he was known as the "silver tongued orator," suffered a nervous collapse early last night.

In ill health for some time, Father Nugent was so overcome with grief that friends at his home who conveyed the message to him in his bed, returned to say that his sorrow was so great that they feared the shock might cause a serious relapse. His condition was such as to make a statement from him impossible.

Father Nugent and Mr. Bryan came into warm personal friendship in the early nineties when Bryan took a leading part in the 16 to 1 silver issue. They spoke from the same lecture platform on numerous occasions thirty years ago.

While Mr. Bryan occupied the office of secretary of state he is said to have offered Father Nugent a post in the diplomatic service.

In recent years, Mr. Bryan has never missed an opportunity of calling on Father Nugent when he was in Des Moines. On his last visit here, the two spent a number of hours together which Mr. Bryan termed "some of the most happy moments in our lives," recalling incidents of the early days of their careers.

Unable to leave his home for some time except for short walks, Father Nugent has read with enthusiasm the arguments of Bryan in the evolution trial at Dayton, and was looking forward to a visit from the great commoner sometime this fall.

**

BRYAN WAS FOND OF RADISHES; ALWAYS HAD SACK WITH HIM

"One of the peculiarities of William Jennings Bryan was his fondness for radishes, which he ate for breakfast whenever it was possible to obtain them," Clyde L. Herring said last night, in speaking of Mr. Bryan's hobbies.

"For fear that he would have to go without them, Bryan during the summer, spring and fall, always carried a sack of radishes along with him."

**

GREAT SORROW IS EXPRESSED BY HOME STATE
News Shocks Friends and His Associates.

Lincoln, Neb., July 26 (A.P.)—Charles E. Pool, secretary of state, said he was too shocked to make any formal statement regarding the death of William Jennings Bryan. "It is indeed a great loss," he declared.

Mr. Bryan and Mr. Pool had been political associates ever since the former came to Nebraska in about 1887. Secretary Pool said he remembered Mr. Bryan's first Fourth of July oration which he delivered at Elk Creek, Neb., and his first political speech in Nebraska at Seward.

His brother, Charles W. Bryan, former governor and candidate for the vice presidency under the democratic banner at the last general election, was said to be somewhere in Colorado and apparently has not been notified of the Commoner's death.

Gov. Adam McCullen, republican and successor to Charles W. Bryan as head of the state government, said:

Suffers Great Loss.

"It is truly a great shock. The state of Nebraska has always considered William Jennings Bryan as a fellow citizen. We suffer a great loss.

"The sympathy of all the people, I am sure, will go out to his devoted wife, who herself is an invalid. This is a time when all political feeling vanishes. William Jennings Bryan was a splendid character. I always admired him personally."

I.J. Dunn of Omaha, who led in the nomination of Mr. Bryan for the presidency at the democratic national convention at Denver in 1908 and who has been a close personal follower of his for more than thirty years was visibly affected by the news.

"His fame will grow with years and history will pronounce his position on the great questions he has championed right.

Mr. Bryan's last campaign in Nebraska, which he had a premonition would be his last, was in the fall of 1922, when he "stumped" thirty-three towns in behalf of his brother Charles, who was running for governor, and Senator Gilbert Hitchcok, who was a candidate for re-election.

**

BRYAN SPOKE IN IOWA 7 SEASONS AS CHAUTAUQUAN

William Jennings Bryan's first tour of Iowa on a chautauqua platform was in 1904 when he appeared on the Redpath circuit, working out of Chicago. He was here with the same circuit again in 1905.

His next visit to Iowa on the chautauqua platform was in 1910, when he took as his subject "The Price of a Soul." He toured the state in 1911, 1912, 1916 and 1918, which was his last appearance in Iowa in the role of a chautauqua lecturer.

In 1923 his daughter, Ruth Bryan Owen, toured Iowa with the Redpath chautauqua.

Tuesday, July 28, 1925
The Des Moines Register

BRYAN FUNERAL SET FOR FRIDAY

WIDOW NAMES WASHINGTON AS BURIAL PLACE

Train Will Leave Dayton Tomorrow for Capital With Body.

Dayton, Tenn., July 27 (A.P.)—Watched by his Dayton friends, the mortal form of William Jennings Bryan, whose spirit fled away as he slept late yesterday, lay in the front room of a simple southern home tonight while the invalid widow worked out plans for bearing the body of the former secretary of state to Washington for ultimate burial in the restful place of the nation's military heroes, Arlington cemetery.

Humble followers of the great commoner came from the Cumberland slopes late today to gaze into the face of him who was their champion of Christian faith and to pay the last tribute of honor and high esteem.

Tomorrow afternoon, under a spreading maple on the lawn of the Richard Rogers residence, where the former democratic chieftain spent his last days and breathed his last breath, a more formal ceremony will take place when the public is invited to view the remains of the dead leader as he lies in state within a casket of bronze.

Mrs. Bryan Bears Up Well.

All details of the last rites for Mr. Bryan will be simple and without display, in accordance with the wishes of Mrs. Bryan.

The bereaved woman has borne her sorrow with unflinching courage and has at all times directed the arrangements for the care and burial of her husband's body.

The schedule of the funeral party, as tentatively outlined late today by the widow and her group of advisers, calls for the departure of the body from Dayton on a special railroad car Wednesday morning at 8:40 o'clock.

After the first part of the long journey, the forty miles to Chattanooga, has been made, the funeral car will be attached to the regular train of the Southern railway which departs for the nation's capital at 11:20 of the same morning. Knoxville, Bristol, Roanoke and Lynchburg are scheduled stops for the sad procession before the body is taken to Washington.

In Washington it is planned to have the body lie in state for another period while thousands of friends and admirers march by to view the face of the man who fought so boldly in behalf of causes he held to be true and honorable.

Burial Planned for Friday.

On Friday, at an hour to be determined as the events of the intervening days unfold, Mrs. Bryan believed tonight the bones of her husband, thrice the presidential nominee of his party, would be laid to final earthly rest. These plans, it was made clear tonight were subject to revision.

From the western states two daughters and William Jennings Bryan, the younger, hastened to join their mother in Dayton or in Washington. Their messages of sympathy and love soothed her aching heart today. From Los Angeles the younger Bryan and his sister, Mrs. Richard Hargreaves, were on their way to the site of burial. Mrs. Ruth Owen is expected here early tomorrow. She left a scheduled chautauqua performance to rush to her stricken mother's side.

Upon the wishes of these three the final decision and planning depends. More definite announcement is expected as to funeral and interment arrangements when Mrs. Owen reaches Dayton.

Gathered around the house of death today, in unceasing vigil since the bold spirit of the commoner left his body, were the members of the prosecution counsel in the Scopes evolution trial in whose association Mr. Bryan spent his last days and efforts. They never left his sleeping form nor removed themselves far from the sight of that placid face whose determined lines had softened into the troubled calm of perfect rest.

Lawyers Stay With Body.

The dead man's constant companions today were the local lawyers. Sue K. Hicks, Herbert Hicks, Ben G. McKenzie, Gordon McKenzie and Wallace Haggard.

Repeated visits were paid to the Rogers home by Atty. Gen. A. T. Stewart, official head of the recent Scopes prosecution, and by Judge John T. Raulston, who presided in that noted cause.

His friends discussed the vigor which Mr. Bryan had shown in the days preceding his unexpected death. At Winchester, Friday, the commoner had spoken to a vast throng of cheering men and women with his accustomed eloquence and power. On the return trip he had declared to the attorney general that he "felt fine."

They spoke, too, of the heat of the long and bitterly contested fight over the Tennessee evolution law. They felt that the strain of the trial with its oppressive weather and intensity of excitement had weakened the fundamentalist leader's system. They recounted the last utterances of Mr. Bryan and showed their deep grief at his departure.

"There lies the noblest hero of these times," was the tribute of his associates as voiced in muffled tones by Ben McKenzie.From all parts of the United States telegrams poured in by hundreds today to tell the widow of the sorrow of millions and the sympathy of uncounted thousands in her loss. Mrs. Bryan, seated in her rolling chair, at intervals throughout the day listened to the reading of these messages by her constant attendants. Her well-controlled grief seemed assuaged by the assurance of loving hearts which turned to her in condolence.

It had been first planned to place the body in state for public viewing this afternoon and announcement was made to this effect. Later when it became evident that thousands who would wish to see again the face of their leader could not arrive today, Mrs. Bryan directed that this opportunity be delayed until tomorrow afternoon.

It was suggested by some of the attendant group that the body should be laid in state upon the Rhea county courthouse lawn and so it was for a time decided. The plan finally agreed upon was that the last viewing of the body in Dayton should be on the lawn of the Rogers residence.

Four books, gifts of Mr. Bryan were being cherished tonight by Judge Raulston and Mr. Stewart, who believed that the commoner's last conscious act was to inscribe his friendly greetings upon their fly leaves. They were found opened upon the scarcely dried pages where the messages of friendship were penned just before death came. Two of the books were copies of a volume of Mr. Bryan's speeches, while the others were volumes of a treatise on the former secretary of state's political career.

Legion Guard of Honor.

As a guard of honor at the viewing of the body tomorrow, the local post of the American Legion has chosen a detail of six former soldiers and sailors who will be on duty in uniform and without arms. The men who will pay this last tribute are: Gordon Darwin, Clay Green, Creed Parham, Ed Morgan, Will Fisher and Wilfred Ault. George W. Rappleyea, friend of the defendant in the recent evolution trial is commander of the Dayton legion.

Mrs. Bryan earlier today declined with expressions of deep appreciation the offer of Dayton men to form a military guard of honor to attend Mr. Bryan on his last earthly journey. She urged that all ostentation and show be avoided.

"We are simple people," the widow of the commoner said, after a brief pause in which she considered the kindly proposal, "and we want all arrangements simply made."

Widow Is Shielded.

The widow was shielded from visitors today by the attorneys who have been constantly in attendance. She would announce to Mr. Hicks or Mr. Haggard her plans, and these would be repeated by her permission to those who represented the world of keenly interested readers.

The scene of the statesman's death was remarkably free from the mourning scarcely so many persons were to be seen around the Rogers home as would indicate that any event of unusual interest or any person of prominence were within the quiet little residence. One or two of the Dayton friends sat on the porch and occasionally a neighbor woman entered to offer her aid and consolation. But the street in front was empty of observers.

In the afternoon, summoned thither by announcement that they might see the dead man's face, 200 or more men and women, of serious countenances and with suppressed voices, quietly visited the house and as quietly withdrew.

No tears were seen to fall though many sighed in sympathy and sorrow. For the most part they echoed the sentiment of Mrs. Bryan when she said:

"I am happy that he died in peace and without pain."

W. E. Thompson, secretary to Mr. Bryan and of recent months his constant companion, reached Dayton tonight after a hurried termination of a visit among friends in Virginia. He was widely sought before he learned of Mr. Bryan's death. He immediately assumed many of the burdens which the widow has been bearing quietly along with the weight of sorrow.

In tribute to the dead, Dayton's flags were flown at half-staff today and Dayton merchants dispensed with the customary business until the late afternoon.

**

SEEK TO QUASH EVOLUTION SUIT

Government Will Ask Dismissal Today.

Washington, July 27 (A.P.)—Formal motions for the dismissal of the Washington evolution case were filed in the District of Columbia supreme court today by the United States government and Washington city authorities.

They will be presented to Justice Siddons tomorrow when the court calls up the injunction proceedings instituted by Loren N. Wittner, a government employee, to stop the payment of salaries to certain Washington city school authorities on the ground that they permit the teaching in the public school here of matter in "disrespect for the holy bible."

Appearing for Frank White, treasurer of the United States, one of the witnesses in Wittner's suit, District Attorney Gordon asked dismissal on several grounds, the chief of which are that Wittner as a taxpayer has no standing in court and that the United States government cannot be sued without its consent.

Other grounds enumerated are:

"That the bill of complaint does not state facts sufficient to constitute a valid cause of action in equity.

"That it is manifest upon the face of the complaint that Treasurer White has no individual interest in the controversy and that the United States alone would be affected by any decree against White."

Corporation Counsel Stevens for the Washington City authorities also took the position that Wittner is without standing and declared that the complaint fails to set forth any specific facts as to the teaching of anything in disrespect of the holy bible.

**

KEEP UP FIGHT LED BY BRYAN ON EVOLUTION

5,000 Lutherans at San Francisco Oppose It in Schools.

San Francisco, July 27 (A.P.)—Delegates to the International Walther League of Lutherans, 5,000 in number, in convention here, today passed a resolution opposing evolution and declaring it "part of a movement for the overthrow of orderly government."

**

Reno, Nev., July 27 (A.P.)—Commenting on the anti-evolution resolutions adopted by the California-Nevada synod of the Presbyterian church, which called on the Nevada state board of education to exclude from the course of study text books teaching that theory, W. J. Hunting, superintendent of public instruction, said that he saw no reason why they should be eliminated.

"It is presented to the pupils as a scientific theory and is laid before them in the same manner that other theories are presented. It is part of the teaching of biology," Mr. Hunting said.

**

Bryan Kept Up Fight.

Dayton, Tenn., July 27 (A.P.)—William Jennings Bryan's confidence in the people as the ultimate directors of the government was revealed here today as friends of the dead leader remembered his last speech in the Scopes trial.

After others concerned in the trial of the Dayton school teacher had expressed their sentiments on the outcome of the case, Mr. Bryan responded to Judge Raulston's invitation and spoke these words, his last in any earthly court:

"The people will determine this issue. They will take sides upon this issue, they will state the question involved in this issue, they—not so much that which has been brought out here, for very little has been brought out here, but this case will stimulate investigation and investigation will bring out information, and the facts will be known and upon the facts, as ascertained, the decision will be rendered.

"I think, my friends, and your honor, that if we are actuated by the spirit that should actuate every one of us, no matter what our views may be, we ought not only desire, but pray that that which is right will prevail, whether it be our way or somebody else's."

**

Bryan's Evolution Stand.

New York, July 27 (A.P.)—William Jennings Bryan's last formal utterance on evolution, entitled "The Bible Is Good Enough for Me," appears in the current issue of Collier's Weekly as an answer to claims for evolution made in the previous issue by Leonard Darwin, son of Charles Darwin.

"The theory of evolution," Mr. Bryan says, "is dangerous to society. When one considers man but a 'bundle of characteristics inherited from brute ancestors,' as many evolutionists do, it not only libels man, the greatest handiwork of the almighty, but it paralyzes all efforts at reform.

"Followers of Darwin have carried this doctrine so far as to declare that pity and sympathy, the greatest and moral forces, are unmanly, and interfere with the coming of their merciless 'superman.' Few people who profess to believe in evolution have ever read Darwin.

Underestimate Environment.

"All Darwinians are prone to underestimate the relative importance of environment. To argue that descendants inherit intelligence because of physical laws is to ignore the fact that intelligent people surround their children with an environment that cultivates intellectual ideals and furnishes educational opportunities to the children.

"There is proof in abundance to support this proposition that a child born into a home where neither parent can read or write may, in spite of such an inheritance, rise to intellectual heights, provided the environment is favorable.

"Most of our great men in the United States come from the common people and it is no reflection upon the parent to say that a child surpasses him in breadth of mental vision or in depth of intellectual enthusiasm.

Not An Evolution.

"And this is not an evolution, because we have examples of ignorant children who were the descendants of intelligent parents. They simply lack the ambition and ideals that inspired industry. This is not a defect that comes in the blood, but is the result of bad companions or bad habits.

"Nothing could be more disastrous to the race than to have parents to act according to the philosophy of evolutionist. If every parent who, lacking education, attributed it to an inherited defect and believed his children would inherit that defect, it would chill the spirit which has led parents to devote themselves to the improvement of their children.

"Darwinism gives us the doctrine of despair; Jesus brought into the world the gospel of hope.

"Darwinism enthrones selfishness; the bible crowns love as the greatest force in the world."

**

Coolidge Pays National and Personal Tributes to Bryan

President Writes His Condolence to Widow.

Washington, July 27 (A.P.)—By direction of President Coolidge, Secretary Kellogg today formally announced for the government the death of William Jennings Bryan. The announcement follows:

"By direction of the president, the undersigned is charged with the sad duty of announcing the death on July 26, 1925, at Dayton,

Tenn., of William Jennings Bryan, a distinguished citizen of the United States, formerly a representative in congress from the state of Nebraska, a colonel in the Spanish-American war, and secretary of state.

"In all these capacities his services were characterized by a faithfulness to duty and a devotion to public interest. His private life was one for the emulation of all American citizens. Thrice the nominee of a great political party, his death will be especially mourned by a large personal following who held him in affectionate esteem.

"As a testimony of this respect, it is ordered by the president that the national flag be displayed at halfstaff on the national buildings at Washington on the date of the funeral.

(Signed) "Frank B. Kellogg."

**

BRYAN BACKERS LACK LEADER TO CONTINUE FIGHT

"Fundamentalist Party" Plan Seem Doomed.

BY THOMAS L. STOKES

Washington, July 27 (U.N.)—The removal of William Jennings Bryan from the national political arena will have a decided effect on the future course of the democratic party, in which he still was a power. More immediately it will affect the fundamentalist campaign he started at Dayton, and which many believe he would have forced into politics, if possible.

"The fundamentalist issue, at the time, crowds the other effects of Bryan's death into the background. The commoner, by his stand at Dayton, was attracting to his religious banner a large following.

The contest at Dayton, Bryan himself indicated was merely the beginning of his fight. Taking to the platform, where his influence was magical, he might have crystallized the effects of his word at Dayton. The issue, as it is, will be raised in congress through the evolution case brought here.

Fundamentalist Party.

If Bryan had lived, many believe he would have made a political issue out of the evolution controversy. A fundamentalist party is not beyond the imagination. The views of Bryan are held by many in both political parties, and he would have drawn from both. He had the ability to dramatize issues, even unpopular issues, before political conventions.

But he is gone. No successor of his zeal or with the desire to take the responsibility appears. The issue will not die out immediately. The fires have been kindled. But lacking a leader the movement will lose its force. It probably will have its tumultuous day or two on the floors of congress, and pass gradually from the foreground.

Politically, Bryan's death will have its effect on the course of the democratic party. What power he still had was demonstrated at the last democratic convention in New York, which placed his brother, Charles W. Bryan, on the national ticket. He sat on the platform committee and helped shape the form of the party's pronouncements.

McAdoo May Be Affected.

Bryan's death may have an effect on the fortunes of William Gibbs McAdoo, in the opinion of some observers. Bryan was McAdoo's chief lieutenant at the New York convention. He fought hard for McAdoo, trying to beat down the opposition from the forces of Gov. A. Smith, and break the deadlock between the two.

Bryan, too, was one of the leaders in the recently inaugurated movement to unite the west and south for the campaign in 1928. McAdoo looked favorably on this effort. Bryan's removal will take away the major influence in this move, which his brother, in an interview here, characteriszed as the hope of democratic victory in the next presidential campaign.

The death of Bryan, following quickly upon that of Senator LaFollette of Wisconsin, is looked upon by some observers as depriving a certain discontented element in the west of its leadership. The men were totally different, but attracted a large following of the same type, which now has no outstanding leader.

**

"GOD'S NAPOLEON," SAYS BILLY SUNDAY IN BRYAN TRIBUTE

Hood River, Ore., July 27 (A.P.)—Rev. William A. Sunday, spending the supper at his country home here, paid the following tribute to William Jennings Bryan:

"The friend of God, the enemy of the devil. To know William Jennings Bryan was an invitation to do right.

"Although he chose politics as a career, he was essentially a crusader for Christianity. He was at his best when fighting on moral rather than religious issues. He fell with his face to the enemy.

"He was Lutheran in his faith, a Napoleon in his battle for God, a Lincoln in his patience. Crown him as one of the world's immortals. He never dipped his colors to compromise. His great hold upon the American people was due to his sincerity of purpose. It was a rare privilege to count him as my friend and co-laborer for God."

**

MOURN BRYAN IN LONDON AS SINCERE MAN

Paris Newspaper Calls Him Bible's Defender

London, July 27 (A.P.)—The news of William Jennings Bryan's death was received here with the greatest surprise, as his recent activities at Dayton gave the impression that he had maintained his fullest vigor.

The Morning Post, which describes Mr. Bryan's death as "A dramatic climax to the Darwin versus Genesis battle," says in a brief obituary:

Possessing sincere convictions, he believed profoundly in himself and the righteousness of the causes he espoused. His integrity and honest belief in his own cause were recognized by those to whom his democratic platform was anathema."

**

Paris, July 27, A.P.)—The newspapers give special prominence to the death of William J. Bryan, recalling that, as secretary of state, he signed the United States' first note of protest after the sinking of the Lusitania.

One paper used this headline over its story:

"Monsieur Bryan, Defender of Bible, Dies Suddenly."

John Baird Bryan, a grandson of the commoner, is studying in Paris.

**

Tokio, July 27 (A.P.)—Prime Minister Shidebara, when apprised of the death of William Jennings Bryan said:

"The death of Mr. Bryan is a great loss, not only to his own country, but to the whole world. His courage in supporting the cause of international peace and friendship has been inspiring, and we in Japan, while continuing to benefit from his example, feel a deep sense of loss of the active sympathy he always displayed towards Japan."

**

Santiago, Chile, July 27 (A.P.)—Editorial tributes to William Jennings Bryan appears in all the morning papers here today. Some of the writers refer to him as "an indefatigable worker for Christianity."

Mr. Bryan visited Chile about fifteen years ago.

**

BRYAN TO REST IN ARLINGTON AS A SOLDIER

Friend Chooses Site for Commoner's Burial

Washington, July 27 (A.P.)—Near the crest of a swelling slope, where sleep a great company of the dead of many wars, the American government today marked out in Arlington National cemetery a final resting place for William Jennings Bryan.

His burial there late Friday afternoon, with simple ceremony, will fulfill his own oft-repeated wish. In life a crusader for peace, he chose in death to lie where the tombs of military men look down upon the capital, amid the beauties of the Virginia hills, but yet nearby the towering memorials reared to Washington and Lincoln.

The right he thus asserted to a place in the nation's citadel of military dead was his by virtue of those stirring days of '98 when he wore the uniform as a colonel of volunteers. His grave will be in that community of death where sleep many comrades of the Spanish-American war, not far from the Dewey mausoleum and the monument that honors those who died on the Maine.

Simple Ceremonies Planned.

Not all of the plans for Friday's funeral services had been arranged tonight, but it seemed certain that the commoner would be committed to his tomb with only those ceremonies which are fitting for a plain and humble citizen. No plans had been made to sound for him the bugle call that says a last farewell to the soldier, nor to heap upon his bier the pompous tribute of a great government for a fallen leader of the people. Those of his friends who are doing for him the last earthly service believe he would approve of no funeral program but the simplest.

In other ways, however, the government and the nation will do what they are permitted to do to honor him. By direction of President Coolidge, flags on the government buildings will fly at half-staff on the funeral day. His body will lie in state for a time, too., after its arrival here Thursday morning, but it is doubtful whether this final public tribute will be paid in any public building.

Not until Friday will the family circle be complete, and the funeral services that afternoon will be held in the Washington place of worship where Mr. Bryan was a constant attendant during the days of his services in the cabinet.

R. G. Davis Chooses Site.

The place of his entombment at Arlington was chosen today by a friend of many years, Ben G. Davis, to whom the former secretary had expressed more than once his desire to sleep in the historic national burying ground. He loved the serenity of the sweep of wooded ridge, rising in gentle fold from the Potomac. He wanted, too, to lie close by the nation's memorial of Abraham Lincoln, whom he loved; and that wish will be fulfilled.

The chosen place is one of the most beautiful in Arlington, within a stone's throw of the summit of the highest ridge, his grave will be upon the bosom of a wide, unshaded sweep, grass-grown and fringed far off with old oaks. Clearly visible across the placid river lies the capital city, a panorama of historic landmarks; the shaft of the Washington monument, the austere colonnade of the Lincoln memorial and the majestic gray-white dome of the capitol.

**

BRYAN, EVERY INCH A MAN, SAYS PRIEST

Father Nugent Speaks Feelingly of Old Friend.

Father J. F. Nugent, who suffered a nervous collapse Sunday night when told of the death of William Jennings Bryan, his intimate friend of the last thirty years, recovered sufficiently yesterday to say a few words of praise for the commoner, with whom he had often occupied the same lecture platform.

"William Jennings Bryan was a man from the ground up," he said. "Every inch of him a man, honest in his own convictions and willing always to fight for that in which he believed."

As he attempted to relate anecdotes of his experiences in the campaign of 1896 with Mr. Bryan, Father Nugent seemed unable to understand that the commoner was dead.

"We are great friends," he said. "I had a great respect for him—I have it yet."

Father Nugent and Mr. Bryan became close friends in 1896 when they met frequently on the lecture platform. In recent years Mr. Bryan had visited Father Nugent at every opportunity and often spoke of the many happy moments that the two of them had spent together.

Early yesterday morning Father Nugent sent a message of condolence to Mrs. Bryan and her family, in which he said:

"I am shocked and deeply grieved by the sudden death of your illustrious husband. As a lifelong admirer of his unswerving devotion to principle, I extend to you and your family my heartfelt sympathy and pray that God, whom he worshipped so devoutly, may sustain you in your bereavement."

**

WHITE DECLARES DEATH OF BRYAN ENDS POPULISM

Says Commoner Was Last of Its Leaders.

Salt Lake City, Utah, July 27.—The death of William Jennings Bryan marks the passing of the generation of populists, leaders of the great cycle in the last two decades of American history that began with Gen. James P. Weaver of Iowa, in the late seventies, and culminated in 1916 with the Wilson administration, said William Allen White, editor of the Emporia, Kan., Daily Gazette, who was a visitor here today.

"One by one the strong men developed by the idea of populism, called variously greenbackers, progressives, liberals and insurgents, have dropped off. Roosevelt, Wilson, La Follette, one by one made exit, and now Bryan goes.

"He is the last of the major figures of that movement. With his death the epoch definitely closes and passes into history and we are now ready for the next adventure in altruism in American politics. It is not due for another decade at least, but when it comes it will be a part of a world movement.

"It was a fine adventure and now that the leaders are off stage and the curtain down, we may begin to estimate its meaning and significance.

"Bryan, the last living leader, contributed to it only the emotion of a great heart. The brains of the movement lay in others."

Abbott Gave Bryan Title.

Chicago, July 27 (A.P.)—The Chicago Herald and Examiner tonight says that the title of "the great commoner," was given to William Jennings Bryan by a newspaper man, Willis J. Abbott, now editor of the Christian Science Monitor, just after Mr. Bryan's nomination in 1896 as the democratic candidate for president.

After Mr. Bryan's famous "Cross of Gold: speech, which brought him that nomination, the secretary of the president of the Burlington railroad, following a standing in those days, came to tender the candidate the use of the railroad president's private car to return home to Nebraska.

"But, Mr. Bryan, you certainly cannot do that," spoke up Mr. Abbott, with the theme of the "Cross of Gold" speech still fresh in his mind. "You are a commoner. You are the great commoner."

Mr. Bryan did not accept the railroad president's offer. Several years later in 1901, he founded his weekly entitled "The Commoner."

**

Theaters Strike Out Lines Satirizing Bryan

New York, July 27 (A.P.)—Out of respect for the memory of William Jennings Bryan, New York theaters have decided to delete scenes satirizing his part in the recent Scopes trial.

A scene in the "Garrick Gaities," portraying Mr. Bryan as the prosecutor in a "monkey trial" will be dropped tonight.

Lines from the Grand Street Follies referring to the commoner are to be deleted, and other comedies in Manhattan theaters which have been satirizing Mr. Bryan by word, suggestion or tableau have had all such parts stricken out.

**

Bryan Called the Work at Dayton "Well Done"

Winchester, Tenn., July 27 (A.P.)—Before leaving here Saturday, after delivering an address, William Jennings Bryan, who died suddenly in Dayton yesterday, made the following statement to a reporter:

"If I should die tomorrow, I should feel that much has been accomplished in the greatest cause for enlightening humanity ever known. I believe that on the basis of the accomplishments of the past few weeks, I could truthfully say, well done."

**

Swampscott, Mass., July 27 (A.P>)—President Coolidge late today sent the following letter of condolence to the widow of William Jennings Bryan:

"My dear Mrs. Bryan:

"The sudden death of Mr. Bryan brought a sense of personal loss to Mrs. Coolidge and myself. It was only the other day that he had been our guest at the White house. We wish to extend to you and your family our most heartfelt sympathy.

"Mr. Bryan has been a prominent figure in public affairs for a third of a century. He has been a leader in the advocacy of many moral reforms and was representative of the effort for purity in our political life. He was endowed with the great gift of eloquence. The sincerity of his motives was beyond dispute. He was three times chosen head of a great political party and held the exalted office of secretary of state.

"His career was another example of what American opportunity affords to those who have the will to industriously apply themselves. It would be difficult to find among his contemporaries, anyone with so large a circle of friends and acquaintances who had so generously bestowed upon him their esteem and confidence.

"I trust that you may be given consolation in remembering all his worth and in the abiding faith that a divine providence has ordered all things well."

**

FOR THE MASSES

It is noted that the student who selects some detail of human knowledge finds himself in a very small group. In politics, in religious thought, in every relation of life the group grows smaller as attention is fixed on the distinctive thing.

These groups, in discovering the more general lines on which they may come together for mutual helpfulness, find themselves considering the fundamentals. As this process is carried on until the whole human family is a unit, the union is found to be on the simplest facts of human experience, and very few even of those. The field is limited indeed in which the whole human family is one.

It is the lot of men to find themselves in the larger or smaller groupings according as their interest runs to the specialties of life, or to the more universal facts. Men as a rule move in one direction or the other. They are exceedingly well informed in specialties, or they are generally well informed, but rarely ever both.

It was plainly the slant of Bryan's mind to turn to the things that interest men in the larger groups. The titles he won are suggestive, the Commoner, the people's oracle. Mr. Bryan talked for men in the mass, and he therefore played upon the emotions men have in common, and debated the things all men can be persuaded to think about. He had himself the character of a people's man. His private life, his home life, his public life were of the sort all people approve. The basic things were his, he did not try to make up with scholarship or talent in some specialty for want of the common virtues.

It is easy for scholars and specialists to berate such a man, he had neither the time nor the talent to become a specialist and in his expositions to the people he frequently showed want of information. And yet in our public life and in our religious life, is there not constant call for men who can come to the larger groupings with a message directed to those common things which all men share together? Must we not have in every generation with our scholars and men of special training the other men who can, as we say, popularize what the others have discovered and fit it in with the moral sanctions on which the community rests?

The problem of human progress does not seem ever to have been a problem of the more advanced. Always it has been a problem of keeping rearguard and vanguard within hailing distance. The triumph of democracy in so far as democracy has triumphed has been in the leadership of men of the masses. They have been of all degrees of talent, but they have never diverted from the main business which was to emphasize the things on which all men can come together in the mutual undertaking.

Bryan was a friend of the masses. He thought their thoughts, he practiced their kindly virtues, he stood for them,. And because he was real in this, it made little difference how many vagaries he sidetracked with, he never lost his hold on the confidence of the common people. And always and everywhere he evangelized for a better, a more humane, a more honest, and a kindlier world. Even the last crusade he had planned, however much we might object to the theory on which he was to make it, would have been a campaign for cleaner living, to magnify the new Adam, to persuade people to dwell more in the spirit.

It would be easy to review such a career and point out the many mistakes. The smaller groups as they come to him will find him singularly wanting in what they have specialized on. But massed as one people, having certain great aims in common do not Americans owe the Commoner a debt of gratitude for his life, his example, his evangelism, his faith? Nobody can fairly ask whether the world is richer or poorer for such a man without finding the answer inevitably in the affirmative.

**

If they get an evolution argument started in Washington, congress may have some trouble attracting its usual attention next winter.

**

Just think what will happen when congress begins chewing the evolution rag!

Wednesday, July 29, 1925
The Des Moines Register

C. W. BRYAN TURNS EVOLUTION FOE

FIGHT GOES ON INTO CONGRESS, HE DECLARES

Commoner's Brother Passes Through Iowa on Way to Funeral.

Creston, Ia., July 28 (Special)—C. W. Bryan, candidate for vice president on the democratic ticket in the last national campaign, and brother to William Jennings Bryan, intends to become the successor of his brother in the leadership of the fight waged by the fundamentalists against the teaching of the theory of evolution.

Passing through here tonight on his way to his brother's funeral in Washington, Mr. Bryan lauded the fight made by William Jennings in the Scopes trial, declared that he was in hearty accord with the commoner in opposition to the scientists, and added that the fight would go on, notwithstanding the commoner's death.

His Heart in Brother's Fight.

Charles W. declared that his heart was with his brother in the fight in Tennessee and asserted that congress eventually will be confronted with the problem of legislation relating to the teaching of evolution. The intention of William Jennings Bryan make the subject an issue in congress-possibly with an eye to its political consequences—figured much in the commoner's political and legal tactics at Dayton. The close comradeship that existed between the Bryan brothers thus gives to the statement of Charles W. here tonight a deep significance.

Mr. Bryan was seen by a correspondent of The Register when the Chicago, Burlington & Quincy train stopped here for a few minutes. The former governor came from his home in Lincoln, Neb.

"Several states already have passed laws prohibiting the teaching of evolution," he said, "and more soon will follow suit.

"Eventually congress will be forced to meet this problem. My brother studied the theory of evolution for ten years and his heart and soul were in the fight against it.

"My brother's death was a very great personal loss to me. In our intimate and close relationship throughout our lives, we were in constant communication by telegraph. My sympathies were all with him in his last great fight, down in Tennessee."

The train bearing the former governor reached here at 9:47 o'clock tonight. His two sisters will pass through here on their way to Washington at the same hour tomorrow evening.

Darrow Answers Commoner.

Lexington, Ky., July 28 (A.P.)—Clarence Darrow, Chicago lawyer, who upheld the theory of evolution at the John T. Scopes trial at Dayton, Tenn., tonight answered very briefly, the final message of William Jennings Bryan, fundamentalist champion and his chief opponent at the Dayton trial. Mr. Darrow came here today for a brief vacation and probably will remain two days.

Like the message of Mr. Bryan, given out through the press today by Mr. Bryan on account of the commoner's death. Mr. Darrow also issued his answer through the press and not in an address.

"I have read what Mr. Bryan intended for his speech at Dayton only hurriedly," Mr. Darrow said, "but it impresses me as only the argumentative statement of a lawyer. He referred again to the Loeb and Leopold case, and the philosophy of Nietzshe. He indicated that, in his belief, such philosophy may have been responsible for their act.

"The trial at Dayton has done several things which are significant. Of the jurors who heard the case at Dayton only one of them had ever heard of evolution. Today in Dayton they are selling more books of evolution than any other kind, and the book shops in Chattanooga and other cities of the state are hardly able to supply the demand for works on evolution. The trial has at least started people to thinking."

To the commoner, whose body will be taken to Washington tomorrow for burial, Mr. Darrow paid a tribute, though the beliefs of the two were far apart.

**

DAYTON HOLDS SIMPLE RITES OVER BRYAN

Hundreds View Body on Eve of Departure for Washington.

Dayton, Tenn., July 28 (A.P.)—The mountain folk of eastern Tennessee, applauding spectators of his last great battle, paid their final tribute today to "Brother Bryan," fearless champion of their Christian faith.

Passing in line, hundreds of men, women and children who watched the last days of the great commoner, looked for the last time today at the placid face of their leader as he lay in an humble Dayton home, and glimpsed through the glass top of his casket those firm-set lips whence eloquence often flowed to stir the hearts of men.

Later, as the shadows lengthened on the sultry summer day, they stood again in a patient multitude upon the lawn to hear a minister speak a funeral paean and praise God for the life and works of William Jennings Bryan.

It was Bryan, the clear voiced herald of religious fundamentalism who received the last rites here today. Thursday and Friday in Washington, his countrymen will pay high honor to the democratic chieftain, presidential candidate and former secretary of state. In Arlington cemetery the colonel of volunteers in the war with Spain will be laid to rest among the military heroes of the nation.

Start Journey Today.

Tonight the widow—embodiment of fortitude in time of sorrow—

from her rolling chair was preparing her household for the departure tomorrow toward the country's capital. The special car for the funeral party arrived in Dayton late today.

In the morning at 8:40 o'clock it will leave for Chattanooga, whence after an interval in which the public there will view the body, the dead leader and his escort will go to Washington by way of Knoxville, Bristol, Roanoke and Lynchburg.

The journey will be all the way over the Southern railway lines on a scheduled train which should cross the Potomac shortly before 7:30 o'clock Thursday morning.

In the party besides Mr. Bryan will be Mrs. Ruth Owen, the commoner's daughter, and her husband, Maj. Reginald Owen of the British army; S. Bryan Jennings, Jacksonville, cousin of the commoner; Col. P. S. Callahan, Louisville; William E. Thompson, secretary to Mr. Bryan; Wallace Haggard, Dayton lawyer and friend of the Bryan family; Mrs. C. C. Stevens, housekeeper, and William H. McCartney, chauffeur for the Bryan family.

Funeral arrangements at Washington had not been definitely fixed tonight. Early today the grief stricken woman announced that her husband's funeral services at Washington would be held in the New York Avenue Presbyterian church. The pastor, Mrs. Bryan said, Rev. Wallace Radcliffe, has been a great friend of the former secretary of state and his family.

Family to Plan Rites.

When Mrs. Bryan learned that Dr. Radcliffe was absent in Europe she told Mr. Thompson that further details of Washington rites would be worked out on arrival at the national capital.

William Bryan, the son, will join his mother and sister in Washington early Friday, accompanied by Mrs. Grace Hargreaves, another daughter of the dead statesman. Funeral and burial hours will then be determined when the family has assembled after their long journeys.

Former service men in army, navy and marine corps uniforms formed a guard of honor at the residence this afternoon while the public viewed the face of the departed advocate of universal peace. The line of sorrowing friends passed in and out quietly under the supervision of these members of the American Legion and two uniformed policemen.

Of the hundreds who gathered from many counties and a few distant states to pay the final tribute to Mr. Bryan today, fully half were women.

Many of these brought their babies. Fathers led in their little sons, who strove to look into the bronze casket which lay at a level with their faces. All expressed in their countenances a general sorrow over the death of their leader and friend.

Occupy Honor Seats.

Rev. C. R. Jones, pastor of the Dayton Methodist Episcopal church, south, in conducting the devotions, stood upon the front porch of the Richard Rogers home and spoke to the hushed throng who crowded the lawn and blocked the street beyond.

The body of the great commoner, lying in the bronze casket inside the front window, was just three feet from the officiating minister outside.

As the preacher poured out a tribute to the champion of Christian faith, local counsel in the Scopes evolution trial, Mr. Bryan's associates and staunch friends in his last great battle occupied seats of honor on the porch in front of Mr. Jones.

For two hours the never-faltering line of men, women and children passed by the flag-draped bier where the great man lay in his last sleep.

They looked intently a moment into the peaceful face of him to whom they had looked—and looked not in vain—as the champion of their Christian faith. They looked upon the proud and noble features under their glazed covering and moved away, passing around a lone sentry of the American Legion, posted with arms folded over his olive drab breast.

Hundreds View Body.

The column formed at the steps of the home at 2 o'clock. A blueclothed officer directed the movement into the hushed chamber of the dead.

Women and children outnumbered the men. Wide-eyed boys and little girls clinging to their parents' hands tiptoed to catch a glimpse of the now immobile features.

**

Bryan Assailed Teaching of Evolution Theory As Great "Crime"

WIDOW REVEALS ADDRESS BARRED IN SCOPES CASE

His "Supreme Effort" to Explain Fith. (faith?)

Dayton, Tenn., July 28 (A.P.)—The anti-evolution speech, in the delivery of which William Jennings Bryan hoped to make his "supreme effort" today was given to the world, despite the fact its author's lips had been sealed by death.

It is Bryan's exposition of religious faith and indictment of the evolutionary hypothesis, set forth in all his brilliant eloquence and philosophical phraseology.

In it christianity is held up as the only means by which "the problems that vex the heart and perplex the world" may be solved. Evolution is branded as only "millions of guesses strung together," disputing the "truth of the bible as the word of God."

The address was to have been delivered in the trial of John T. Scopes, convicted of violating Tennessee's law prohibiting the teaching of evolution in its schools, but by agreement between counsel, closing arguments were dispensed with.

Then the great commoner prepared to deliver his message at an early date, when it would have been released for publication throughout the country. But tonight he lies silent within a bronze casket.

Chattanoogan Has Address.

Following the death of her husband Sunday, Mrs. Bryan placed the speech in the hands of George F. Milton, president and editor of the Chattanooga News, a devoted friend of the commoner, who admired his courage and sincerity in his last great battle. Mr. Milton decided to make the address public today.

"The right of the state to control the public schools is affirmed in the recent decision in the Oregon case, which declares that the state can direct what shall be taught and also forbid the teaching of anything 'manifestly inimical to the public welfare,'" Mr. Bryan asserted. "The above decision goes even further and declares that the parent not only has the right to guard the religious welfare of the child, but is in duty bound to guard it."

After adding that it was hardly necessary to state that the anti-evolution law did not have "its origin in bigotry," Mr. Bryan asked, "What right has a little irresponsible oligarchy of self-styled 'intellectuals' to demand control of the schools of the United States, in which 25,000,000 children are being educated at an annual expense of nearly $2,000,000,000?"

Appreciates Science's Part.

Further discussion of legal phases of the case and the evidence introduced by the state was given by Mr. Bryan, who then declared that Tennessee did not undervalue the service rendered by science.

"Religion is not hostile to learning: Christianity has been the greatest patron learning has ever had," he continued. "But Christians know that the 'fear of the Lord is the beginning of wisdom' now, just as in the past, and they therefore oppose the teaching of guesses that encourage godlessness among the students."

Further on:

"Christianity welcomes truth from whatever source it comes and is not afraid that any real truth from any source can interfere with the divine truth that comes by inspiration from God himself. It is not scientific truth to which Christians object, for true science is classified knowledge, and nothing therefore can be scientific unless it is true.

"Evolution is not truth; it is merely an hypothesis—it is millions of guesses strung together. It had not been proven in the days of Darwin."

Science Balks Evolution.

"Chemistry is an insurmountable obstacle in the path of evolution. It is one of the greatest of sciences; it separates the atoms—isolates them and walks about them, so to speak. If there were in nature a progressive force, an internal urge, chemistry would find it. But it is not there. All of the ninety-two original elements are separate and distinct; they combine in fixed and permanent proportions. Water is H2-O as it has been from the beginning. It was here before life appeared and has never changed; neither can it be shown that anything else has materially changed."

In support of his position, the following excerpts are noted in the Commoner's address:

"There is no more reason to believe that man descended from some inferior animal than there is to believe that a stately mansion has descended from a small cottage."

"Resemblances are not proof—they simply put us on inquiry."

"There is a spiritual gravitation that draws all souls toward heaven, just as surely as there is a physical force that draws all matter on the surface of the earth towards the earth's center."

"Most of the people who believe in evolution do not know what evolution means."

Teaches Children Wrongly.

"Whatever may be said in favor of teaching evolution to adults, it surely is not proper to teach it to children who are not yet able to think."

"Evolution not only offers no suggestion as to a creator, but tends to put the creative act so far away as to cast doubt upon creation itself."

"While it is shaking faith in God as a beginning, it is also creating a doubt as to a heaven at the end of life."

"Christ has made of death a narrow starlit strip between the companionship of yesterday and the reunion of tomorrow; evolution strikes out the stars and deepens the gloom that enshrouds the tomb."

"Before accepting a new philosophy of life, built up as a materialistic foundation, we have reason to demand something more than guesses."

"Our first indictment against evolution is that it disputes the truth of the bible account of man's creation and shakes faith in the bible as the word of God."

"It (evolution) not only contradicts the Mosaic records of the beginning of human life, but it disputes the bible doctrine of reproduction according to kind—the greatest scientific principle known."

Disputes Entire Bible.

"The evolutionary hypothesis, carried to its logical conclusion, disputes every vital truth of the bible. Its tendency, natural if not inevitable, is to lead those who really accept it, first to agnosticism, and then to atheism."

"He (Darwin) drags man down to the brute level and then, judging man by brute standards, he questions whether man's mind can be trusted to deal with God and immorality."

"The people of Tennessee have been patient enough; they have acted none too soon. How can they expect to protect society, even the church, from the deadening influence of agnosticism and atheism, if they permit the teachers employed by taxation, to poison the minds of the youth with this destructive doctrine?"

Another indictment of "the evolutionary hypothesis" is that if taken seriously and made the basis of a philosophy of life, it would eliminate love and carry man back to a struggle of tooth and claw.

"Evolution is a bloody business, but civilization tries to make it a pink tea."

"If civilization is to be saved from the wreckage threatened by intelligence not consecrated by love, it must be saved by the moral code of the meek and lowly Nazarene."

"A sudden decision of the defense to submit the case without argument, and permit a verdict of guilty, prevented the delivery of the speech," says an introductory note to Mr. Bryan's address.

The text of Mr. Bryan's address follows:

"May it please the court and gentlemen of the jury:

"Demosthenes, the greatest of ancient orators, in his 'Oration on the Crown,' the most famous of his speeches, began by supplicating the favor of all the gods and goddesses of Greece. If, in a case which involved only his own fame and fate, he felt justified in petitioning the heathen gods of his country, surely we, who deal with the momentous issues involved in this case, may well pray to the ruler of the universe for wisdom to guide us in the performance of our several parts in this historic trial.

"Let me in the first place, congratulate our cause that circumstances have committed the trial to a community like this and entrusted the decision to a jury made up largely of the yeoman of the state. The book in issue in this trial contains on its first page two pictures contrasting the disturbing noises of a great city with the calm serenity of the country. It is a tribute that rural life has fully earned.

Lauds Tennessee Folk.

"I appreciate the sturdy honesty and independence of those who come into daily contact with the earth, who, dealing with the myriad mysteries of earth and air, seek to learn from revelation about the bible's wonder-working God. I admire the stern virtues, the vigilance, and the patriotism of the class from which the jury is drawn, and am reminded of the lines of Scotland's immortal bard, which, when changed but slightly, describe your country's confidence in you:

"O Scotia, my dear, my native soil!
"For whom my warmest wish to heaven is sent,
"Long may thy hardy sons of rustic toil
"Be blest with health, and peace, and sweet content.
"And, oh, may heav'n their simple lives present,
"From luxury's contagion, weak and vile,
"Then, howe'er crowns and coronets be rent,
"A virtuous populace may rise the while,
"And stand, a wall of fire, around their much loved isle."

Cites Misrepresentation..

"Let us now separate the issues from the misrepresentations, intentional or unintentional, that have obscured both the letter and the purpose of the law. This is not an interference with freedom of conscience. A teacher can think as he pleases and worship God as he likes, or refuse to worship God at all. He can believe in the bible or discard it;

he can accept Christ or reject him. This law places no obligations or restraints upon him. And so with freedom of speech, he can, so long as he acts as an individual, say anything he likes on any subject. This law does not violate any rights guaranteed by any constitution to any individual. It deals with the defendant, not as an individual, but as an employee, an official or public servant, paid by the state, and therefore under instructions from the state.

"The right of the state to control the public schools is affirmed in the recent decision in the Oregon case, which declares that the state can direct what shall be taught and also forbid the teaching of anything 'manifestly inimical to the public welfare.' The above decision goes even farther and declares, that the parent not only has the right to guard the religious welfare of the child, but is in duty bound to guard it. That decision fits this case exactly. The state had a right to pass this law and the law represents the determination of the parents to guard the religious welfare of their children.

Law Not Founded on Bigotry.

"It need hardly be added that this law did not have its origin in bigotry. It is not trying to force any form of religion on anybody. The majority is not trying it—it is trying to protect itself from the effort of an insolent minority to force religion upon the children under the guise of teaching science. What right has a little irresponsible oligarchy of self-styled 'intellectuals' to demand control of the schools of the United States, in which 25,000,000 children are being educated at an annual expense of nearly $2,000,0000,0000?

"Christians must, in every state of the union, build their own colleges in which to teach Christianity; it is only simple justice that atheists, agnostics and unbelievers should build their own colleges if they want to teach their own religious views or attack the religious views of others.

"The statute is brief and free from ambiguity. It prohibits the teaching, in the public schools, of any theory that denies the story of divine creation as taught in the bible and teaches, instead, that man descended from a lower order of animals. The first sentence sets forth the purpose of those who passed the law. They forbid the teaching of any evolutionary theory that disputes the bible record of man's creation and, to make sure that there shall be no misunderstanding, they place their own interpretations on their language and specifically forbid the teaching of any theory that makes man a descendant of any lower form of life.

Pupils Accused Scopes.

"The evidence shows that defendant taught, in his own language as well as from a book outlining the theory, that man descended from lower forms of life. Howard Morgan's testimony gives us a definition of evolution that will become known throughout the world as this case is discussed. Howard, a 14-year-old boy, has translated the words of the teacher and the textbook into language that even a child can understand. As he recollects it, the defendant said 'a little germ of one cell organism was formed in the sea; this kept evolving until it got to be a pretty good sized animal, then came on to be a land animal, and it kept evolving, and from this was man.

"There is no room for difference of opinion here, and there is no need of expert testimony. Here are the facts, corroborated by another student, Harry Shelton, and admitted to be true by counsel for defense. Mr. White, superintendent of schools, testified to the use of Hunter's Civic Biology, and to the fact that the defendant not only admitted teaching evolution, but declared that he could not teach it without violating the law. Mr. Robinson, the chairman of the school board, corroborated the testimony of Superintendent White in regard to the defendant's admissions and declaration. These are the facts; they are sufficient and undisputed; a verdict of guilty must follow.

"But the importance of this case requires more. The facts and arguments presented to you must not only convince you of the justice of conviction in this case but, while not necessary to a verdict of guilty, they should convince you of the righteousness of the purpose of the people of the state in the enactment of this law.

Tennessee Values Learning.

"The state must speak through you to the outside world and repel the aspersions cast by the counsel for the defense upon the intelligence and the enlightenment of the citizens of Tennessee. The people of this state have a high appreciation of the value of education. The state constitution testifies to that in its demand that education shall be fostered and that science and literature shall be cherished. The continuing and the increasing appropriations for public instruction furnish abundant proof that Tennessee places a just estimate upon the learning that is secured in its schools.

"Religion is not hostile to learning: Christianity has been the greatest patron learning has ever had. But Christians know that 'the fear of the lord is the beginning of wisdom' now, just as it has been in the past, and they therefore oppose the teaching of guesses that encourage godlessness among the students.

"Neither does Tennessee undervalue the service rendered by science. The Christian men and women of Tennessee know how deeply mankind is indebted to science for benefits conferred by the discovery of the laws of nature and by the designing of machinery for the utilization of these laws. Give science a fact and it is not only invincible, but it is of incalculable service to man. If one is entitled to draw from society in proportion to the service that he renders to society, who is able to estimate the reward earned by those who have given to us the use of steam, the use of electricity, and enabled us to utilize the weight of water that flows down the mountainside?

Inventions Invaluable.

"Who will estimate the value of the service rendered by those who invented the phonograph, the telephone and the radio? Or, to come more closely to our home life, how shall be recompense those who gave us the sewing machine, the harvester, the threshing machine, the tractor, the automobile, and the method now employed in making artificial ice? The department of medicine also opens an unlimited field for invaluable service. Typhoid and yellow fever are not feared as they once were. Diphtheria and pneumonia have been robbed of some of their terrors, and a high place on the scroll of fame still awaits the discoverer of remedies for arthritis, cancer, tuberculosis and other dread diseases to which mankind is heir.

"Christianity welcomes truth from whatever source it comes, and is not afraid that any real truth from any source can interfere with the divine truth that comes by inspiration from God himself. It is not scientific truth to which Christians object, for true science is classified knowledge, and nothing therefore can be scientific unless it is true.

"Evolution is not truth; it is merely an hypothesis—it is millions of guesses strung together. It had not been proven in the days of Darwin; he expressed astonishment that with two or three million species it had been impossible to trace any species to any other species. It had not been proven in the days of Huxley and it has not been proven up to today.

Scientist Admitted Defeat.

"It is less than four years ago that Professor Bateson came all the way from London to Canada to tell the American scientists that every effort to trace one species to another had failed—every one: He said he still had faith in evolution but had doubts about the origin of species. But of what value is evolution if it cannot explain the origin of species? While many scientists accept evolution as if it were a fact, they all admit, when questioned, that no explanation has been found as to how one species developed into another.

"Darwin suggested two laws—sexual selection and natural selection. Sexual selection has been laughed out of the classroom, and natural selection is being abandoned, and no new explanation is satisfactory even to scientists. Some of the more rash advocates of evolution are wont to say that evolution is as firmly established as the law of gravitation or the Copernican theory. The absurdity of such a claim is apparent when we remember that anyone can prove the law of gravitation by throwing a weight into the air, and that anyone can prove the roundness of the earth by going around it, while no one can prove evolution to be true in any way whatever.

Chemistry Balks Theory.

"Chemistry is an insurmountable obstacle in the path of evolution. It is one of the greatest of the sciences; it separates the atoms—

isolates them and walks about them, so to speak. If there were in nature a progressive force, an eternal urge, chemistry would find it. But it is not there. All of the ninety-two original elements are separate and distinct; they combine in fixed and permanent proportions. Water is H-2O, as it has been from the beginning. It was here before life appeared and has never changed; neither can it be shown that anything else has materially changed.

"There is no more reason to believe that man descended from some inferior animal than there is to believe that a stately mansion has descended from a small cottage. Resemblances are not proof—they simply put us on inquiry. As one fact, such as the absence of the accused from the scene of the murder, outweighs all the resemblances that a thousand witnesses could swear to, so the inability of science to trace any one of the millions of species to another species outweighs all the resemblances upon which evolutionists rely to establish man's blood relationship with the brutes.

"But while the wisest scientists cannot prove a pushing power, such as evolution is supposed to be, there is a lifting power that any child can understand. The plant lifts the mineral up into a higher world, and the animal lifts the plant up into a world still higher.

Man Drawn Upward.

"So, it has been reasoned by analogy man rises, not by a power within him, but only when drawn upward by higher power. There is a spiritual gravitation that draws all souls toward heaven, just as surely as there is a physical force that draws all matter on the surface of the earth towards the earth's center. Christ is our drawing power; he said, 'I, if I be lifted up from the earth, will draw all men unto me,' and his promise is being fulfilled daily all over the world.

"It must be remembered that the law under consideration in this case does not prohibit the teaching of evolution up to the line that separates man from the lower form of animal life. The law might well have gone farther than it does and prohibit the teaching of evolution in lower forms of life; the law is a very conservative statement of the people's opposition to an anti-biblical hypothesis. The defendant was not content to teach what the law permitted; he, for reasons of his own, persisted in teaching that which was forbidden for reasons entirely satisfactory to the law makers.

"Most of the people who believe in evolution do not know what evolution means. One of the science books taught in the Dayton High school has a chapter on 'the evolution of machinery.' This is a very common misuse of the term. People speak of the evolution of the telephone, the automobile, and the musical instrument. But these are merely illustrations of man's power to deal intelligently with inanimate matter; there is no growth from within in the development of machinery.

Now Evolution in Plants.

"Equally improper is the use of the word 'evolution' to describe the growth of a plant or a seed, the growth of a chicken from an egg, or the development of any form of animal life from a single cell. All these give us a circle, not a change from one species to another.

"Evolution—the evolution involved in this case, and the only evolution that is a matter of controversy anywhere—is the evolution taught by defendant, set forth in the books now prohibited by the new state law, and illustrated in the diagram printed on page 19 of Hunter's Civic Biology. The author estimates the number of species in animal kingdom at 518,900. These are divided into eighteen classes, and each class in indicated on the diagram by a circle, proportionate in size to the number of species in each class and attached by a stem to the trunk of the tree. It begins with protozoa and ends with the mammals.

"Passing over the classes with which the average man is unfamiliar, let me call your attention to a few of the larger and better known groups. The insects are numbered at 360,000, over two-thirds of the total number of species in the animal world. The fishes are numbered at 13,000, the amphibians at 1,400, the reptiles at 3,500 and the birds at 13,000, while 3,500 mammals are crowded together in a little circle that is barely higher than the bird circle.

Man Called a Mammal.

"No circle is reserved for man alone. He is, according to the diagram, shut up in the little circle entitled 'mammals,' with 3,499 other species of mammals. Does it not seem a little unfair not to distinguish between man and lower forms of life? What shall we say of the intelligence, not to say religion, of those who are so particular to distinguish between fishes and reptiles and birds, but put a man with an immortal soul, in the same circle with the wolf, the hyena and the skunk? What must be the impression made upon children by such a degradation of man?

"In the preface of this book, the author explains that it is for children and adds that 'the boy or girl of average ability, upon admission to the secondary school, is not a thinking individual.' Whatever may be said in favor of teaching evolution to adults, it surely is not proper to teach it to children who are not yet able to think.

"The evolution does not undertake to tell us how protozoa moved by interior and resident forces, sent life up through all the various species, and cannot prove that there was actually any such compelling power at all. And yet, the school children are asked to accept their guesses and build a philosophy of life upon them.

No Laughing Matter.

"If it were not so serious a matter, one might be tempted to speculate upon the various degrees of relationship that, according to evolutionists, exist between man and other forms of life. It might require some very nice calculation to determine at what degree of relationship the killing of a relative ceases to be murder and the eating of one's kin ceases to be cannibalism.

"But it is not a laughing matter when one considers that evolution not only offers no suggestions as to a creator but tends to put the creative act so far away as to cast doubt upon creation itself. And while it is shaking faith in God as a beginning, it is also creating doubt as to a heaven at the end of life.

"Evolutionists do not feel that it is incumbent upon them to show how life began or at what point in their long drawn out scheme of changing species man became endowed with hope and promise of immortal life. God may be a matter of indifference to the evolutionists and a life beyond may have no charm for them, but the mass of mankind will continue to worship their creator and continue to find comfort in the promise of their savior that he has gone to prepare a place for them.

"Christ has made of death a narrow, starlit strip between the companionship of yesterday and the reunion of tomorrow. Evolution strikes out the stars and deepens the gloom that enshrouds the tomb.

"If you, your honor, and you, gentlemen of the jury, would have an understanding of the sentiment that lies back of the statute against the teaching of evolution, please consider these facts:

Marine Vertebrata First.

"First, as to the animals to whom evolutionists would have us trace our ancestry, the following is Darwin's family tree, as you will find it set forth on pages 180-181 of his "Descent of Man":

"'The most ancient progenitors in the kingdom of vertebrata at which we are able to obtain an obscure glance apparently consisted of a group of marine animals, resembling the larvae of existing ascidians. These animals probably gave rise to a group of fishes, as lowly organized as the lancelot; and from these the ganoids, and other fishes like the lepidosiren, must have been developed. From such fish a very small advance would carry us on to the amphibians.

"'We have seen that birds and reptiles were once intimately connected together; and the monotremata now connect mammals with reptiles in a slight degree. But no one can at present say by what line of descent the three higher and related classes—namely, mammals, birds and reptiles—were derived from the two lower vertebrate classes, namely amphibians and fishes.

"'In the class of mammals, the steps are not difficult to conceive which led from the ancient monotremata to the ancient marsupials; and from these to the early progenitors of the placental mammals. We may thus ascend to the lemuridae; and the interval is not very wide from these to the simiadae. The simiadae then branched off into two great stems, the new world and old world monkeys; and from the latter, at a remote period, man, the wonder and glory of the universe, proceeded. Thus we have given to a man a pedigree of prodigious length, but not, it may be said, of noble quality.'"

"(1874, Hurst)

"Note the words implying uncertainty—'obscure glance,' 'apparently,' 'resembling,' 'must have been,' 'slight degree,' and 'can conceive.'

First Man in Africa.

"Darwin on page 171 of the same book, tries to locate his first man—that is, the first man to come down out of the trees—in Africa. After leaving man in company with gorillas and chimpanzees, he says:

"'But it is useless to speculate on this subject.'

"If he had only thought of this earlier, the world might have been spared much of the speculation that his brute hypothesis has excited.

"On page 79, Darwin gives some fanciful reasons for believing that man is more likely to have descended from the chimpanzee than from the gorilla. His speculations are an excellent illustration of the effect that the evolutionary hypothesis has in cultivating the imagination. Prof. J. Arthur Thomson says that the 'idea of evolution is the most potent thought economizing formula the world has yet know.' It is more than that; it dispenses with thinking entirely and relies on the imagination.

"On page 141. Darwin attempts to trace the mind of men back to the mind of lower animals. On pages 113 and 114, he endeavors to trace man's moral nature back to the animals. It is all animal, animal, animal, with never a thought of God or of religion..

"Our first indictment against evolution is that it disputes the truth of the Bible account of man's creation and shakes faith in the Bible as the word of God. This indictment we prove by comparing the processes described as evolutionary with the text of Genesis. It not only contradicts the Mosaic record as to the beginning of human life, but it disputes the Bible doctrine of reproduction according to kind—the greatest scientific principle known.

Evolution Leads to Atheism.

"Our second indictment is that the evolutionary hypothesis, carried to its logical conclusion, disputes every vital truth of the Bible. Its tendency, natural, if not inevitable, is to lead those who really accept it, first to agnosticism and then to atheism. Evolutionists attack the truth of the Bible, not openly at first, but by using weazel words like 'poetical,' 'symbolical,' and 'allegorical' to suck the meaning out of the inspired record of man's creation.

Bundle of Characteristics.

"We call as our first witness, Charles Darwin. He began life a Christian. On page 39, Vol. 1, of the 'Life and Letters of Charles Darwin,' by his son, Francis Darwin, he says, speaking of the period from 1828 to 1831, 'I did not in the least doubt the strict and literal truth of every word in the Bible.' On page 412 of Vol. 2 of the same publication, he says, 'When I was collecting facts for "the origin" my belief in what is called a personal order was as firm as that of Dr. Puzey himself.' It may be a surprise to your honor and to you, gentlemen of the jury, as it was to me, to learn that Darwin spent three years at Cambridge studying for the ministry.

Later Changed His Views.

"This was Darwin as a young man, before he came under the influence of doctrine that man came from a lower order of animals. The change wrought in his religious views will be found in a letter written to a German youth in 1879. The letter begins: 'I am engaged, an old man, and out of health, and I cannot spare time to answer your question fully—nor indeed can they be answered. Science has nothing to do with Christ, except insofar as the habit of scientific research makes a man cautious in admitting evidence. For myself, I do not believe that there has ever been any "revelation." As for a future life, every man must judge for himself between conflicting vague probabilities.'

"Note that 'science has nothing to do with Christ, except in so far as the habit of scientific research makes a man cautious in admitting evidence.' Stated plainly, that simply means that 'the habit of scientific research' makes one cautious in accepting the only evidence that we have of Christ's existence, mission, teachings, crucifixion, and resurrection, namely the evidence found in the Bible. To make this interpretation of his words the only possible one, he adds, 'for myself, I do not believe that there ever has been any revelation.' In rejecting the Bible as a revelation, 'I cannot pretend to throw the least light on such abstruse problems. The mystery of the beginning of all things is insoluble by us; and I for one must be content to remain an agnostic.'

Had Been a Christian.

"When Darwin entered upon his scientific career, he was 'quite orthodox and quoted the Bible as an unanswerable authority on some point of morality.' Even when he wrote 'The Origin of Species,' the thought of 'a first cause, having an intelligent mind in some degree analogous to man,' was strong in his mind. It was after that time that 'very gradually, with many fluctuations,' his belief in God became weaker. He traces this decline for us and concludes by telling us that he cannot pretend to throw the least light on such abstruse above referred to us then comes the flat statement that he 'must be content to remain an agnostic'; and to make clear what he means by the word, agnostic, he says that 'the mystery of the beginning of all things is insoluble by us,'—not by him alone but by everybody. Here we have the effect of evolution upon its most distinguished exponent; it led him from an orthodox Christian, believing the word of the Bible and in a personal god, down and down and down to helpless and hopeless agnosticism. But there is one sentence upon which I reserved comment—it throws light upon his downward pathway. 'Then arises the doubt, can the mind of man which has, as I fully believe, been developed from a mind as low as that possessed by the lowest animals, be trusted when it draws such grand conclusions?'

Drags Man Down.

"Here is the explanation; he drags man down to the brute level, and then, judging man by brute standards, he questions whether man's mind can be trusted to deal with God and immortality!

"How can any teacher tell his students that evolution does not tend to destroy his religious faith? How can an honest teacher conceal from his students the effect of evolution upon Darwin himself? And is it not stranger still that preachers who advocate evolution never speak of Darwin's loss of faith, due to his belief in evolution? The parents of Tennessee have reason enough to fear the effect of evolution upon the minds of their children. Belief in evolution cannot bring to those who hold such a belief any compensation for the loss of faith in God, trust in the Bible, and belief in the supernatural character of Christ. It is belief in evolution that has caused so many scientists and so many Christians to reject the miracles of the Bible, and then give up, one after another, every vital truth of Christianity. They finally cease to pray and sunder the tie that binds them to their heavenly father.

Were Miracles Performed?

"The miracle should not be a stumbling block to anyone. It raises but three questions: First—Could God perform a miracle? Yes, the God who created the universe can do anything he wants to with it. He can temporarily suspend any law that he has made or he may employ higher laws that we do not understand.

"Second—Would God perform a miracle? To answer that question in the negative one would have to know more about God's plans and purposes than infinite mind can know, and yet some are so wedded to evolution that they deny that God would perform a miracle merely because a miracle is inconsistent with evolution.

"If we believe that God can perform a miracle and might desire to do so, we are prepared to consider with open mind the third question, namely, did God perform the miracles recorded in the Bible? The same evidence that establishes the authority of the Bible establishes the truth of the record of miracles performed. Do these evolutionists stop to think of the crime they commit when they take faith out of the hearts of men and women and lead them out into a starless night? What pleasure can they find of robbing human beings of the 'hallowed glory' of that creed that Romanes once cherished and in substituting the lonely mystery of existence as he found it? Should the fathers and mothers of Tennessee be blamed for trying to protect their children from such a tragedy?

"If anyone has been led to complain of the severity of the punishment that hangs over the defendant, let him compare this crime and its mild punishment with crimes for which a greater punishment is prescribed. What is the taking of a few dollars from one in day or night in comparison with the crime and leading one away from God and away from Christ? He who spake as never man spake, thus describes the crimes that are committed against the young. 'It is impossible but that offenses will come. But woe unto him through whom they come. It were better for him that a millstone were hanged about his neck, and be cast into the sea, than that he should offend one of these little ones.'

"Christ did not overdraw the picture. Who is able to set a price upon the life of a child—a child into whom a mother has poured her life and for whom a father has labored? What may a noble life mean to the child itself, to the parents, and to the world?

Existence Here a Small Arc.

"And, it must be remembered, that we can measure the effect on only that part of life which is spent on earth; we have no way of calculating the effect on that infinite circle of life of which existence here is but a small arc. The soul is immortal and religion deals with the soul; the logical effect of the evolutionary hypothesis is to undermine religion and thus affect the soul.

"I recently received a list of questions that were to be discussed in a prominent eastern school for women. The second question in the list read 'Is religion an obsolescent function that should be allowed to atrophy quietly, without arousing the passionate prejudice of outworn superstition?' The real attack of evolution, it will be seen, is not upon orthodox Christianity, or even upon Christianity, but upon religion—the most basic fact in man's existence and the most practical thing in life.

"But I have some more evidence of the effect of evolution upon the life of those who accept it and try to harmonize their thought with it.

"James H. Leuba, a professor of psychology at Bryn Mawr college, Pennsylvania, published a few years ago, a book entitled 'Belief in God and Immortality.' In this book he relates how he secured the opinions of scientists as to the existence of a personal God and a personal immortality. He used a volume entitled, 'American Men of Science,' which he says, included the names of 'practically every American who may properly be called a scientist.' There were 5,500 names in the book. He selected one thousand names as representative of the 5,500 and addressed them personally. Most of them, he said, were teachers in schools of higher learning. The names were kept confidential. Upon the answers received, he asserts that over half of them doubt or deny the existence of a personal God and a personal immortality, and he asserts that unbelief increases in proportion to prominence, the percentage of unbelief being greatest among the most prominent. Among biologists, believers in a personal God numbered less than 31 per cent, while believers in a personal immortality numbered only 37 per cent.

Unbelief Increases.

"He also questioned the students in nine colleges of high rank and from 1,000 answers received, 97 per cent of which were from students between 18 and 20, he found that unbelief increased from 15 per cent in the freshmen class up to 40 to 45 per cent among the men who graduated. On page 280 of this book, we read 'the students' statistics show that young people enter college, possessed of the beliefs still accepted, more or less perfunctorily, in the average home of the land, and gradually abandon the cardinal Christian belief.' The change from belief to unbelief he attributes to the influence of the persons 'of high culture under whom they studied.'

"The people of Tennessee have been patient enough; they acted none too soon. How can they expect to protect society, and even the church, from the deadening of the church, from the deadening influence of agnosticism and atheism if they permit the teachers employed by taxation to poison the minds of the youth with this destructive doctrine? And remember, that the law has not heretofore required the writing of the word 'poison' on poisonous doctrines. The bodies of our people are so valuable that druggists and physicians must be careful to properly label all poisons; why not be as careful to protect the spiritual life of our people from the poisons that kill the soul?

"There is a test that is sometimes used to ascertain whether one suspected of mental infirmity is really insane. He is put into a tank of water and told to dip the tank dry while a stream of water flows into the tank. If he has not sense enough to turn off the stream, he is adjudged insane. Can parents justify themselves if, knowing the effect of belief in evolution, they permit irreligious teachers to inject skepticism and infidelity in the minds of their choice?

"Do bad doctrines corrupt the morals of students? We have a

case in point. Mr. Darrow, one of the most distinguished criminal lawyers in our land, was engaged about a year ago in defending two rich men's sons who were on trial for as dastardly a murder as was ever committed. The older one, "Babe" Leopold, was a brilliant student, 19 years old. He was an evolutionist and an atheist. He was also a follower of Nietzsche, whose books he had devoured and whose philosophy he had adopted. Mr. Darrow made a plea for him, based upon the influence that Nietzsche's philosophy had exerted upon the boy's mind. Here are extracts from his speech:

Quotes From Darrow.

" 'Babe took to philosophy. . .He grew up in this way; he became enamoured of the philosophy of Nietzsche. Your honor, I have read almost everything that Nietzsche ever wrote. A man of wonderful intellect; the most original philosopher of the last century. A man who made a deeper imprint on philosophy than any other man within a hundred years, whether right or wrong. More books have been written about him than probably all the rest of the philosophers in a hundred years. More college professors have talked about him. In a way he has reached more people, and still he has been a philosopher of what we might call the intellectual cult.

"'He wrote a book called "Beyond the Good and Evil," which was a criticism of all moral precepts, as we understand them, and a treatise that the intelligent man was beyond good and evil, that the laws for good and the laws for evil did not apply to anybody who approached the superman. He wrote on the will to power.

"'I have just made a few short extracts from Nietzsche that show the things that he (Leopold) has read and these are short and almost taken at random. It is not how this would affect you. It is now how it would affect me. The question is, how it would affect the impressionable, visionary, who should never have seen it—too early for him.'

"Quotation from Nietzsche: 'Why so soft, oh, my brethren? Why so soft, so unresisting and yielding? Why is there so much disavowal and abnegation in your heart? Why is there so little fate in your looks? For all creators are hard and it must seem blessedness unto you to press your hand upon millenniums and upon wax. This new table, oh, my brethren, I put over you.

"'To be obsessed by moral consideration presupposes a very low grade of intellects. We should substitute for morality the will to our own end, and consequently to the means to accomplish that. A great man, a man whom nature has built up and invented in a grand style, is colder, harder, less cautious and more free from the fear of public opinion. He does not possess the virtues which are compatible with respectability, with being respected, nor any of those things which are counted among the virtues of the herd.'

"Supermen Fill Colleges."

"Mr. Darrow says that the superman, a creation of Nietzsche, has permeated every college and university in the civilized world.

"'There is not any university in the world where the professor is the not familiar with Nietzsche, not one. . .Some believe it and some do not believe it. Some read it as I do and take it as a theory, a dream, a vision, mixed with good and bad, but not in any way related to human life. Some take it seriously. . .There is not a university in the world of any high standing where the professors do not tell you about Nietzsche and discuss him, or where the books are not there.

"'If this boy is to blame for this, where did he get it?

"'Is there any blame attached because somebody took Nietzche's philosophy seriously and fashioned his life upon it? And there is no question in this case but what that is true. Then who is to blame? The university would be more to blame than he is. The publishers of the world are more to blame than he is. Your honor, it is hardly fair to hang a 19-year-old boy for the philosophy that was taught him at the university. It does not meet my ideas of justice and fairness to visit upon his head the philosophy that has been taught by university men for twenty-five years.'

"In fairness to Mr. Darrow, I think I ought to quote two more paragraphs. After this bold attempt to excuse the student on the ground that he was transformed from a well-meaning youth into a murderer by the philosophy of an atheist, and on the further ground that this philosophy was in the libraries of all the colleges and discussed by the professors—some adopting the philosophy and some rejecting it—on these two grounds, he denies that the boy should be held responsible for the taking of human life. He charges that the scholars in the universities were more responsible than the boy, and that the universities were more responsible than the boy, because they furnished such books to the students, and then he proceeds to exonerate the universities and the scholars, leaving nobody responsible. Here is Mr. Darrow's language:

Universities Too Large.

"'Now I do not want to be misunderstood about it. Even for the sake of saving the lives of my clients, I do not want to be dishonest and tell the court something that I do not honestly think in this case. I do not think that the universities are to blame. I do not think they should be held responsible. I do think, however, they are too large and that they should keep a closer watch, if possible, upon the individual.

"'But you cannot destroy thought, because forsooth, some brain may be deranged by thought. It is a duty of the university, as I conceive it, to be the greatest storehouse of the wisdom of the ages, and to have its students come there and learn and choose. I have no doubt but that it has meant the death of many, but that we cannot help.'

"This is a damnable philosophy, and yet it is the flower that blooms on the stalk of evolution. Mr. Darrow thinks the universities are in duty bound to feed out this poisonous stuff to their students, and when the students become stupefied by it and commit murder, neither they nor the universities are to blame. I protest the adoption of any such a philosophy in the state of Tennessee. A criminal is not relieved from responsibility merely because he found Nietzsche's philosophy in a library which ought not to contain it. Neither is the university guiltless if it permits such corrupting nourishment to be fed to the souls that are entrusted to its care. But, go a step farther, would the state be blameless if it permitted the universities under its control to be turned into training schools for murderers? When you get back to the root of this question, you will find that the legislature not only had a right to protect the students from the evolutionary hypothesis but was in duty bound to do so.

Another Angle.

"While on this subject, let me call your attention to another proposition embodied in Mr. Darrow's speech. He said that Dicky Loeb, the younger boy, had read trashy novels of the blood and thunder sort. He even went so far to commend an Illinois statute which forbids minors reading stories of crime. Here is what Mr. Darrow said:

"'We have a statute in this state, passed only last year, if I recall it, which forbids minors reading stories of crime. Why? There is only one reason; because the legislature in its wisdom thought it would have a tendency to produce these thoughts and this life in the boys who read them.'

"If Illinois can protect her boys, why cannot this state protect the boys of Tennessee? Are the boys of Illinois any more precious than yours?

"But to return to the philosophy of an evolutionist, Mr. Darrow said: 'I say to you seriously that the parents of Dicky Loeb are more responsible than he, and yet few boys had better parents'. . . .Again he says, 'I know that one of two things happened to this boy; that this terrible crime was inherent in his organism, and came from some ancestry, or that it came through his education and his training after he was born.' He thinks the boy was not responsible for anything; his guilt was due, according to this philosophy, either to heredity or environment.

"But let me complete Mr. Darrow's philosophy based on evolution. He says: 'I do not know what remote ancestor may have sent down the seed that corrupted him, and I do not know through how many ancestors it may have passed until it reached Dicky Loeb. All I know is, it is true, and there is not a biologist in the world who will not say I am right.'

"Psychologists who build upon the evolutionary hypothesis teach that man is nothing but a bundle of characteristics inherited from brute ancestors. That is the philosophy which Mr. Darrow applied in this celebrated criminal case. 'Some remote ancestor'—he does not know how remote—'sent down the seed that corrupted him.' You cannot punish the ancestor—he is not only dead, but, according to the evolutionists, he was a brute and may have lived a million years ago. And he says that all the biologists agree with him—no wonder so small a per cent of the biologists, according to Leuba, believe in a personal God.

"This is the quintessence of evolution, distilled for us by one who follows that doctrine to its logical conclusion. Analyze this dogma of darkness and death. Evolutionists say that back in the twilight of life a beast, name and nature unknown, planted a murderous seed and that the impulse throbs forever in the blood of the brute's descendants, inspiring killings innumerable, for which cause coerced by a fate fixed by the laws of heredity! It is an insult to reason and shocks the heart. That doctrine is as deadly as leprosy; it may aid a lawyer in a criminal case, but it would, if generally adopted, destroy all sense of responsibility and menace the morals of the world. A brute, they say, can predestine a man to crime, and yet they deny that God incarnate in the flesh can release a human being from this bondage or save him from ancestral sins. No more repulsive doctrine was ever proclaimed by man; if all the biologists of the world teach this doctrine—as Mr. Darrow says they do—then may heaven defend the youth of our land from their impious babblings.

Causes Trifling Speculation.

"Our third indictment against evolution is that it diverts attention from pressing problems of great importance to trifling speculation. While one evolutionist is trying to imagine what happened in the dim past another is trying to pry open the door of the distant future. One recently grew eloquent over ancient worms, and another predicted that 75,000 years hence everyone will be bald and toothless. Both those who endeavor to clothe our remote ancestors with hair and those who endeavor to remove the hair from the heads of our remote descendants ignore the present with its imperative demands. The science of 'how to live' is the most important of all the sciences. It is desirable to know the physical sciences, but it is necessary to know how to live. Christians desire that their children shall be taught all the sciences, but they do not want them to lose sight of the rock of ages while they study the age of the rocks; neither do they desire them to become so absorbed in measuring the distance between the stars that they will forget him who holds the stars in his hand.

"While not more than 2 per cent of our population are college graduates, these, because of enlarged powers, need a heavenly vision even more than those less learned, both for their own restraint and to assure society that their enlarged powers will be used for the benefit of society and not against the public welfare.

"Evolution is deadening the spiritual life of a multitude of students. Christians do not desire less education, but they desire that religion shall be entwined with learning so that our boys and girls will return from college with their hearts aflame with love of God and love of fellow men, and prepared to lead in the altruistic work that the world so sorely needs. The cry in the business world, in the industrial world, in the professional world, in the political world—even in the religious world—is for consecrated talents—for ability plus passion for service.

Beneficent Changes.

"Our fourth indictment against the evolutionary hypothesis is that, by paralyzing the hope of reform, it discourages those who labor for the improvement of man's condition. Every upward looking man or woman seeks to lift the level upon which mankind stands and they trust that they will see beneficent changes during the brief span of their own lives. Evolution chills their enthusiasm by substituting aeons for years. It obscures all beginnings in the mists of endless ages. It is represented as a cold and heartless process, beginning with time and ending in eternity, and acting so slowly that even the rocks cannot preserve a record of the imaginary changes through which it is credited with having carried an original germ of life that appeared some time from somewhere. Its only program for man is scientific breeding, a system under which a few supposedly superior intellects will direct the mating and the movements of the mass of mankind—an impossible system. Evolution, disputing the miracle and ignoring the spiritual in life, has no place for the regeneration of the individual. It recognizes no cry of repentance and scoffs at the doctrine that one can be born.

"It is thus the intolerant and unrelenting enemy of the only process that can redeem society through the redemption of the individual. An evolutionist would never write such a story as the prodigal son; it contradicts the whole theory of evolution. The two sons inherited from the same parents and, through their parents, from the same ancestors, proximate and remote. And these sons were reared at the same fireside and were surrounded by the same environment during all the days of their youth; and yet they were different.

"If Mr. Darrow is correct in the theory applied to Loeb, namely, that his crime was due either to inheritance or to environment, how will he explain the difference between the elder and wayward son? The evolutionist may understand from observation, if not by experience, even though he cannot explain, why one of these boys was guilty of every immorality, squandered the money that the father had laboriously earned and brought disgrace upon the family name; but his theory does not explain why a wicked young man underwent a change of heart, confessed his sin, and begged for forgiveness. And because the evolutionists cannot understand this fact, one of the most important in the human life, he cannot understand the infinite love of the heavenly father who stands ready to welcome home any repentant sinner, no matter how far he has wandered, how often he has fallen, or how deep he has sunk in sin.

Quotes From Poem Judge Read.

"Your honor has quoted from a wonderful poem written by a great Tennessee poet, Walter Malone. I venture to quote another stanza which puts into exquisite language the new opportunity which a merciful God gives to everyone who will turn from sin to righteousness.

"'Though deep in mire, wring not your hands and weep;
I lend my arm to all who say, 'I can.'
No shame-faced outcast ever sank so deep
But he might rise and be again a man.'

"There are no lines like these in all that evolutionists have ever written. Darwin says that science has nothing to do with the Christ who taught the spirit embodied in the words of Walter Malone, and yet this spirit is the only hope of human progress. A heart can be changed in the twinkling of an eye and a change in the life follows a change in the heart. If one heart can be changed, it is possible that all hearts can be changed—that a world can be born in a day. It is this fact that inspires all who labor for man's betterment. It is because Christians believe in individual regeneration and the regeneration of society through the regeneration of individuals that they pray. 'Thy kingdom come, thy will be done on earth as it is in heaven.' Evolution makes a mockery of the Lord's prayer!

"To interpret the words to mean that the improvement desired must come slowly through unfolding ages—a process with which each generation could have little to do—is to defer hope and hope deferred maketh the heart sick.

"Our fifth indictment of the evolutionary hypothesis is that, if taken seriously and made the basis of a philosophy of life, it would eliminate love and carry man back to a struggle of tooth and claw. The Christians who have allowed themselves to be deceived into believing that evolution is a beneficent, or even a rational process, have been associating with those who either do not understand its implications or dare not avow their knowledge of these implications. Let me give you some authority on this subject. I will begin with Darwin, the high priest of evolution, to whom all evolutionists bow.

"On pages 149 and 150, in 'The Descent of Man' already referred to, he says:

"'With savages, the weak in body or mind are soon eliminated; and those what survive commonly exhibit a vigorous state of health. We civilized men, on the other hand, would do our utmost to check the process of elimination; we build asylums for the imbecile, the maimed, and the sick; we institute poor laws; and our medical men exert their utmost skill to save the life of everyone to the last moment. There is reason to believe that vaccination has preserved thousands who from a weak constitution would formerly have succumbed to smallpox. Thus the weak members of civilized society propagate their kind. No one who has attended to the breeding of domestic animals will doubt that this must be highly injurious to the race of man. It is surprising how soon a want of care, or care wrongly directly, leads to the degeneration of a domestic race; but, excepting in the case of man himself, hardly any one is so ignorant as to allow his worst animals to breed.

"The aid which we feel impelled to give to the helpless is mainly an incidental result of the instinct of sympathy, which was originally acquired as part of the social instincts, but subsequently rendered, in the manner previously indicated, more tender and more widely diffused.

How could we check our sympathy, even at the urging of hard reason, without deterioration in the noblest part of our nature? . . .We must therefore bear the undoubtedly bad effects of the weak serving and propagating their kind.'

Analyzes Darwin Statement.

"Darwin reveals the barbarous sentiment that runs through evolution and dwarfs the moral nature of those who become obsessed with it. Let us analyze the quotation just given. Darwin speaks with approval of the savage custom of eliminating the weak so that only the strong will survive and complains that 'we civilized men do our utmost to check the process of elimination.' How inhuman such a doctrine as that! He thinks it injurious to 'build asylums for the imbecile, the maimed, and the sick,' or to care for the poor. Even the medical men come in for criticism because they 'exert their utmost skill to save the life of everyone to the last moment.' And then note his hostility to vaccination because it has 'preserved thousands who, from a weak constitution would, but for vaccination, have succumbed to smallpox.' All of the sympathetic activities of civilized society are condemned because they enable 'the weak members to propagate their kind.' Then he drags mankind down to the level of the brute and compares the freedom given to man unfavorably with the restraint that we put on barnyard beasts.

"The second paragraph of the above quotation shows that his kindly heart rebelled against the cruelty of his own doctrine. He says that we 'feel impelled to give to the helpless,' although he traces it to a sympathy which he thinks is developed by evolution; he even admits that we could not check this sympathy 'even at the urging of hard reason, without deterioration of the noblest part of our nature.' We must therefore bear what he regards as 'the undoubtedly bad effect of the weak surviving and propagating their kind.' Could any doctrine be more destructive of civilization? And what a commentary on evolution! He wants us to believe that evolution develops a human sympathy that finally becomes so tender that it repudiates the law that created it and thus invites a return to a level where the extinguishing of pity and sympathy will permit the brutal institute to again do their progressive (?) work.

New Book More Brutal.

"Let no one think that this acceptance of barbarism as the basic principle of evolution died with Darwin. Within three years a book has appeared whose author is even more frankly brutal than Darwin. The book is entitled 'The New Decalogue of Science.' And has attracted wide attention. One of our most reputable magazines has recently printed an article by him defining the religion of a scientist. In his preface he acknowledges indebtedness to twenty-one prominent scientists and educators, nearly all of them 'doctors' and 'professors'. One of them who has recently been elevated to the head of a great state university, read the manuscript over twice 'and made many invaluable suggestions.' The author describes Nietzsche, who, according to Mr. Darrow, made a murderer out of Babe Leopold, as 'the bravest soul since Jesus.' He admits that Nietzsche was 'gloriously wrong,' not certainly, but 'perhaps' 'in many details of technical knowledge' but he affirms that Nietzsche was 'gloriously right in his fearless questioning of the universe and of his own soul.'

"Jungle Products."

"In another place the author says 'most of our morals today are jungle products' and then he affirms that 'it would be safer, biologically, if they were more so now.' After these two samples of his views, you will not be surprised when I read you the following (see page 34):

"Evolution is a bloody business, but civilization tries to make it a pink tea. Barbarism is the only process by which man has ever organically progressed and civilization is the only process by which he has ever organically declined. Civilization is the most dangerous enterprise upon which man ever set out. For when you take man out of the bloody, brutal, but beneficent hand of natural selection, you place him at once in the soft, perfumed, dainty-gloved, but far more dangerous hand of artificial selection. And, unless you call science to your aid and make this artificial selection as efficient as the rude methods of nature, you bungle the whole task.'

"This aspect of evolution may amaze some of the ministers who have not been admitted to the inner circle of the iconoclasts whose theories menace all the ideals of civilized society. Do these ministers know that 'evolution is a bloody business?' Do they know that 'barbarism is the only process by which man has ever organically declined?' Do they know that 'the bloody, brutal hand of natural selection' is 'beneficent?' And that the 'artificial selection' found in civilization is 'dangerous?' What shall we think of the distinguished educators and scientists who read the manuscript before publication and did not protest against this pagan doctrine?

Reads Kidd's Version.

"To show that this is a worldwide matter, I now quote from a book issued from the press in 1918, seven years ago. The title of the book is 'The Science of Power,' and its author, Benjamin Kidd, being an Englishman, could not have any national prejudice against Darwin. On pages 46 and 47 we find Kidd's interpretation of evolution:

"'Darwin's presentation of the evolution of the world as the product, that is to say, of a struggle in which the individual efficient in the fight for his own interests was always the winning type—touched the profoundest depths of the psychology of the west. The idea seemed to present the whole order of progress in the world as the result of a purely mechanical and materialistic process resting on force. In so doing it was a conception which reached the springs of that heredity born of the unmeasured ages of conquest out of which the western mind has come. Within half a century "The Origin of the Species" has become the bible of the doctrine of the omnipotence of force.'

"Kidd goes so far as to charge that 'Nietzche's teaching represented the interpretation of the popular Darwinism delivered with the fury and intensity of genuineness.' Neitzsche, be it remembered, denounced Christianity as the 'doctrine of the degenerate' and democracy as 'the refuge of weaklings.'

"Kidd says that Nietzsche gave Germany the doctrine of Darwin's efficient animal in the voice of his superman, and that Bernhardi and the military textbooks in due time gave Germany the doctrine of the superman translated into the national policy of the super-state aiming at world power. (Page 67).

"And what else but the spirit of evolution can account for the popularity of the selfish doctrine, 'each one for himself, and the devil take the hindmost,' that threatens the very existence of the doctrine of brotherhood.

"In 1900—twenty-five years ago—while an international peace congress was in session in Paris, the following editorial appeared in L'Univers:

"'The spirit of peace has fled the earth because evolution has taken possession of it. The plea for peace in past years has been inspired by faith in the divine nature and the divine origin of man; men were then looked upon as children of apes, what matters it whether they are slaughtered or not?'

Assails Southern Magazine.

"When there is poison in the blood, no one knows in what part of the body it will break out but we can be sure that it will continue to break out until the blood is purified. One of the leading universities of the south (I love the state too well to mention its name) publishes a monthly magazine entitled 'Journal of Social Forces.' In the January issue of this year, a contributor has a lengthy article on 'sociology and ethics' in the course of which he says:

"'No attempt will be made to take up the matter of the good or evil of sexual intercourse among humans aside from the matter of conscious procreation, but as an historian, it might be worth while to ask the exponents of the impurity complex to explain the fact that, without exception, the great periods of cultural afflorescence have been those characterized by a large amount of freedom in sex relations, and that those of the greatest cultural degradation and decline have been accompanied with greatest sex repression and purity.'

"No one charges or suspects that all or any large percentage of the advocates of evolution sympathize with this loathsome application of evolution to social life, but it is worthwhile to inquire why those in charge of a great institution of learning allow such filth to be poured out for the stirring of the passions of its students.

"Just one more quotation: The Southeastern Christian Advocate of June 25, 1925, quotes five eminent college men of Great Britain as joining in an answer to the question, 'Will civilization survive?' Their reply is that:

Science Needs Religion.

"'The greatest danger facing our civilization is the abuse of the achievements of science. Mastery over the forces of nature has endowed the twentieth century man with a power which he is not fit to exercise. Unless the development of morality catches up with the development of technique, humanity is bound to destroy itself.'

"Can any Christian remain indifferent? Science needs religion to direct its energies and to inspire with lofty purpose those who employ the forces that are unloosed by science. Evolution is at war with religion because religion is supernatural; it is, therefore, the relentless foe of Christianity which is a revealed religion.

"Let us, then, hear the conclusion of the whole matter. Science is a magnificent material force, but it is not a teacher of morals. It can perfect machinery, but it adds no moral restraints to protect society from the misuse of the machine. It can also build gigantic intellectual ships, but it constructs no moral rudders for the control of storm tossed human vessels. It not only fails to supply the spiritual element needed but some of its unproven hypotheses rob the ship of its compass and thus endanger its cargo.

"In war, science has proven itself an evil genius; it has made war more terrible than it ever was before. Man used to be content to slaughter his fellow men on a single plane—the earth's surface. Science has taught him to go down into the water and shoot up from below and to go up into the clouds and shoot down from above, thus making the battle field three times as bloody as it was before; but science does not teach brotherly love. Science has made war so hellish that civilization was about to commit suicide; and now we are told that newly discovered instruments of destruction will make the cruelties of the late war seem trivial in comparison with the cruelties of wars that may come in the future. If civilization is to be saved from the wreckage threatened by intelligence not consecrated by love, it must be saved by the moral code of the meek and lowly Nazarene: His teachings, and his teachings alone, can solve the problems that vex the heart and perplex the world.

"The world needs a savior more than it ever did before, and there is only one 'name under the heaven given among men whereby we must be saved.' It is this name that evolution degrades, for, carried to its logical conclusion it robs Christ of the glory of a virgin birth, of the majesty of his deity and mission, and of the triumph of his resurrection. It also disputes the doctrine of the atonement.

"It is for the jury to determine whether this attack upon the Christian religion shall be permitted in the public schools of Tennessee by teachers employed by the state and paid out of the public treasury. This case is no longer local; the defendant ceases to play an important part. The case has assumed the proportions of a battle royal between unbelief that attempts to speak through so-called science and the defenders of the Christian faith, speaking through the legislature of Tennessee. It is again a choice between God and Baal; it is also a renewal of the issue in Pilate's court. In that historic trial—the greatest in history—force, impersonated by Pilate, occupied the government, mistress of the world, and behind the Roman government were the legions of Rome. Before Pilate stood Christ, the apostle of love. Force triumphed; they nailed him to the tree and those who stood around mocked and jeered and said, 'He is dead.' But from that day the power of Caesar waned and the power of Christ increased. In a few centuries the Roman government was gone and its legions forgotten; while the crucified risen Lord has become the greatest fact in history and the growing figure of all time.

Force and Love Meet.

"Again force and love meet face to face, and the question 'What shall I do with Jesus? must be answered. A bloody, brutal doctrine—evolution—demands, as the rabble did 1,900 years ago, that he be crucified, that cannot be the answer of those representing a Christian state and sworn to uphold the laws of Tennessee. Your answer will be heard throughout the world; it is eagerly awaited by a praying multitude. If the law is nullified, there will be rejoicing wherever God is repudiated, the Savior scoffed at and the Bible ridiculed. Every unbeliever of every kind and degree will be happy. If, on the other hand, the law is upheld, children protected, millions of Christians will call you blessed and, with hearts full of gratitude to God, will sing again that grand old song of triumph:

"'Faith of our fathers, living still,
In spite of dungeon, fire and sword;
Oh, how our hearts beat high with joy,
Whene'er we hear that glorious word,
Faith of our fathers—holy faith;
We will be true to thee till death.'
**

AGREE TO DELAY EVOLUTION SUIT IN WASHINGTON

New Attorney for Wittner Obtains Stay.

Washington, July 28 (A.P.)—A hearing in Washington's evolution suit was postponed today until Friday.

On that day the motion of the government to dismiss the case will have preferred status as the question before the court.

This delay was agreed to by Justice Siddons of the District of Columbia supreme court, when counsel for Loren H. Wittner, who brought the suit in an effort to stop the pay of local school authorities, insisted that more time was needed to study the government's motion to dismiss, filed yesterday.

The decision to postpone came after District Attorney Gordon had begun his argument for the defense, and was made possible by the appearance of a new attorney for Wittner—Crandall Mackey. The latter, announcing his entry, demanded his legal right of two days in which to study the government's motion, and the court held that his demand could not be denied. Justice Siddons, a few minutes before, had indicated he would not grant the request when it was made by Wittner's original lawyers.

To Determine Wittner's Standing.

It was made clear by the court that there would be no hearing on any other question until it was determined whether Wittner had a standing in court as a taxpayer which entitled him to press the case.

Both the district attorney and counsel for the city insisted he had no such right in the injunctions proceedings he has brought to stop the salaries to certain Washington school teachers, on the ground that in teaching scientific subjects, they have violated an act of congress prohibiting the teaching here of any matter in "disrespect for the holy bible."

Ringgold Hart, assistant corporation counsel, informed the court that late yesterday, Wittner and one of his counsel had informed the city's counsel that they had decided to withdraw the suit, but that later Wittner changed his mind.

B. H. Dolby, one of Wittner's lawyers, in asking the court for a continuance until Friday, said that his client had under consideration dropping the case and that he would decide between now and Friday whether he would pursue that cause, or would amend the original bill to meet objections raised against it.

Cites Famous Case.

District Attorney Gordon opened the argument today by citing the decision of the United States supreme court in the famous Frothingham case, involving the maternity law, in which the court held that the plaintiff had no standing in court in the capacity of federal taxpayer because of inability to show immediate danger of material damage as a result of the operation of the law.

An answer to Wittner's original complaint was filed by counsel for Daniel J. Donovan, auditor, and James R. Lusby, disbursing officer, for the District of Columbia, denying Wittner's charges in general. Nothing is taught in the schools concerning the bible, the defendants say, or the doctrine of the bible or the evolution of man, except as theories and facts, "which are known to ordinarily intelligent persons who have read or studied such subjects." The respondents also say they will continue to pay the school salaries without damage to Wittner, who they assert has no interest which would entitle him to a standing in a court of equity.

**

SAYS EVOLUTION GIVES BEAUTIFUL CONCEPT OF GOD

Dr. D. W. Morehouse, president of Drake university, gave an address to students on the origin of the solar system on the campus of the university last night.

The talk was illustrated by telescopic photographs. In his closing remarks, he said: "Call it evolution, progress or what you will, to me it is a grander concept of an omnipotent God, than calling the universe a special act of creation in a given space of time. The man who has not studied astronomy does not really appreciate the all wonderful God."

On Tuesday evening, Aug. 4 at 8 o'clock, Prof. L. S. Ross will give a lecture on "The Supposed Religion," and Thursday, Aug. 6, Dean Caldwell will talk on "The Development of Religions."

EVOLUTION

The Register cannot too cordially urge its readers to get "The Evolution of Man," published by the Yale University Press, if they would know what the evolutionary theory of man" descent (descent is always used in this connection as we use the related word descendant) really is.

The book consists of six chapters. "The Antiquity of Man," by Professor Lull of Yale; "The Natural History of Man," by Professor Ferris of Yale; "Evolution of the Nervous System," by Professor Parker of Harvard; "Evolution of Intelligence," by President Angell of Yale; "Societal Evolution," by Professor Keller of Yale; "The Trend of Evolution," by Professor Conklin of Princeton.

Probably in no one volume can so authoritative or so plain a statement of the evolutionary theory be found.

**

Young Mr. Scopes is getting more offers of marriage than offers to pay his $100 fine.

**

Presumably business has fallen off somewhat at the Robinson drug store since the Scopes trial ended.

Thursday July 30, 1925
The Des Moines Register

BRYAN FUNERAL TRAIN IS ON WAY TO WASHINGTON

Throngs View Remains at Many Stops; Reach Capital Today.

On Board Funeral Train En Route to Washington, Bristol, Va.-Tenn., July 29 (A.P.)—Kind hearts tonight kept watch over the body of William Jennings Bryan and tender hands ministered to the comfort of his widow as the train bearing the burdened casket moved out of Tennessee into Virginia on its journey to Washington.

Early on the morrow the funeral party with the body was expected to reach Washington, where his countrymen wait to bestow last honors. In the national capital, where Mrs. Bryan and her daughter, Mrs. Ruth Owen, were to await the coming of the other daughter, Mrs. Grace Hargreaves, and her brother, William, jr., final plans for the funeral and burial in Arlington cemetery Friday had yet to be completed.

Mrs. Bryan, sitting upright near her husband's casket, was overwhelmed by the crowds of men and women who appeared along many hundreds of miles of the commoner's last journey to do silent homage to the dead.

Hundreds View Body.

Leaving Dayton early in the day after the friends of his last days and spectators of his last great fight had demonstrated their regard in every form of service, the body of the fundamentalist champion was witnessed throughout the day by throngs of sorrowing friends who showed their grief in unmistakable emotion. At Chattanooga and at Knoxville, hundreds were admitted into the rear compartment of the special pullman to view the set face of the fallen leader.

At Chattanooga where, in transferring the special car from one train to another, a halt of an hour was made, city officials, civic organizations and the public joined in a demonstration of esteem, to which Mrs.

Bryan returned grateful thanks.

In the small towns traversed by the funeral train the inhabitants flocked to the track side. Stores were closed and flags flew low in token of respect. In many villages observers estimated that the crowds exceeded the normal populations. At Knoxville, where Mrs. Bryan permitted a waiting crowd to view the body, many evidences of love and devotion were shown to both herself and Mr. Bryan.

Presented With Bible.

The Knoxville Chamber of Commerce presented her with a bible, attached to which was a ribbon bearing an inscription of one of the commoner's favorite quotations: "I have enough religion to live by and to die by."

From the citizens of Lenoir City, a colorful bouquet of simple garden grown blossoms told of the deep feelings of the givers, a penned message announcing:

"A token of our appreciation of his upright life and fearless defense of truth."

The Associated Bible classes of Knoxville presented a large wreath of roses and a resolution expressing sorrow over the death of their bible leader. It was signed by a committee of members and said in part:

"Last Great Champion."

"In the death of the commoner the world has lost a great champion of the right; the Christian religion an untiring defender; the nation an eloquent platform orator and all bible study classes a true and noble friend."

At Jefferson City roadside watchers expressed their tribute in song. A male quartet from Carson-Newman college stood at the door where the Christian leader's body lay and sang one of Mr. Bryan's favorite songs.

As the train slowly drew away the crowd joined in with the singing. From the train a large sign could be seen. It read:

"We honor the memory of William Jennings Bryan."

Large Crowds View Bier.

Knoxville, Tenn., July 29 (A.P.)—The train bearing the Bryan funeral party reached Knoxville at 2:35 o'clock this afternoon. The dead leader's remains were viewed by hundreds during the brief scheduled stop.

So dense was the crowd at the station and so eager the desire to view the body of the dead statesman, that the police on the rear platform had difficulty in restraining their advance.

Rapidly the massed watchers climbed to the special car and passed in rapid succession past the quiet face of the once great party chieftain.

A giant wreath of red roses, gift of the Associated Bible class of the city was carried into the car where flowers already were heaped against the windows.

Hundreds despairing of seeing the body because of the press of humanity and the brief halt of the train ranged themselves upon the overhead viaduct and watched their fellows below.

Stop at Chattanooga

Chattanooga, Tenn., July 29—The Bryan funeral party arrived in Chattanooga at 10:15 a.m., central standard time. The public was admitted to the special pullman where in single file they viewed the remains of the dead statesman.

The car with its sorrowing passengers was transferred here to the fast Southern train which would reach Washington early Thursday after stops in Knoxville, Bristol, Roanoke and Lynchburg.

Conductor G. W. Mitchell of Knoxville was in charge of the train which drew the funeral car northward. Mr. Mitchell for four winters had been a member of Mr. Bryan's Sunday school class in the First Presbyterian church at Miami.

"Everybody loved him," Mr. Mitchell said. "He was the greatest speaker that ever lived. And I believe he was right."

J. G. Collette, fireman, has known Mr. Bryan for twenty years, he said. He, too, had been during three winters a member of the commoner's Sunday school class in Miami.

I differed from Mr. Bryan in politics," said the flagman on the funeral train, "but we know that he was a truly great man. If what his Sunday school pupils think of him is true, he certainly has without doubt passed to his happy home."

H. H. Weaver was the engineer on the train which left Chattanooga shortly before noon. The fireman was Frank Booker.

Richard Rogers, host to the great leader in his last days, joined the funeral party at Chattanooga, having decided to make the trip to Washington with other friends of Mr. Bryan.

A crowd estimated at above 1,500 persons pressed against the iron barrier of the station as the train from Dayton pulled in. Capt. W. L. Baker of the Chattanooga police restrained the eager throng, and his men formed in double lines to expedite the orderly review.

In single file men and women, with a few children, passed into the car where the statesman lay, and looked down into the metal casket where the peaceful leader's countenance was seen. They moved on without halting leaving the coach at the other entrance.

Flowers Fill Car.

Flowers, the tributes of patriotic and civic organizations, were brought and placed within the compartment where the body reposed. Room was lacking to hold them all.

The widow remained in her seat in the rear section of the car. Her face showed the strain of the sorrowful burden which she has resolutely sustained.

During the trip from Dayton, Mrs. Bryan sat in her section, the one next the flag-draped casket. She maintained her composure so remarked upon by her associates since the death of her husband.

The resting-place of the commoner was heaped with flowers. A truck load had been conveyed to the train at Dayton in addition to the wreaths put in the car here.

Dayton Pays Final Tribute.

Dayton, Tenn., July 29 (A.P.)—The body of William Jennings Bryan began its long journey to the national capital early today when the bronze casket in which the Commoner lay was removed from the Rogers residence at 7:40 o'clock.

The widow followed, as the remains of her distinguished husband were placed aboard the special pullman on a siding near the place of Mr. Bryan's death.

Citizens of Dayton attended the funeral carriage on the short march through the streets of the town. A guard of six uniformed men formed the simple escort.

In Dayton loving tribute was paid to the fundamentalist chief by the friends among whom he passed, men and women to whom he was the defender of the faith bred in them by God-fearing forebears of the southland. Here he received the homage of the hills, rendered in the simple fashion of those who dwell among them.

To Be Honored at Capital.

In Washington will come the laudations of those who knew him best as he moved among them, the political leader, the orator, statesman.

As the funeral car headed toward Washington news came from different sections of the country of the homage to be paid the memory of the silver tongued orator of the past.

Pledges of his comrades in the fight against evolution came in far-separated corners of the land. Opponents of the evolution theory will drive it from the tax-supported schools of the nation, they said.

Telegrams and letters continued to flood the little home at Dayton, bringing to the bereaved widow notes of consolation from hundreds of admirers and friends of the dead.

From other sections of the country came news of a tribute to be paid the memory of the dead man. In North Carolina, Gov. Angus McLean issued a proclamation ordering all flags on state, county and municipal buildings in the state to fly at half-staff Friday, while the people of the state laid aside their activities for thirty minutes during the funeral.

Bells Will be Tolled.

This was supplemented by additional instructions from mayors of different cities. In Charlotte, N. C., a request was made by the mayor to the pastors of the city's churches to toll their bells for five minutes at the hour of the funeral.

From other sections, announcements came of memorial services to be conducted at the hour of the funeral. Chief among these was the announcement of a meeting to be held in Royal Palms Park at Miami, Fla., where the voice of the commoner had been heard so many times in Bible classes, under the direction of his former pastor.

The funeral party included Mrs. Bryan, Mrs. Ruth Owen, her daughter and her husband Major Reginald Owen, of the British army; Colonel P. H. Callahan Louisiana; Wm. E. Thompson, secretary to Mr. Bryan; Wallace Haggard, member of the prosecution counsel in the Scopes trial; Mrs. C. C. Stevens, housekeeper and William H. McCartney, chauffeur for the Bryan family.

William Jennings Bryan, the younger, will join his mother and sister in Washington Friday, accompanied by Mrs. Grace Hargreaves, another daughter.

**

Expect Bryan's Body to Lie in State at Capital Church

FUNERAL PLANS AWAIT WISHES OF HIS WIDOW

Will Assign Troops if Mrs. Bryan Permits.

Washington, July 29 (A.P.)—Tentative arrangements for the funeral of William Jennings Bryan here Friday, all subject to the approval of his widow, were made toady as the body of the commoner was being brought to Washington from Dayton, Tenn.

There will be services both at the New York Avenue Presbyterian church, where Mr. Bryan worshipped when secretary of state, and at the grave at Arlington national cemetery, but the whole ceremony will be as simple as might be that of the humblest citizen.

Few Military Honors.

Save possibly for the artillery caisson on which the body will be conveyed from the church to the Potomac hills, and the sounding of taps, the soldiers' requiem, at the grave, there will be no hint of military honors. That will be as Mr. Bryan had wished.

Immediately upon the arrival of the funeral train at union station early tomorrow, the bronze casket will be taken to an undertaking establishment, but if Mrs. Bryan approves, it will be moved a few hours later to the New York Avenue church to lie in state during the afternoon and the early hours of Friday.

Funeral services at the church will begin at 3 p.m. Friday and will be conducted by Rev. Dr. Joseph R. Sizoo, the pastor, who is returning here from his vacation in New York state.

At the conclusion of these services, the funeral procession will move across the mall and Potomac park to the Virginia hills beyond the river, where the body will be interred on the side of a hill dominated by the Dewey mausoleum.

Rites at "President's" Church.

The edifice, in which the services will be held, is a red brick structure three-quarters of a century old, tucked in among buildings in the heart of the city's business district. It is known as "the church of the presidents."

Here it was that the martyred Lincoln, whose life Bryan so much admired, worshipped. The pew which he and his family occupied is still preserved and upon it is a silver plate bearing these words:

"Abraham Lincoln. 1861-65."

Andrew Jackson, Franklin Pierce, James K. Polk, James Buchanan and Andrew Johnson were other presidents whose names have been enrolled as members of the church, either since the construction of the present building or between that period and the year 1803, when the congregation first was organized.

Accommodates 1,000 Persons.

The building can accommodate about 1,000 persons in the main auditorium and in the old fashioned balcony above, but most of the seats will be reserved for government officials, diplomats and friends of the commoner.

Because of the usual congestion of traffic in the vicinity, the police have made elaborate arrangements to handle the thousands who are expected to visit the church if the body lies in state tomorrow and Friday. With exit doors on each side as well as the main entrance, the quick passage of those who would pay a last tribute to Mr. Bryan would be facilitated.

Arrangements have been made to care for thousands who are expected to attend the service at the grave but because of the physical contour of the ground, only a few hundred will be able to see the interment. The plot is on a hillside facing to the north, with huge oaks to the right and a fringe of smaller trees rearing their heads upward from the valley between this and an adjacent hill.

**

Harrison Calls Bryan Greatest Law Maker

Clinton, Ia., July 29 (A.P.)—"No man in this generation has contributed more toward having laws passed that work equitably and justly to the masses, nor wielded a greater influence toward the moral uplift," said Senator Pat Harrison of Mississippi, of the late William Jennings Bryan, when the senator arrived here today to fill a speaking engagement.

**

NORMAN E. MACK SAYS CONSISTENCY WON BRYAN'S PLACE

Buffalo, N.Y., July 29 (A.P.)—Norman E. Mack, former chairman of the democratic national committee and present New York state member of that body, today asserted that William J. Bryan's consistency is one of the main reasons for the homage he is receiving and is destined to be one of the main factors in the verdict of history.

"He was not only a brilliant but he was a constructive statesman," Mr. Mack said. "This is demonstrated by the fact that he lived to see accomplished so many of the causes in which he was a pioneer. A single instance in point is the direct election of United States senators.

Another is the worldwide affirmation of the principle of arbitration of international disputes."

**

Berlin, July 29 (A.P.)—Chancellor Luther of Germany today paid tribute to William Jennings Bryan for his advocacy of international arbitration of the differences of governments.

He did this in receiving a party of clergymen, editors of religious publications and professors from the United States making a tour of Europe.

**

IN POLITICS ALSO

Very few of those who comment on Bryan seem to recognize that he was a fundamentalist in politics as he was in religion. The tendency is to picture him an innovator in politics, because it so happened that silver coinage came as an innovation at the time he championed it.

But the fact of the silver debate was that it was Bryan who was urging the good old policies of the fathers, and the gold men who were the innovators and progressives.

So far did Bryan go to sustain the fathers that he stuck for 16 to 1 as the ratio, solely because that had been the ratio, although the market demonstrated that that ratio was not logical or possible without a world union to maintain it.

The people had always used silver, as money, they were accustomed to the size of the silver dollar, silver was a habit with them just as much as gold, in fact they recognized silver first because it was in the smaller denominations. The men who proposed to abandon silver were the radicals and the innovators.

In the matter of state rights Mr. Bryan was always a conservative. Our federal reserve bank system is divided into districts, instead of being a central bank as proposed by Senator Aldrich because Bryan would not consent to it but on the state rights theory.

Bryan was intensely conservative in his party relations. He countenanced no breaking away from the democratic party, no matter what the issues were. His pride was always to be a democrat in all weathers.

No independent movement got a good word from him.

He was in a rather aggressive and affirmative way what used to be known as a "before the war democrat," a democrat who was born that way and never changed. Nearly all the "before the war democrats" were negative even to being balky in the postwar years. Bryan had the fire of youth and was naturally a leader. But his mental attitude was like that of the others. He held back to the good old ways.

What made Bryan seem the innovator was his intense moral purpose? He introduced prayer at democratic meetings in Iowa and talked temperance in the anti-prohibition liquor days, and that made him seem intensely a radical. But in that he was merely bringing things back to the earlier standards.

He was a fundamentalist all his life and in every relation. The fundamentalist conserves the wisdom of the ages. If he sometimes makes old ways hold after they have outlived their usefulness, he never let the world break away from the really valuable lessons of the past. When he tried to hold silver as a money metal he was probably blocking progress. His fight to discredit scientific investigation will not be to his credit in the end. But he stood fast, and merely standing fast has its lesson for an unstable world.

With all his seeming radicalism and progressivism Bryan was everywhere and always an old-fashioned advocate of what had been. It was the wisdom of the past he stood for.

Possibly the reported rush toward Florida was started by the rumor that William J. Bryan run his fortune up to seven figures in real estate there.

**

Speaking of evolution, we sometimes wonder what the genuine, honest-to-goodness pert flapper evoluted from.

**

Of course, some doctors will point to a moral in the fact that Mr. Bryan ate a heavy meal before lying down and dying in his sleep.

**

The tomb of Bryan will become a shrine, but not as that of another "unknown warrior."

**

Four Leaders

Grundy Center, Ia.—To the Editor: The past thirty years developed four outstanding personal characters in the public life of America—William Jennings Bryan, Robert M. LaFollette, Woodrow Wilson and Theodore Roosevelt—and now the greatest of them all has just passed on, and yet this man originated the sentiment and popularized the cause that made possible the careers of Roosevelt Wilson and LaFollette.

Abraham Lincoln in 1842 in closing an address said of the fame of George Washington, "In solemn awe pronounce the name, and in its naked, deathless splendor leave it shining on."

Today as millions contemplate the career of Bryan, dead, and reflect upon the glorious fact of his life and take note of the conviction that the close of his earthly toil took place just when his work was done, and at a moment when humanity can learn the lesson of his life "In solemn awe pronounce the name, and in its naked, deathless splendor leave it shining on." William G. Kerr.

**

Is This Still Sunday?

Pleasantville, Ia.—To the Editor: Since one day with God is said to be 1,700,000 years, isn't it possible that Bryan, Darrow, and Scopes are all right in their assertions and beliefs?

If the above thereby holds true, then the animals and plants were made 8,500,000 years before he made man. If God then did rest on the seventh day after making man it is possible that he is resting now and the age we are living in is but a small fraction of the last 1,700,000 years of time or the seventh day with God. Loren C. Minnick.

**

BRYAN'S DOWNFALL

BY MARK SULLIVAN.
(Copyright, 1925)

Washington, July 28. —What may best serve the reader today is a coherent account, as ample as space permits, that will provide the backbone and framework into which the reader can fit the interesting anecdotes and the collections now coming out of Bryan's career.

The forces that gave rise to Bryan and how he mounted and rode them, compose the thing that readers under the age of fifty never knew as a personal experience, and that even older readers in the cast did not fully understand. Some months ago, I put some pains into an attempt at describing Bryan's start. Bryan read it, and while disagreeing with some judgments, said of it as a whole:

"Creature of His Age."

"You are entirely correct in describing public men as the creatures of their age. I have often used the same explanation with regard to myself. I lived in the very center of the country out of which the economic reforms grew and was quite naturally drawn to the people's side. My father's teachings and my early associations all tended to ally me with that side."

The principal ones of the conditions that gave rise to Bryan may be summarized in three paragraphs, although the compression is much the same as condensing a whole book into each paragraph. They were:

The coming to an end of the period of free land—the end of those opulent American days when anyone could go west and acquire a 160-acre farm with no more trouble than squatting on it and no more expense than a nominal registration fee.

The government's management of the currency. During the civil war, the government doubled the number of dollars. After the war, it cut the number in half. The result was that farmers who mortgaged their land for a thousand dollars when a thousand dollars was equal to a thousand bushels of wheat, had to pay off the mortgage when a thousand dollars called for two thousand bushels of wheat.

Gold Output Decreased.

Allied to the government's reduction of the currency was a reduction in the amount of gold coming from the mines of the world. For twenty-five years preceding 1890, the first year Bryan ran for any office, the world's gold production steadily lagged. In each of those years the supply was less than it had been the first year. During the same period, by some whimsical irony of nature, the silver mines of the United States went the other way and increased their output by more than 10,000 per cent.

These and some other factors gave rise to a condition in the west that was described by William Allen White in a classic, entitled, "What's the Matter With Kansas." That editorial, by the way, written hastily for the Emporia Gazette, as the editor was leaving for a vacation, gave White a sudden boost into fame that Bryan later acquired through his oratorical description in the "Cross of Gold" speech. Some of White's unsympathetic description of the state of the west in the early nineties read:

Passions Ran Amuck.

"It was a fanaticism like the crusades. Indeed, the delusion that was working on the people took the form of religious frenzy. Sacred hymns were torn from their pious tunes to give place to words which defied the cause and made gold—and all its symbols, capital, wealth, plutocracy—diabolical. It was a season of shibboleths and fetishes and slogans. Reason slipped, and the passions, the jealousy, covetousness, hatred, ran amuck."

Out of that Bryan sprung. Twice, in 1890 and 1892, he ran for congress, successfully. In 1894 he tried for the senate but was beaten. Thereupon, he determined to leap that step and aim higher. During the next two years he had a connection with the Omaha World-Herald, but devoted most of his time to speaking up and down the Missouri valley, trying out on country schoolhouse audiences biblical figures of speech about gold being a cross that was crucifying mankind, a crown of thorns upon the brow of labor.

Perfected Master Oration.

Slowly he wove and perfected the passages of a speech destined to be an epoch-making oration. At the same time he kept in touch with local democratic leaders, former associates in congress, and others. To one, Charles S. Thomas of Colorado, later a senator, he wrote on April 16, 1896, less than three months before the national convention that would nominate the democratic candidate for president, "I don't suppose your delegation is committed to any candidate—our delegation may present my name. Whether it goes further than a compliment will depend on the feeling of other states. I am not saying this to the public, but writing you in confidence."

The recipient of that letter read it and wondered whether he would ever again encounter such superlative assurance—the very seriousness of the suggestion emphasized its absurdity."

As the convention approached, Bryan had himself elected a delegate. But the gold democrats of Nebraska sent a competing delegation. On the opening day the convention being at that stage under the domination of the older, pro-gold organization of four years before, unseated Bryan, and by one of the most picturesque ironies in American history, Bryan spent the first day as a mere onlooker in the galleries.

Convention Reorganized.

On the second day the reorganized convention seated Bryan. He arranged through friends with the chairman for the opportunity to make the closing speech, strategically important to an orator, on the adoption of the free silver standard.

On the day before that speech, July 9, 1896, the correspondent of the New York World wrote: "The silverites have neither machine nor boss—the opportunity is here; the man is lacking."

That was printed on the morning of July 10, 1896. Before night of that day, before a good many subscribers to the World had had time to read it, William Jennings Bryan, through a single speech, had made himself spokesman and master of the silver wing of the party—had utterly routed the shrewd, old leaders who had commanded the democratic party for a generation—and, in the confident self-possession with which he handled himself in the victory was restraining the exalted delegates from changing the order of the program so as to give him the presidential nomination by acclamation instantly, a day before the balloting was scheduled.

This whole issue of this paper could be filled with descriptions of that triumph of Bryan himself who was "handsome as Apollo," Senator Stone of Missouri said. John Clark Ridpath said, "That the few inspired utterances of a human soul rising to a great occasion and pouring out the vehement river of truth."

Began to Undermine Him.

That was the day of Bryan's highest reach. As natural and economic forces had produced him, so did they destroy him. They had already begun silently to undermine him before his "Cross of Gold" speech had made him a national figure.

Two mining engineers in south Africa who had never heard of Bryan, and of whom Bryan had never heard, invented the cyanide process of extracting more gold from low grade ores. New mines were discovered in Australia and elsewhere. The annual increment of gold reversed its course and began to mount. Prices of wheat, wages, and commodities began to rise. Mortgages and other debts became easier to pay.

Bryan, having practiced the device, sound from the standpoint of political strategy, focusing his whole fight on one issue, and economic forces having turned that issue against him, Bryan was not only destroyed for that campaign and that period, but was injured permanently. In the new issues he embraced in subsequent years anti-imperialism in 1900 and anti-trust in 1908 voters recalled the silver issue, and felt a vague distrust of his judgment.

There was always left to Bryan, however, a sympathetic instinct for the "underdog" in all sorts of economic issues and for the idealistic in moral issues. In these people trusted him.

As audiences and readers, they applauded him and were his loyal followers. But as voters their memories recalled the fate of the issue with which he was completely identified when he first burst upon the country.

As voters they retained a lack of confidence in the soundness of his intellectual judgments which forever kept Bryan from the presidency.

Friday July 31, 1925
The Des Moines Register

Military Will Participate in Bryan's Funeral at Washington Today

CAPITAL BOWS IN TRIBUTE TO THE COMMONER

Reverent Crowds Stream Past His Bier.

Washington, July 30 (A.P.)—Close to the pulpit before which he worshipped in the brief years of his official life in Washington, William Jennings Bryan lay tonight wrapped in the calm dignity of the long sleep into which he slipped so quietly at the close of his last crusade in far away Dayton.

There was a great peace in the face upon which thousands looked down in reverent silence as the stream of great and little folk, came to do him honor, moved slowly by through the quiet church. Among them were many who had known him in life, who had seen him in his great moments, pleading the causes he championed with a fire and eloquence that is given few men to invoke.

To these it seemed that death had touched with softening hand the familiar, rugged features; had smoothed away lines on the wide forehead etched by the crowding years and the more than three decades of ceaseless warfare for the ideals he preached in religion and politics.

Doors Left Open.

Well into the night the church doors stood open that all who would might come to stand a moment beside the bier. Again tomorrow the grieving family will share their sorrow with the public until the hour strikes for the last journey to the grave that awaits the commoner on a little hillside across the Potomac in Arlington national cemetery.

There was nothing of pomp or official ceremony about the scene in the little red brick church that long has survived the crowding down-town bustle of a growing city.

At the head and foot of the casket, which lay close against the raised step of the chancel, the motionless figure of an army comrade of the Spanish war kept ceaseless vigil, a vigil that continued after the doors had closed out the noise from the busy streets to await the coming of another day.

Three Floral Wreaths.

Beside the casket stood the first of the three floral pieces that had been set in place. It was a great wreath of yellow roses, orchids and lilies and bore the card of the secretary of state. On the casket itself, resting on the vivid coloring of the draping flag, lay a little cluster of pink rosebuds, set there in the name of the dead man's only great grandchild, Ruth Meeker of Philadelphia.

To the right of the casket on the raised floor of the chancel stood a huge floral pedestal surmounted with an open bible worked in pink and white asters. It was a tribute to a fallen leader from the Jackson Democratic club of Washington and it bore the inscription in white bloom, "The Prince of Peace."

That was all, except for the steady stream of young and old, rich and poor, white and black Americans, who seized a moment in their busy lives to look once more on the face that has been known from ocean to ocean for more years than many of them have lived.

Tomorrow there will come a change in the form of the last tributes. A group of old friends, colleagues of the dead leader in many a bitterly fought political battle were busy through the day with plans for the last service they could do for their fallen comrade. Among these was Ben G. Davis, chief clerk of the state department when Mr. Bryan ruled there as secretary, and Josephus Daniels, secretary of the navy in the cabinet in which the commoner was censor advisor to President Wilson.

After consultation with Mrs. Bryan it was determined that a military escort should meet the funeral procession at the south gate of the cemetery tomorrow afternoon. Noncommissioned officers of the regular garrison at Fort Meyer will lift the casket from the hearse and lower it into the grave and an army bugler will sound taps, but there will not be triple crash of rifle fire in deference to the wishes of the widow.

Will Sleep in Arlington.

The change in plan which gave the military a place in the ceremonies was due to the feeling that up to the time that the casket passes into the cemetery, the funeral will be simply that of a plain American who held no office or appointment of state at the time of his death, who claimed no special distinction save such tribute as his fellow citizens cared to render him in their own way.

He will then sleep in Arlington cemetery, however, by virtue of the single requirement—that he held an honorable discharge from the military service of his country. It is pride of the army that its dead shall be rendered due military honors when they come to their last bivouac, so it will give this last great service to the commoner, who wore the eagles of a colonel of infantry in the Spanish-American war.

The last family reunion will be held tomorrow in the church.

The doors will be closed to the public at noon and the dead be given back to the keeping of his loved ones for a little space before the religious services that precede the funeral are opened at 2:50 p.m.

Family Circle Present.

It was so arranged since the son from California, William Jennings Bryan, jr., and the daughter, Mrs. Grace Hargreaves, could reach Washington only in time for this last assembly of the family circle. No others will share in these moments of parting before the casket is closed for the last time. When they are over, the very few who can be admitted to the little church will take their places and the funeral service of the Presbyterian faith will follow supplemented by the reading of those bible passages in which the dead man found his greatest comfort and strength, and the singing by the church choir of his favorite hymns, "Lead Kindly Light," "One Sweetly Solemn Thought," and "Faith of Our

Fathers."

Brought here from Tennessee where he died Sunday, his body was taken just before noon to the New York Avenue Presbyterian church, to lie in state until noon tomorrow. Then, after a short religious service it will be entombed at Arlington with military honors.

Police Divert Traffic.

Special details of police were placed about the church to divert traffic and to guide the continuous slow procession that tramped in at the door and past the silent figure at the altar. Half of the top of the casket had been removed and an American flag draped the remainder.

Until after the church services tomorrow, the flag was to be the only emblem of his service to his country, but plans approved by his widow during the morning, insured that a military touch would be given to his actual burial, in remembrance of the days when he wore the uniform as a colonel of volunteers during the Spanish-American war.

Mr. Kellogg announced that the state department would be closed during the afternoon tomorrow as a mark of respect and to permit as many as possible of Mr. Bryan's former colleagues in the department to attend the funeral. As an additional tribute the flags on all government buildings will fly at half staff tomorrow.

The church where the body lay in state today was but a few blocks distant from the state department, and many employed there utilized their luncheon period to obtain a last look at the long-familiar features of the former secretary.

Crowds Stream Into Church.

Early in the afternoon the waiting lines in front of the church had disappeared, though others came in twos and fours as the hours passed, ever replenishing the quiet, solemn stream that flowed past the sleeper at the chancel. The temporary halts enabled some of his older friends to linger a moment or two, and gaze intently upon his placid face or offer silent prayer.

Congressmen, other government officials, labor union officials and war veterans were represented. Frank Morrison, secretary of the

American Federation of Labor, was an early visitor.

The Spanish-American war veterans who formed the guard of honor, relieved each other every half hour. As the late afternoon came on, the size of the crowd increased until there was a steady stream flowing through the church.

Ashurst First to View Body.

The line of men and women that had formed to the north of the church began to pass through the east entrance as soon as the doors were thrown open. It moved down the long aisle to the chancel, back again to the main entrance and down a winding stairway to make its exit from a door on New York avenue.

The first to pass by the body was Senator Ashurst of Arizona, one of those selected as an honorary pall bearer.

Charles W. Bryan, the dead man's brother and perhaps his closest confident during his long years of political battle, came to the church at noon to look upon his features for the first time since death. With welling eyes, the brother stood for a moment beside the silent form and then passed on.

**

PALL BEARERS FOR FUNERAL OF COMMONER

Washington, July 30 (A.P.)—The official list of active and honorary pallbearers at the funeral of William Jennings Bryan was announced tonight as follows:

Active pallbearers:

Josephus Daniels, former secretary of the navy; Senator Fletcher of Florida; Col. P. H. Callahan, Louisville, Ky.; Charles A. Lord, Lincoln, Neb.; N. F. Dunlap, Jacksonville, Ill., and State Senator Charles E. Hull of Illinois.

Honorary pallbearers:

Senator Swanson of Virginia, Senator Ashurst of Arizona, Senator Sheppard of Texas, Senator McKellar of Tennessee, Senator Norris of Nebraska, Representative Oldfield of Arkansas, Representative Upshaw of Georgia, Representative Yates of Illinois, Governor Donahey of Ohio, William B. Wilson, former secretary of labor; Bishop Thomas Nicholson of Michigan, former Senator Hitchcock of Nebraska.

John Skelton Williams of Virginia, former comptroller general; Clem Shaver of West Virginia, chairman of the democratic national committee; Edwin F. Goltra of Missouri, James Kirby Risk of Indiana, Normal E. Mack of New York, Howard Russell of Ohio, Charles E. Douglass of Washington, D. C., Charles F. Horner of Missouri, and Manton W. Yvell of Washington, D. C.

**

BRYAN'S WIDOW WILL CHRONICLE HUSBAND'S LIFE

Will Be Guided by His Initial Draft.

Chattanooga, Tenn., July 30 (A.P.)—The Chattanooga News, in a story published today says the memories of William Jennings Bryan will be written by his widow.

The story says:

"At the time of his death Mr. Bryan had started on the framework of his recollections. He had intended to devote to the writing of this chronicle of American life for the past half century, the rest of the summer and fall and in fact all the time up to his leaving for the Holy Land in February of 1926.

"He had dictated in the rough to his secretary, Walter E. Thompson, the first drafts of six or seven chapters of the memoirs. Thompson now has these on yellow typewritten sheets. The headings include such copies as the great commoner's childhood and youth, the Chicago convention of 1896, the Baltimore convention of 1912, his work with peace treaties while he was secretary of state and one or two other incidents in his busy life.

"These guideposts for his memoirs, for, according to Thompson, they were more of a framework giving the general trend of events rather than the detailed particularized account the commoner had expected to make by amplifying the first draft, were among the material which Mrs. Bryan will have at her disposal for her task.

"When the widow of the great commoner passed through Chattanooga Wednesday morning, en route to Arlington with the bier of her husband, she told friends that she intended to give her attention to these memoirs as soon as conditions permitted. She said she would be aided in the writing by her daughter, Mrs. Ruth Owen, and the latter's husband, Maj. Reginald Owen.

"Mrs. Bryan is a gifted writer, and for many years assisted her husband in his literary endeavors. She is the author of the biography of Mr. Bryan which introduced the collected volume of his speeches. She is also the author of the account of the Baltimore democratic convention of 1912 as throughout their married life she was in intimate touch with the innermost details of her husband's political career; with the train of thought leading to his notable political decisions, with his significant conversations and with his correspondence and files.

"It is likely that her work will be done at Marymont, the Bryan home at Cocoanut Grove, near Miami, Fla."

**

ORDER OF SERVICES FOR FUNERAL TODAY

Washington, July 30 (A.P.)—The order of services of the funeral of William Jennings Bryan tomorrow is:

At the church, 2:45 p.m.

"Lead Kindly Light," by mixed quartet.

"On Sweetly Solemn Thought," quartet.

Reading of the Presbyterian services for the dead by the Rev. Dr. Joseph R. Sizoo, pastor of the New York Avenue Presbyterian church.

The Twenty-third Psalm, read by Dr. Sizoo.

Invocation by the pastor, followed by the Lord's prayer, repeated in unison by the congregation.

Reading of the Ninetieth Psalm by Dr. Sizoo, also a portion of I Corinthians xv, 50-58.

Reading of portion of fourteenth chapter of the gospel of St. John.

Pastoral prayer.

Hymn, "Faith of Our Fathers."

Funeral address, by Dr. Sizoo.

Benediction.

Chopin's funeral march on the pipe organ as the casket is carried from the church.

At Arlington National cemetery:

Funeral train met at south gate by military escort composed of the band of the Third cavalry, dismounted, and batteries A, B and C, Sixteenth field artillery, dismounted, which will lead the way to the grave.

Reading there from the Presbyterian burial service by Dr. Sizoo.

Benediction.

"Taps."

**

THE DAYTON SPEECH

It will be unfortunate if the honors paid to Bryan in Washington are interpreted to sustain his Dayton speech as an effective indictment of the theory of evolution.

It is as easy to judge the speech at one point as another. If we take the point on which the orator laid most stress it is the agnosticism of Charles Darwin and incidentally of Clarence Darrow. But Voltaire and Thomas Paine were much more aggressive opponents of current Christian doctrine than Darwin and Darrow, and they lived long before evolution had been so much as mentioned. It is plain therefore that the agnosticism of Darwin and the theory of evolution have no necessary connection.

In our own time the most aggressive enemy of current religious beliefs has been Ingersoll. And yet evolution had nothing whatever to do with the Ingersoll argument. He devoted all his talent to exposing what he regarded the inconsistencies of the Bible

In the same way it may be said of Nietzsche, to whom Bryan referred, by far most powerful of all the enemies of Christianity, that his fundamental theory is that of the Roman empire days, and not at all of modern scientific days. Nietzsche magnified the superman, he believed in the right of the strong, he despised all appeals for the weak, his hostility to Christianity was because Christianity wastes its sympathies on the weak, the helpless, the forlorn. The strong, he preached, alone are entitled to attention. There are evolutionists of the Nietzsche persuasion. But it is not because of evolution.

All anybody need do to catch the distinction is to turn to one example. Dr. Thomas H. McBride, president emeritus of the state university, for fifty years a teacher in the university, is if we mistake not a communicant of Bryan's denomination, in any event an ardent and eloquent champion of Christianity and at the same time an ardent teacher of evolution as the explanation of God's method.

In yesterday's Register Dr. Haggard of Drake university subscribes himself, "I, an evolutionist."

One of the most vigorous champions of evolution was the venerable Bishop Bashford of the Methodist church.

It would be easy to multiply the examples, but one example is enough to suggest that Darwin's religious beliefs have no bearing on the theory of evolution, until in some very concrete way a connection is established. Every college in America is teaching evolution, whether the college be a state or a church school. They are not teaching it to sustain agnosticism, we may be sure.

The next point on which Bryan put great emphasis was a canvass of the teachers of the sciences in the United States showing a large percentage of unbelievers, as that word is ordinarily used. But suppose the canvass had been made of lawyers? Or of Doctors? Or of editors? Nobody would think of saying the law supports unbelief, because a number of lawyers are unbelievers. Nor would medicine be held responsible for the unbelief of doctors.

The fact is a large part of the preachers if canvassed on the particular tenets on which Bryan insisted would be found to be in the doubting class.

It may as well be said frankly the Bryan speech was written more to prejudice the case of evolution than to try evolution by legal processes. There was nowhere in the speech any evidence of an effort to fairly estimate the discoveries of science running now over more than seventy years and accepted by the scholarship of the world, the Christian scholarship.

This is not in any way to question the integrity of Bryan's purpose. It is merely to suggest that in his arguments Bryan could connect things together in such a way as to suggest cause and effect when as a matter of fact that connection is not established. As a rule that is the temperamental defect of the oratorical mind. The oratorical mind reflects on everything in figures of speech. Bryan could say "I am much more concerned with the Rock of Ages than with the age of rocks: with tremendous effect. And yet it might happen that the age of rocks is the very thing on which the Rock of Ages rests.

Not all the students are sound in all their opinions. But we must not because of that discourage the student attitude of inquiry into the facts of the universe. It will not do to connect some individual opinion of even Charles Darwin with any law of the universe he may have discovered in such a way as to discredit the law of the universe. Jean Jacques Rousseau had many views Americans would not subscribe to. And yet it is likely that Thomas Jefferson found the inspiration for the Declaration of Independence in Rousseau.

Evolution is not true or false because Darwin was this or that, any more than gravitation turns on what Newton believed, or relativity on what Einstein believes. The Bryan argument at Dayton did not go to the merits of the proposition.

**

MILITARY BURIAL.

"As colonel of the Third Nebraska volunteers, a regiment he raised in 1898, Mr. Bryan served in the Spanish-American war. It has always been his desire to lie in Arlington, and preparations were begun here tonight to accord him a resting place with other distinguished Americans who lie in the national cemetery."—Washington correspondent Public Ledger.

Probably this is more unexplainable than any one thing in the whole life of the commoner.

Why he should set his heart on a military burial when his military part was so incidental, and his life devoted to "peace on earth good will toward men" will be hard for his biographers.

It has been pointed out that frequently people are most insistent about recognition for the things they subconsciously feel they lack.

In any event a military burial for Bryan puzzles.

**

Young Mr. Scopes still gets his name into print occasionally, but it doesn't figure in any exciting news.

**

Eulogies and words of grief follow the invective and denunciation of partisans at the Scopes trial.

**

BRYAN'S SUCCESSES

By Mark Sullivan.
(Copyright, 1925.)

Washington, July 30.—Bryan goes to his grave under circumstances appealing to his sense of personal triumph. This would be accounted for by the circumstances of his death if not by other means. That the last functioning of his life should have been in a field so intimately personal to him as religion, that he should have died making a fight for it, that the circumstances of his death enabled him to put before the world a passionate plea for his religion under conditions that gave it the impressiveness of a literal message from the grave—all these things would have been enough to fulfill the picture of triumph.

But aside from that, taking into account only the purely political part of his career, Bryan was not embittered nor even much disappointed. The comments on his end, even those that are in the nature which compare him with Henry Clay, do not coincide with Bryan's own feeling about his political career. The points of similarity between Bryan and Clay were many.

Never Greatly Downcast.

But Bryan had given up his ambition for the presidency at an earlier age than Clay did. Also Bryan was never cast down by his defeats for the presidency. Most of the narratives of Clay's career picture him as giving more emotion to his defeats for the presidency than to the triumphs he had in some of his fights for policies. But with Bryan that was not so. The one occasion where Bryan's gallant fighting spirit left him for a moment and caused him to give out an expression of woe, was not one of his defeats for the presidency, but a setback from one of his pet causes. It was when the 1920 democratic convention nominated a candidate whom Bryan regarded as not sufficiently "dry" that Bryan said, "My heart is in the grave."

Bryan had too much vitality, too much humor, too much exuberance of spirit to be greatly cast down by his failure in his own ambitions for office. He had a stock attitude about this, and some stock phrases he loved to repeat.

His Policies Won.

Whenever strangers met him who blundered into condolences about his never having been president. Bryan would draw aside, and according to the period, draw a picture of Roosevelt advocating the initiative and referendum, or the republicans tumbling over themselves to join in a final triumph of prohibition. He would show that with humorous gloating, and end the picture with a broad grin and an engaging question:

"Madam, why should I bother about losing the offices when my opponents are steadily adopting my policies?"

A good deal of that sort of thing happened. Bryan was a pioneer in several causes, of which others became belated converts and instruments of final success.

Pictures of Roosevelt and of the republicans stealing planks from Bryan's platform were frequent incidents of gridiron dinners. Bryan wearing a barrel to hide the nakedness thrust upon him by the theft of his policies was one of the most frequent variations of cartoons. The innovations that Bryan advocated, when they were innovated, were often forlorn strangers, but later became part of our government's structure.

Twelve Notable Innovations.

During the twenty-five years from 1900 to 1925, twelve important innovations were made in the structure of American government and in the field of judicial decisions. For the moment it is sufficient to enumerate the ones with which Bryan was identified.

The first was the direct primary. Bryan did not invent that. He was rarely an inventor. But in this, as in many other cases, he became an instant convert when his attention was called to it. The men who more than anyone else, were the originators of the direct primary, were two whose names would mean nothing to the present day public; one a member of the Minnesota legislature in the late nineties, the other a private citizen in Oregon.

Bryan, through his steady advocacy of the direct primary on the lecture platform and through personal urging of friends in office, contributed as much as any other one man to the final spread of this innovation.

Another change in our governmental procedure to which Bryan had the same relation was the direct election of United States senators. A third was the income tax. The first graduated income tax was written by a ways and means committee of congress of which Bryan was a member. When it was invalidated by the supreme court in 1895, Bryan made agitation against that decision one of his own steps to power. Thereafter, he was a steady advocate of it, until it finally came in 1913.

Fought Prohibition

Yet another of Bryan's policies was national prohibition. He was late in coming to that. All the pioneer work was done by others. Bryan for years regarded national prohibition as impracticable. As late as 1910 he threw his weight against putting a national prohibition plank into democratic national and state platforms.

There could be little doubt, however, that Bryan's help, when he took up prohibition on the platform and urged it upon his followers in congress, was an indispensable agency in the final victory.

Bryan's advocacy of woman suffrage was longer. When both prohibition and woman suffrage came, within practically a year of each other, Bryan had a broad smile of satisfaction in a saying he used to repeat about how much more elevated politics is "since we threw booze out and invited the ladies in."

Bryan's contribution to all these causes was by no means limited to his lecturing, powerful as that was. The more vivid memory many people will have of Bryan, friends and opponents alike, will be the recollection of the whirlwind way with which he would drop into Washington from a midnight train, in an interval between his trips, get half a dozen of his friends in congress to take breakfast with him, spend a whole feverish day calling on others, and in twenty-four or forty-eight hours bring victory to a fight that before his coming had little promise.

Lost on Anti-Imperialism.

In mentioning the Bryan causes that won, anti-imperialism is not included. On that, the superficial record is that Bryan lost. He did lose the 1900 presidential campaign in which anti-imperialism was his issue. Apparently McKinley's republican policy of annexation was adopted by America.

But it is to be observed that after 1900, after the nation had incorporated the various annexations to which it had been committed as an unanticipated result of the Spanish war—thereafter America clearly discarded the policy of expansion. We completed, many years later in one case, annexations we had already tentatively begun, in 1900, like the Panama Canal zone, and the Virgin islands; but after 1900 America never initiated another step. When the other nations tried to thrust dependencies on us in the shape of mandates, there was nothing more clear about American state of mind than our conviction that we wanted no more, that we preferred to withdraw rather than expand.

**

THE OUTSIDE VIEW.

Editorial in Winnipeg Free Press:— W. J. Bryan died just after winning his case in the Scopes trial in Tennessee, Scopes having been found guilty of teaching evolution in the Tennessee schools, and fined $100 as a penalty. And then Bryan dies, with the Scopes trial fresh and amazing in the whole world's mind, and the name of William Jennings Bryan on the lips of millions and in the headlines of every newspaper in the western hemisphere. For a man who was a headliner for thirty years what a consistency there is in the accident of his demise! He played one of the star parts while he held the boards and he died out in front, in full character, with the blaze of publicity unquenched, the central figure of a thousand brilliant spotlights, and the world itself for audience. It was, we may be sure, the death he would have chosen.

It would not be fair to say Bryan's life was a personal failure because he lost all his causes. He stepped from failure to failure, but he stepped higher each time, and each of his failures attracted a wider circle of public attention; the more absurd he became the more conspicuous he became. We can now only conjecture the heights to which he might still have attained, but as it is he did well; as a champion of muddle-headed movements his achievement is unique, it is almost splendid.

He sounded first upon the public ear as the melodious advocate of the free coinage of silver; an issue which is now remembered principally because Bryan was for it. He thrice was offered by the democratic party the nomination for the presidency of the United States and thrice he did accept it; and thrice he was rejected by the people; but it can still be said that if he had not even one term he had three nominations. He was secretary of state from 1913 to 1915, Woodrow Wilson's first cabinet; but he resigned when his peculiar conception of pacifism was rejected by the president as a suitable policy for the United States to adopt towards the belligerents in Europe; but Bryan could still depart, with his white flag flying, and at least be a martyr to his condemnation of imperialism.

He was one of the shining lances in the campaigns against intoxicating liquor; his unrivalled energy, his unending oratory, helped to make rum an outlaw and the bootlegger a figure of international fame; and he has passed to his reward while his countrymen are still earnestly studying the phenomenon of prohibition and wondering what this thing really is that Bryan and his cohorts succeeded in fastening upon the life of the United States.

These constitute great works, but more remain. Like Gladstone, but with an impetuosity, an ardor, that even Gladstone never had, Bryan leaped upon the impregnable rock of holy scripture, and made his platform on its summit; from which vantage he hurled defiance at the scientists of the world. He did not climb his heights by the laborious steps of thought; he reached them at a bound; he spurned learning as the dust in which pedants grope and went up the precipices of knowledge like a balloon on the winds of his own eloquence. His position was curious, it was even ridiculous; but it was—who could deny it?—commanding. He denounced Charles Darwin. It was an inspiration of genius, and his fame expanded to its fullest glow; evolution, after all, had not been without its use.

And there he died; on his height, full in the world's eye; his energy not abated and his silver tongue still going; conspicuous to his last moment, and his last moment making him conspicuous still. The great Commoner. He will be remembered for his nerve when better men have not been preserved for their wisdom.

Saturday August 1, 1925
The Des Moines Register

SIMPLE RITES MARK FUNERAL OF COMMONER

Buried As Soldier of the Flag with "Taps" at Arlington.

Washington, July 31 (A.P.)—Beneath a peaceful grass-grown hillside William Jennings Bryan lies tonight to sleep time away. No special guard keeps watch beside his grave.

In common with the valorous company of soldier and sailor dead among whom he rests in Arlington national cemetery, only the quiet tread of troopers on their regular patrol of the great field of the fallen resounds above the commoner's burial plot.

He is in the keeping of the God and of the nation to whose service his life was given. In common, too, with the veteran dead about him, a simple white painted wooden marker, placed at the head of the grave, notes that here lies William Jennings Bryan, colonel of infantry. The form and inscription of the stone tribute to his memory that will ultimately replace that marker still is to be planned by the grieving widow and the many dear friends who would do him honor.

The long, last journey of the commoner from the Tennessee village where he fell asleep ended under the tight drawn canvas of an army tent spread to shelter his grave from the driving rain that had fallen since morning, to cease only a moment before the funeral party arrived at the cemetery. Within that small inclosure there was no room save for the casket, wrapped about with the glowing colors of the flag the dead man had served in peace and war, the little group of nearest kin, and a handful of the many friends of his three decades of stirring life.

Bugler Sounds Taps.

These and the ministers of the gospel who said above him the rites for the dead, and who a little time before had given him the last benediction of the church, alone saw the casket sink slowly down into the earth as the soft calling of an army bugle lulled the sleeper to his long repose with the tender notes of "taps," the soldier requiem.

Even the sorrowing woman who was his dearest care and who had sat beside his casket throughout the funeral service in a Washington church, did not see that last scene of the career in which she had so large a share. Gripped by her infirmities, she remained in her closed motor car a hundred yards from the tented grave until the bugle notes brought to her the message that the long strain was over, and her dead at peace at last.

Outside the shelter around the roped inclosure and among many newly made graves on the tree-bordered sweep of sodden sward, crowded the hundreds who had trudged or ridden the long way from Washington, despite the earlier deluge of rain, to bid the commoner their own farewell. There, too, stood the double rank of artillerymen from Fort Myer, caps and raincoats dark with the watery downpour through which they had waited to form the last escort.

No Volley Fired.

As the simple service was said, the troops, carrying only side arms, stood at rigid salute, until the bugle notes had died away over the gentle, wooded hills about. There was no drumming of rifle fire to pay last honors to the dead. But as the column formed to swing away and the mourners turned back up the slope to the waiting motors, the distant muffled thunder of a single cannon shot came from the post beyond. It was the sunset gun, marking the lowering of the garrison colors for the night, the soldier signal that another day's toil is ended, and the hours of rest at hand.

Before the fallen leader, now come to his last military honors, was surrendered to soldier keeping at the south gate of the old cemetery, he had received, down in the haze-covered city beyond the river, the solemn service that men of his religious faith had designed in reverence to their dead. It was to the simple citizen that this benediction was offered. Through it ran the deep consolation that the Christian faith holds out to the dear ones left behind.

Within the cramped auditorium of the New York Avenue Presbyterian church, where the commoner lay in state in death and where he had worshipped in life, the funeral scene was dim and shadow in the half light of the clouded, rain washed day. The few who could find room had taken their places and the echoes of the two old hymns Mr. Bryan most loved, "Lead Kindly Light" and "One Sweetly Solemn Thought," still lurked in the recess of the high roof when the family came in, led by Rev. Dr. Joseph R. Sizoo, the pastor.

"I am the resurrection and the life," the minister slowly repeated, as he moved down the aisle toward the flag draped casket. Behind him was Mrs. Bryan, her pale face clear against her black gown, with her son, who now alone bears the distinguished name of the dead, gently pushing forward the wheel chair to which her infirmities confine her. As it came to rest close to the casket, other members of the family took their places in the long pew at the left.

Through the services that followed, the brief prayers, the readings from the psalms that her husband most loved. The short eulogy by the pastor, the widow sat with eyes intent on the speaker's face. He had moved around through the flower-bordered chancel to take his place in the pulpit above the casket, and he talked as to that sorrowing woman alone.

There was little in the brief funeral ceremony in the church that any plain, God-fearing man might not have known. Only the presence of a little cluster of high officials of the government, and a few diplomats, struck a note of remembrance for his years of distinguished public service.

But at the church it was to Bryan, the friend and neighbor and man of faith, that those who loved him best gave their memories and tears.

Read Scripture Lesson.

Remaining seated in the wheel chair, Mrs. Bryan kept her gaze intently upon the face of the pastor as he read the opening scripture lesson and pronounced the invocation:

"Ever living, ever loving God in whom we live and move and have our being, we thank thee we are not strangers to thy mercy and we are not aliens to thy constant love.

"We invoke thy divine blessing upon us as we come with heavy hearts to worship thee in the beauty of holiness. Give us the consciousness of thy radiant presence and may the assurance of thy goodness give us peace.

"Grant that the words of our mouths and the meditations of hearts may be acceptable in thy sight, Oh Lord, our strength and our redeemer."

The congregation joined in the Lord's prayer and the scriptural reading continued with the fourteenth chapter of the gospel of St. John.

The audience knelt as the pastor delivered the pastoral prayer and once more the pealing notes of the organ arose with the strains of "Faith of Our Fathers," from which the dead had quoted in his now famous undelivered speech.

The funeral address began amid a great hush. In a soft, even voice Dr. Sizoo praised the fallen one for the "three fold splendor" of his upright life, his love of man and God and his great faith.

Then to the strains of Chopin's "Funeral March" the body was borne gently down the central aisle. The members of the family followed closely and stood on the church steps while it was lifted into a motor hearse to begin the journey to Arlington. A string of motor cars fell in behind and the mourners found place within them just as the heaviest downpour of the day broke over the capital and the waiting crowd in the cemetery across the river.

The rain became a drenching deluge as the cortege passed down Thirteenth street from the church on New York avenue and entered the highway bridge from the Mall, and took its way through winding Virginia roads that lead up to Arlington ridge tops. Water saturated the caps and even the raincoats of the waiting soldiery inside the cemetery gate and pounded its way through the umbrellas and wrappings of onlookers, driving many back to the shelter of street cars and waiting automobiles.

**

HAD CONFIDENCE AND AFFECTION OF THE PEOPLE

Dr. Sizoo Declares His Life an Open Book.

Washington, July 31 (A.P.)—The text of Dr. Joseph R. Sizoo's funeral address at the bier of William Jennings Bryan follows:

"Some years ago—it seems only like yesterday—Mr. Bryan delivered a lecture to a group of some 500 students in a midwestern college.

His theme was 'The Value of An Ideal.' He spoke with that amazing clarity which so characterized all his addresses not only of the place of an ideal in life but also of the various ideals which man may hold, and then that highest of all ideals—Christian service.

"How profoundly he moved that group of young men, Mr. Bryan never knew. There was one student in that audience for whom he changed the whole program of his life. This student was a freshman at college that year with the plan of preparing for some professional career. The plea for Christian service, made by this great heart of faith, never left and following that urge he later entered the Christian ministry. I was that student. That stirring plea marked the beginning of a whole new attitude to life, and I bring my testimony to the memory of a man who never knew how greatly he had changed that life.

Ways of God Strange.

"Surely it is unique that as he lies here dead among us, I should bear my witness to his influence in this most solemn hour.

"How strange are the ways of God, and how otherwise from our desires. Had it been given to us to control the affairs of life, how different would it have been. Earth can ill spare such noble souls. His ability was so striking, his sincerity was so genuine, his personality was so winsome and his faith so serene that we had hoped to have him longer with us. We seem to need him so.

"But God willed otherwise, and until the daybreak when shadows flee away we reverently kneel in submission to pray, 'Father, Thy will be done.' The end came quickly. He did not suffer, he did not know pain. A merciful providence guarded over that hour. Serenely and in the home of a friend he made his last great venture of faith on the first day of the week which, to the Christian, is the unforgettable symbol of the resurrection.

Life Never Unfinished.

"We talk about unfulfilled dreams and incomplete lives and broken circles; but with God there is no unfinished life and there are no broken circles. Jesus—dead at thirty-three—cried out exultantly from the cross;

"It is finished." So is every life that follows God's will. When is a life finished, you ask? When the seeds of its influence have dropped into the lives of others, enriching them. A life is finished when other lives are lit up by it and walk in its strength. A life is finished when those around it have caught the splendor of its power and lived happier, nobler and truer. If that is true, then this great heart lived a finished life. The heritage of that life it may take long to measure. Multitudes have caught the splendor of it and lived by its guiding light.

"It is to rehearse this splendor that we have come today. Praise or blame do not affect him now. They never disturbed his convictions. He was far above all that on earth and he is far beyond all that now. Nothing we say or do can in any way add or detract from him. It is for us to see again the glory of that life and heed its heritage.

"There was three-fold splendor about this noble man which will ever challenge those who have lived in his day and who are to carry on in the days to come.

"He had a capacity for noble living. He was a man with an upturned face and an upward life. His life was an open book beyond all possible reproach. His character was unsullied to the very end. You can turn the searching light of a critical publicity on any page of his past through all manner of personal and political fortunes of later life and not one page is smutted or soiled or stained. There was no shadow of self-seeking or gain in him.

"There was no skeleton in the closet. You do not have to tread softly over any episode. Friend or foe call him a man whose great concern was the causes he espoused and to those causes he came with clean hands and a pure heart.

Name Is Treasured.

"Not only for what he said but for what he was will his name be treasured. It was because of this unsullied life that he held the confidence and affection of the nation for more than thirty years. So often one hears it said that men in public life and leadership are inspired by sinister motives of self gain or for ulterior ambitions of self-aggrandizement, that many questions everyone who aspires to serve his country. Then God gives us a man like this to give that philosophy the lie, a man 'whom the just of office could not buy and whom the spoils of office could not kill.'

"1. His upstanding integrity, his high sense of honor, his devotion to duty, his sense of gratitude, his remembrance of the humblest, his freedom from all cant make his life today an inspiration and a challenge to all the nation. Like so many great hearts of earth, and like his master, he met hate without bitterness, defeat without vengeance, ill thought with forgiving love, and misunderstanding with charity.

"Oh, all you who mourn and are left stranded upon the shores of time, what a comfort and what a heritage is yours. Death takes many things from us. Truly it is the great destroyer. But one thing, thank God, death can never take away from you, and that is the imperishable memory of his fine manliness, courage and humble sincerity. He did not live in vain. Thousands are made better because he passed this way.

Deep Capacity for Love.

"2. He had a deep capacity for love. He was a great friend and never played fast and loose with friendship. Some men are not big enough to have friends because they are not big enough to be friends, but not so with him. Political opposition never lost him personal friendships. His love was genuine with rich and poor alike, it knew no border, breed or birth. Differing from men who held contrary convictions he still held them within the grasp of life long affections.

"But his capacity for love reached beyond the border of the individual. He did not live like a star apart from his fellow men. He always spoke with, and of and for the people. He was not only an architect but also the builder of a better world. He never lost sight of humanity. His heart and his pulse throbbed for the needs of his fellow men. He kept many a weary vigil on the hilltop of the world, wondering what might be done to help, never resting till the crown of thorns had been lifted and the golden crown of happiness and peace put in its place. It may take decades to measure the urge and hope for peace which he provided for the nation in his day and generation.

"3. He had a rich capacity for faith. Any summary of the heritage of his life, however, brief, would be utterly unworthy if it did not bear witness to his unfaltering faith in God. You will never know this man until you know him there. He was essentially a religious man.

Knew About the World.

"He was not disillusioned about the world. He knew its ills and its failures. He was acquainted with its griefs and its heart-burnings, he saw its anguish and wan hopelessness. He saw all this but he also saw that the way out was not by some strange hysterical solution. How often he said that happiness will be restored, prosperity will beat again with its angel wings and peace will come with its eternal abiding, when men come back to the simple elemental forces of life like honesty, reverence and faith in God. Not by the pronunclamentoes of plenipotentiaries, not by legislative enactment alone, but only as men climb the storm swathed sides of Sinai and hear again the voice, 'Thus saith the Lord God,' will prosperity be promoted and peace dawn at last.

"Nothing else explains the greatness of the man like the greatness of his faith. That was unchallengeable, irresistible, and burned with a quenchless fire.

Rebuilt Altar of Faith.

"Some day perhaps we may see that that was his great contribution to life and the final heritage that he has come to leave. He has rebuilt the altar of faith in God and covered that altar with his very life. It was faith that gave such sweep to his helpful service, such depth to his character. In the last analysis an unsullied life and an unchallengeable faith in God is life's final argument and has no answer. In a day full of intellectual bewilderment when many Christians are growing uncertain of their convictions, when multitudes have misgivings lest the things they have believed may prove false: in a day when many become obsessed with despair like that of a man who has played his last card and lost, Mr. Bryan grew more sure and his faith more profound. God be praised for the tonic of this man's trust in God. Would that the cloak of his simple faith might fall upon us. He was never disturbed by criticism, he was never distracted by praise because with the faith of a great prophet he held his course close to God. Say what you will about him, he has rethought and restated for multitudes the meaning of life in terms of God.

"For all the saints, who from their labor rest,
Who thee, by faith, before the world confessed,
Thy name, O, Jesus, be forever blest.
Hallelujah."

"What a challenge in such a life to all who falter; what a comfort to all who believe; what an indictment upon all who reject it; what a prophecy of power to all who make it real.

Shall See Him Again.

"We shall see him again, for such a life cannot die. I like to believe that somewhere in that better country where the sun goes not down, where twilight breaks into eternal dawn, where God wipes away all tears from our eyes, where there is no pain, and where flowers fade not away, he is still carrying on with the same sweet faith and same noble spirit into an ever glowing fullness and likeness of his God and our God.

"Somewhere beyond, life still runs on without the imperfections and impediments of this life. We bury our dead with their faces to the east for sunrise eternal has broken over their souls where 'Nearer, My God, to Thee" is not longer a hymn of hope but an everlasting experience.

"Sunset and evening star.
And one clear call for me;
And may there be no moaning of the bar
When I set out to sea.
"For though from out the bourne of time and place.
The floods may bear me far.
I hope to see my Pilot face to face.
When I have crossed the bar."

"God bless and hallow the heritage and memory of William Jennings Bryan."

**

KLANSMEN SEND FLORAL TRIBUTE FOR BRYAN RITES

Chapters Hold Memorial Services.

Washington, July 31 (A.P.)—Among the floral tributes sent to the church where the body of William Jennings Bryan lay in state today was one in the form of a cross, bearing a card on which was written "Ku-Klux klan, Realm of Ohio."

The piece was about five feet high and was composed of red roses. It was placed near the pulpit.

**

Columbus, O., July 31 (A.P.)—Klansmen in three Ohio cities tonight held memorial services for William Jennings Bryan, closing each with the burning of memorial crosses.

At Dayton the cross carried the inscription: "In memory of the greatest klansman of our time; he stood at Armageddon and battled for the Lord."

At Toledo the cross had written on it: "In memory of the greatest klansman."

The Columbus meeting was featured by memorial addresses, after which a memorial cross for Mr. Bryan was lighted.

**

Commoner's Bible Class Holds Memorial Service

Miami, Fla., July 31 (A.P.)—From the same platform in Royal Palm park where he had taught the world's largest Sunday school class, speakers today eulogized the life of William J. Bryan, while his friends of the masses braved a downpour of rain in final tribute to their teacher and friend.

Crowds thronged the park long before the hour set for the services. Never before has such an audience, representative of wider interests and conceptions, gathered here, and never was such a gathering more attentive or more reverent. Rumbling thunder and flashing lightning failed to disturb them and the following downpour found them unmoved.

**

AN ENGLISH ONLOOKER

George Mccready Price in London Times.

It has occurred to me that the people of England would really be interested in seeing the other side of the case in that matter of the trial in Tennessee. As a British subject who has spent some twenty years in very extensive travel throughout America, mostly while engaged in educational and research work, I think that I ought to be fairly familiar with the tone of public feeling in that country.

Of course, there are many extreme religionists, represented by such books as "God or Gorilla" and "Hell and the High Schools," both of which (with many others) have had a considerable circulation among certain classes. There are also many extreme evolutionists, of the type of the last Ernst Haeckel, who consider themselves the special apostles of the evolution doctrine. If these two classes alone were concerned, with the latter already in the places of power and influence, as is the case in some places, the contest might not be tried out in the courts; for history shows that there are other ways of settling extreme religious differences.

The great majority of the American people are not on either of these extremes. But a moderate amount of scientific training in botany, zoology, and general biology is very much more commonly given in the high schools and in the first two years of college; for the American system of aiming at a "balanced" kind of education has tended to make some science almost universal; and then a high school and college training are much more nearly universal among the common people than they are in England.

Accordingly, the average American man or woman is very much more likely to be familiar with the ordinary facts on which the theory of organic evolution is based than would be the case with the average man or woman in this country. But knowing these facts, he is also much better prepared to say that the evolution idea is at best only a theory; while the facts of these various sciences can be taught without any theory whatever as to origin; just as the facts of chemistry can be taught without any theory as to the evolution of the elements, or as the facts of cytology and biology can be taught without any speculation as to spontaneous generation. Thus, when such a man sees the intense feelings which are stirred up by this controversy, he says at once that, if evolution is not a religion, it seems to have all the symptoms of a religion on both sides; and therefore he concludes that it is a question that the state must not interfere with.

For one here in England must never lose sight of the fact that one of the chief characteristics of the American system of education is its absolutely neutral or non-religious character. While each state controls its own system of education, in a large number of them even the simple act of reading the bible before the school has long been banned; in every one of them no form of sectarian teaching is allowed. And the American considers that these laws of long standing which forbid sectarian teaching in the public schools are merely acts of fairness, since all pupils have to go to schools of some kind under compulsory education, and there are very few privately maintained elementary schools. These ancient laws against sectarianism are regarded as protecting the taxpayer against the possibility of having his child taught some creed that he does not like. And a friend of mine, who is an editor in the capital of Tennessee, has put the case as follows, in a recent editorial:—

But now comes along a new teaching, unknown to our forefathers, which is in reality a religion or anti-religion; and yet because its advocates call it a science and nothing else, it is allowed to be taught freely in state-supported schools. We are protected from all creeds we may not want, except the evolution creed. Is it not in keeping, then, with the principles we have always followed to debar the evolution creed along with all the others, from a positive teaching as truth in public schools? . . . Neutrality in such questions is the only safe stand for the civil power to take.

This characteristically American spirit and attitude is, it seems to me, the real reason why some four other states besides Tennessee have already passed laws or issued executive decrees of about the same character forbidding the teaching of the theory of man's animal origin. And this is why some twelve more states have the matter under consideration, and why, as I believe, it is only a matter of time when almost all of the others will follow suit. America has done many things which seem strange to an Englishman; the act of "going dry" was considered wholly incredible until it was an accomplished fact. And whether we like it or not, we are, in my opinion, quite likely to see not only a "dry" America, but one that will not permit a taxpayer to be taxed to have his child taught something regarding origins which he considers wrong and contrary to his religion.

I notice that Nature, in its current issue of July 11, has issued a supplement dealing with the expressions of opinion by some thirty-odd leading scientists and educationists. And it is quite suggestive that some at least of these men look at the matter quite differently from the way in which the newspapers have been presenting the case. Thus, Sir Ray Lankester, who certainly will not be suspected of secretly opposing the theory of evolution, says that, while the "law" in Tennessee ought to be changed, he sees no reason for disobeying the law instead of repealing it. And he goes on to say: —

> The whole affair is being worked by journalistic enterprise in the states on a misleading basis. There is no "trial" of the advertised teacher. He is no martyr. He is simply a case of the very ordinary failure of an employee who will not carry out the terms of his engagement and is dismissed accordingly. He is under no compulsion. He can teach according to contract, or he can go elsewhere. He prefers to go. (Supplement, p. 72.)

Dr. F. A. Bather of the geology department of the British museum also has some sensible remarks about the essential difference between the teaching of facts and the teaching of theories. For no law in any of these states, as now in force or as planned for, contemplates the prohibition of teaching any concrete fact of any of the biological or geological sciences. Thus Dr. Bather says:

> Evolution is a theory of creation. There are other theories, and some of them, held by thousands of well-meaning people, may not be taught in the state schools of certain countries. Perhaps it is just as well not to teach any theories. A teacher who is not himself an investigator is liable to be too dogmatic and to bring forward a theory as a ready-made explanation of matters which he is really (like the rest of us) unable to explain. The right of free thought and free speech is one thing; the guidance of the young is another. . . .
>
> Are not Americans a little too ready to substitute theory for fact in their educational courses? Perhaps this attack is the inevitable reaction,

and it may prove not unwholesome. It would do us all good to drop "that blessed word evolution" for fifty years. (Supplement. P. 77).

But I think I have already trespassed too far on the limits of your space. It is an interminable subject; yet I wished to indicate that there are phases of the problem which do not seem to have been hitherto presented to the people of England.

**

What Do YOU Think?

Issues Then, Personality Now.

Storm Lake, Ia.—To the Editor: Yesterday he stood at bay defiant, unyielding, making his last stand, ridiculed and reviled by editors, statesmen, poets, satirists, cartoonists, vaudeville artists, Christians, communists, educators, fools—in fact the whole world. Talk of the world growing better! Their shafts are more delicate and refined but just as fatal as the nails they drove into the feet of the man on the cross. They crucified him spiritually on his cross of gold, but they killed him.

Today behold those same editors, statesmen, Christians and the world exalting his name to the highest notes of praise with whole pages of encomiums and eulogies. Never in our history has there been such a reversal in a day by the press and public and not even Lincoln, Roosevelt or Wilson received so much space in our dailies and current literature.

Now if the world knows today that he was such a sincere, honest and able man, it knew it yesterday, and why does the world taunt and berate its great men while they live and praise and laud them when they are dead? Nineteen hundred years ago they said "Crucify him and give us Barabbas." Yesterday they said, "Nail him to his cross and give us Darrow."

But Bryan is not dead. The mortal body is all there in its leaden box, but who can believe that a dynamic fighting spirit that directed the hands, vocal chords, and brain of that lump of flesh has been obliterated in a second of time? Somewhere he must be resting and today his last utterances will be read with respect. Like Lincoln, "He now belongs to the ages." J. R. Barkley

**

Government in Religion.

Avoca, Ia.—To the Editor: I notice the article on legislated religion by Mr. Perry Engle of Newton. His statement, "The religion of the future will not be based on authority, either spiritual or temporal," is certainly broad enough to suit the most radical anarchist.

We all know that everything that passes through the hands of man is at some time abused, but shall we discard all because man abuses it? What law has man not abused? Shall we say no law, because at some time man has misused it?

Now we have the proposition of no authority in religion. If God is to have no authority, who shall have authority? Then you have no government with authority. No law that has authority. What more could the most radical anarchist ask for? W. E. Sauerman.

Sunday, August 2, 1925
The Des Moines Sunday Register

MRS. W. J. BRYAN STARTS RETURN TRIP TO FLORIDA

Capital Friends Bid Commoner's Wife Goodby.

Washington, Aug., 1 (A.P.)—Mrs. William Jennings Bryan tonight began her sad journey back to Marymont, the coconut grove, Florida home which the commoner built and named for her.

She was accompanied by her son, William Jennings Bryan, jr., her nurse, Mrs. C. C. Stephans, and her late husband's secretary, W. E. Thompson.

Mrs. Bryan's departure from Washington was relatively quiet, the throngs that crowded about the funeral party Thursday morning when it arrived with the body of her husband being absent today.

Few recognized her as the widow of the commoner as, during a forty minute wait for her train, she chatted with the small group of relatives and friends who came to say goodby.

Within this circle was Mrs. Bryan's daughter, Mrs. Reginald Owen, Josephus Daniels, the former secretary of the navy, and intimate friend of Mr. Bryan, who left on the same train for Raleigh, N. C.

**

Washington, Aug. 1 (A.P.)—A nationwide campaign for fundamentalism was inaugurated today by the Seventh Day Adventists at their headquarters at Takoma park with a sermon by the Rev. Charles A. Longacre, in which he replied to the questions propounded by Clarence Darrow to William Jennings Bryan during the Scopes trial at Dayton, Tenn.

**

LOSS OF BRYAN WILL BE FELT BY DEMOCRATS

Party's Future Will Be Seriously Affected

BY ROBERT T. SMALL.
(Special Dispatch to the Register.)
(Copyright, 1925, by the C.P.A.)

Washington, Aug. 1.—Now that the so-called Bryan "blight" has been removed from it, what will the democratic party do?

Many times during the last twenty-five years the followers of national conventions have heard the exclamation: "We can't do anything with Bryan and we can't do anything without him."

Certain classes of democrats certainly regarded the commoner as a "blight," while his friends always insisted he was a savior of the party, their argument being it was better to keep the party pure and unsullied by adopting Mr. Bryan's views than to gain success at the polls.

In this respect Mr. Bryan unquestionably did yeoman service. But the rank and file of democrats have been restive and have wanted to win in their own way rather than to continue to lose in the Bryan way.

Bryan's Influence Gone.

Mr. Bryan is dead, and his influence, so largely personal, has gone with him. It is a great tribute to Bryan that he was so feared within his party. He had a power of expression and a hold upon the people which could not be overestimated. The national conventions of the future will not be the same without him. He hovered over the party gatherings always as an influence which must be met and dealt with. To the "Bryan shouters" he was always an influence for good. To the Bryan "haters" he was always just about to throw a monkey wrench any time the machinery seemed to be working smoothly.

Mr. Bryan's death will be felt as a distinct loss to those democrats who believed and believed sincerely that the future hope of the party rested upon an amalgamation of the south and west to fight against the east. Mr. Bryan believed with them. At Dayton he told the writer that this was his deliberate judgment and he promised to say more along that line as soon as he could get the evolution case temporarily out of his mind.

The friends of William Gibbs McAdoo were soliciting the support of Mr. Bryan in such a scheme of organization, and he was constantly in consultation with them.

Championed South and West.

"We must have a southern or a western man as our next candidate," said Mr. Bryan.

The skeptics, who always seemed to follow Mr. Bryan as closely as the true believers, immediately saw a "catch" in this statement. They argued that Mr. Bryan had been of the west and was now of the south. Consequently, he would fill the bill himself as the party's candidate in 1928. The McAdoo followers insisted, however, that the former secretary of the treasury really filled the bill, for he was at one time of the south and was now of the very far west.

Mr. Bryan's opponents have seen in his political activities only an effort to obtain the presidency for himself. The late Champ Clark and those about him openly charged that, when Mr. Bryan deserted the Clark camp at the Baltimore convention in 1912, his object was not to bring about the nomination of Woodrow Wilson, but to throw the convention into an uproar and gain the honor for himself. The move proved fatal to Mr. Clark, who had received a majority vote and was holding on for the necessary two-thirds.

But there was no stampede for Bryan. Mr. Wilson gradually wore down the Clark forces and eventually was proclaimed the nominee, to go forward to two world-stirring terms in the white house. Whatever Mr. Bryan's real purpose was in the convention, his move brought about the Wilson nomination, and that is why he was made secretary of state in the Wilson cabinet. It is easy to sketch Mr. Bryan's record at the national conventions of the last thirty years.

Bryan's Career.

1896—Won the presidential nomination with his "Cross of Gold" oration.

1900—Again nominated and again defeated.

1904—Opposed nomination of Alton B. Parker. Parker nominated and defeated.

1908—Nominated for the third and last time and defeated.

1912—Broke away from Clark instructions and voted for Wilson.

1916—Had broken with Wilson but made no open move to prevent the latter's renomination, which was a foregone conclusion.

1920—Urged prohibition plank upon party, and when this was defeated, declined to support nominee of party.

1924—Advocated Mr. McAdoo under instructions and opposed those who wanted to denounce Ku-Klux klan by name in platform.

"What will Bryan do?" has been a common question at the conventions of the last thirty years. There was a wild cheer in Madison Square garden last summer when the commoner prophetically declared from the speaker's stand that it was his last convention. He met the hostile cheer by saying that he might change his mind. But it was his last, and new forces within the party may fight it out in 1928 with no Bryan to bother them. The "blight" is removed forever.

**

WHAT SHALL OR SHALL NOT BE TAUGHT

BY MARK SULLIVAN
(Copyright, 1925)

It is painfully evident that for some time there is going to be before us the question of the right of each state, through its legislature, to prescribe what shall be taught and what shall not be taught in public schools. The passing of Bryan will not alter this tendency; to some extent, the tendency will be accelerated by the emotions arising out of Bryan's death. It was not Bryan who started this movement and it will go on without him.

The Tennessee case, so far as it has gone, instead of bringing this question to a conclusion, has merely accelerated its momentum. Six states already have passed statutes roughly identical with the Tennessee one. From information received from over the country no one need doubt that in the next session of the various legislatures proposals of this kind will be presented in increasing numbers. Fortunately—if you look at it that way—next winter happens to be one of the years in which comparatively few legislatures meet. Most state legislatures meet, not every year, but once in every two years; and 1926 happens to be, for most states, one of the off years. Eighteen months from now, however, during the first week of January, 1927, or during the early months of that year, upward of forty legislatures will meet.

Meantime it is just possible that the Tennessee case may have found its way to the supreme court of the United States and that the supreme court will have affirmed or denied the right of the states to pass this kind of statute. Until that happens it can be taken as certain that there will be increasing interest in this subject, increasing pressure from those who believe in this kind of statute, increasing tenseness of opposition from those who oppose it.

*

In a dispatch in this paper one day last week the writer said something to the effect that "the right of the states to dictate what shall or shall not be taught in public schools is generally admitted." That statement was interpreted as meaning to prophesy that the supreme court would sustain the right of the state to pass a statute like the Tennessee one. As such the statement has been hotly controverted.

For that off-hand statement the writer had only casual authority. It was based partly on a letter from one of the leading scientists of the a United States who had written me a letter in which the following passage occurred:

"The laws or authorities of all states prescribe what the pupils in the public schools shall be taught and shall not be taught, and, so far as I know, the constitutional right of such authority has never been challenged. The laws in some states require the reading of a chapter of the bible, and in other states prohibit the reading of the bible in the public schools. Both laws, I suppose, are constitutional, but if the government has the right to prohibit the reading of the biblical account of creation I do not see but what they have the right to prohibit the reading of the Darwinian account of creation. The case will doubtless go against the defendant in the Tennessee courts, and if it is carried to higher courts they will have to decide exclusively on the constitutional question, and, it seems to me, must decide in favor of the constitutionality of the law."

In addition to this passage in a letter from a distinguished scientist, the only other authority I had for saying that the right of the states to dictate what shall or shall not be taught in the public schools is generally admitted, was a casual conversation with a well known constitutional lawyer, a former member of the United States senate. He is strongly opposed to the Tennessee statute, but he said that he did not see how the higher courts could fail to sustain it—he did not see how the right of the state to prescribe what shall or shall not be taught can be denied.

*

The assertion that the states have a right through their legislatures or otherwise to dictate what shall or shall not be taught in the public schools was based rather more on logic than on legal precedents. The sound argument seems to run thus: Somebody must say what shall and what shall not be taught in the public schools. There is no escape from that. Some man or group of men is and must be the final arbiter of the curriculum of every institution of education. There must be somewhere a governing man or governing body. Occasionally one must probe through several layers of authority to find the final one, but always there is a final one. Harvard university, for example, is a familiar type of educational institution in which the final authority rests on a self-perpetuating corporate body. This corporate body, this final authority, usually does not exert itself. In many colleges thus governed wide latitude is given in the matter of fixing the curricula to intermediate authorities, to the president, to the faculty, to some kind of advisory body; but always the final authority is there. In church institutions, parochial schools and the like, the final authority is the church hierarchy. In state universities the final authority is the legislature. The legislature may delegate its authority to the state university president or to a board of regents. But when any real question arises, it is the state legislature that is the final authority.

As to the public schools, clearly the state legislature is the body that has final authority to say what shall or shall not be taught. State legislatures did not commonly exercise this authority or pay much attention to it until the present contest arose between fundamentalism and modernism.

Somebody must say what is to be taught in the public schools. Somebody must have the discretion and must exercise it. It cannot readily be the local teacher, because that is more authority than we are commonly willing to give to any one person. More accurately, we are willing to let the local teacher have a good deal of authority until a controverted question arises, and then we quickly discover that the individual teacher's authority has no real basis. It might be argued that the local school board should have the question, because the local school board can only get its authority from the state legislature. Logically there seems no escape from the assertion that the final authority to dictate what shall or shall not be taught in the public schools rests in the state legislature.

If the state legislature has not the power, who has? We may question the wisdom of what subjects the state prescribes or bans, but we can hardly deny its power. We cannot assert the power is somewhere else. About the only alternative would be a referendum in states where the mechanism of referendum exists. A referendum might be no more pleasing to the modernists than a legislature. The Oregon law (recently declared void by the United States supreme court) which forbade, in effect, all private schools, was adopted in a popular referendum by a vote of 115,506 in favor, to 102,685 opposed.

*

Of course, the power of the legislature in this as in all matters is subject to review by the courts. Just what are the limitations on the right of a legislature to dictate the teachings of one thing and bar the teachings of another is, one presumes, the question that shortly will come before the supreme court of the United States. It will be a wholly new question. The guarantees of the federal constitution unquestionably place a limitation on the right of the legislatures to dictate the curricula of public schools. Whether this Tennessee statute and others of the kind invade the guarantees of the constitution is the question the supreme court will be called on to decide.

Even deeper than the written guaranties of the constitution, it is to be presumed that the supreme court would recognize that in nature there are some things no legislature can do. There is a story about an action once undertaken by an early legislature in Kansas. Whether a search of the legislative records would confirm the veracity of this story I do not undertake to say. In any event, the story is to the effect that a Kansas legislature, during those days of discontent with many things that prevailed during the flame of populism that spread over the west in the seventies and early eighties of the last century, passed a statute beneficently designed to relieve mature men, as well as children in the schools, from one of the most vexatious institutions that trouble the human mind. The statute, according to legend, read:

"Whereas, in our public schools, much time is wasted and much difficulty is encountered in multiplying by 3.1416; therefore be it

"Resolved, that on and after the first day of January, next, the circumference of a circle shall be three times the diameter, and no longer shall be 3.1416 times."

*

For the problem now about to be put before the supreme court, the question of the right of the states to forbid the teaching of certain subjects in schools, there is no precedent. There is, however, one recent case that may be called to some extent analogous. It is only analogous, however. The reader should understand clearly that the case about to be described had to do with private schools and not public schools. To that extent it is not a precedent, but merely has interest and possibly some bearing.

Just about the time the recent war was ending the state of Nebraska became excited over the "foreign language question." (In addition to Nebraska, some twenty other states passed legislation similar to the statute about to be described. The laws of two of these states, Ohio and Iowa, went before the supreme court of the United States along with the Nebraska case).

Nebraska really started out with the purpose of outlawing all private schools, of making the attendance of children in public schools compulsory. A bill to that effect passed the house, but after a bitter contest was defeated in the state senate by a majority of one.

Defeated in this broad purpose, the Nebraska legislature thereupon proceeded to achieve part of its purpose in another way. They passed a statute making it unlawful to teach foreign languages below the ninth grade in private, parochial or denominational schools. The law was directed primarily at the teaching of German. Immediately after the passage of this act the Nebraska district of the Evangelical Lutheran synod, acting on behalf of the Lutheran parochial schools, and the Omaha Catholic bishop, acting on behalf of the Catholic parochial schools, retained an Omaha lawyer, a leader of the local bar and an exceptionally forceful man, Arthur F. Mullen. Mr. Mullen, acting for the Lutheran and Catholic private schools, brought proceedings in the Nebraska state courts to enjoin the governor and other state officials from putting the act in force. The pleadings filed by the counsel for the governor contended that the state, under its police power, has complete control of the subject of education; that the state has the power to prohibit the study of foreign languages or any other subject in private schools. (Here again let it be emphasized that it was private, not public schools that figured in this case.)

The supreme court of Nebraska decided against the constitutionality of the act. Some of the words of the decision of the supreme court in Nebraska have pertinence here:

"The state should control the education of its citizens far enough to see that it is given in the language of their country, and to insure that they understand the nature of the government under which they live, and are competent to take part in it. Further than this education should be left to the fullest freedom of the individual."

*

When the Nebraska legislature reconvened in 1921 they proceeded to overcome the decision of the supreme court by passing another language law in which the legislature showed its determination to "put teeth" in the act. This act was passed on April 14, 1921, with an emergency clause putting the law into effect at once.

Immediately after this second act the same defendants, the Evangelical Lutheran synod and the Catholic bishop, with the same counsel, Arthur F. Mullen, renewed their proceedings in the Nebraska courts to enjoin the governor and other officials from enforcing the act. In the meantime, a teacher in a private school named Meyer was arrested and convicted in a local court for the offense of teaching Bible stories to children in a Lutheran school in the German language, "between 1 and 1:30 in the afternoon." This conviction was sustained in a divided opinion by the supreme court of Nebraska.

Thereupon the two cases, one seeking an injunction to forbid the governor to put the law into effect, and the other the conviction of Meyer, were consolidated, were appealed to the supreme court of the United States, and were argued together in February, 1923. The counsel for the state took the familiar ground that the state of Nebraska had the right, if it chose, to require everybody to attend public schools, and that therefore the state through its police power could prohibit the study of foreign languages in private schools.

The counsel for the Lutheran and Catholic schools, Mr. Mullen, recited the history of compulsory education in the United States, which began only as late as 1852. In his argument he included not only the legal aspects of the case but cited authorities on the philosophy of education and liberty from Plato down to John Stuart Mill. In the course of his argument he was interrupted by upward of fifty questions from justices of the court. It was evident that the court realized the importance of the case. In fact, the case is occasionally described as one of the four or five most important ever decided by the supreme court.

In the end the court decided against the state and in favor of the right of the Lutheran and Catholic parochial schools to teach German. The decision, though it did not attract wide attention at the time, was largely the basis of the decision handed down a year later on the Oregon school case, about which every one knows.

*

As I have said, this case had to do with public, not with private schools. So far as one might gather from it, an inference that the supreme court would decide against a law, for example, forbidding the teaching of German in public schools, one might readily be mistaken. In fact, Mr. Mullen in his argument conceded repeatedly that the state has a larger power to dictate what shall be taught and not be taught in public schools than in private ones. He said:

"The right of the state to regulate public schools maintained by taxes is broader than its right to regulate private schools maintained by the funds of those who patronize these schools. The state cannot exercise the same control over private schools that it does over public schools. The state has power to outline a complete course of study in public schools and to prevent the study of any subject not in that course of study."...

At the same time, Mr. Mullen's argument contained some pungent passages against a too great autocracy on the part of the state in education, passages that give comfort to those who oppose the Tennessee statute:

"The right to study any subject is a personal right which is protected by the constitution of the state. If the state has an absolute right to prescribe a mental regime, why not a physical? Why not enact a national bill of fare based on the most approved medical principles? The act in question is based on the discarded philosophy of Plato. It is in line with the code of the Spartans that deprived the parents of any control over the education of their children and vested it exclusively in the state. . . The consensus of civilized thought is in favor of a general supervision by the state, but lodging in the parents the power to control and direct the education of their children. . .The present American life demands not only technical education but an education which develops the mind and enables those possessing it to take a broad, comprehensive view of the affairs of the state, the nation and the world. The school of thought that believes that the first concern of government is the state proceeds on the theory that the state has the power and the right to do anything it deems necessary. In the old days it was said 'The king can do no wrong.' In these modern days it is said that a majority of the legislature can do no wrong."...

*

In this whole commotion about the Tennessee case and others there is one lesson so clear that few will deny it.

Just after the Tennessee trial was closed it was discovered that among the statutes passed by congress last year, 1924, is one that applies to teachers in the District of Columbia, over which congress has jurisdiction. The provision is attached to an appropriation bill and reads:

"Provided, that no part of this sum shall be available for the payment of the salaries of any superintendent. . .of intermediate instruction. . .who permits the teaching of partisan politics, disrespect of the holy Bible or that ours is an inferior form of government."

The very existence of that provision was practically unknown until a government clerk dug it up and started a test suit under it. The law was unknown to the teachers, unknown to the public. It was practically unknown to the congress that passed it.

It developed that this "rider" to an appropriation bill, which has all the effect of law, was passed by congress without ever having been considered by any committee, near the close of a late afternoon session, at a moment when fewer than twenty out of the 435 members of the lower house were present.

The lesson is this: There is frequent complaint of the supreme court. That complaint was one of the chief tenets of La Follette's third party last year. They proposed that the power of the supreme court should be abrogated in effect, that congress should be superior to the court, that the court should no longer have power to invalidate laws passed by congress.

To try to make the lesson more pointed would be to leave too little to the perspicacity of the reader. Whatever may be said of the supreme court, it does not take action on fundamental matters "in the late afternoon without adequate discussion and with less than a tenth of the membership present."

Tuesday, August 4, 1925
The Des Moines Register

TWO FACTIONS STILL DIVIDE THE DEMOCRATS

With Bryan Dead, It Still Is McAdoo vs. Smith.

By: MARK SULLIVAN
(Copyright, 1925.)

Washington, Aug. 3. —With Bryan in his grave, a survey of his party reveals two strongly antagonistic factions. One has its home in New York, the New England states, New Jersey and Pennsylvania, plus parts of Illinois, Ohio, Indiana and Wisconsin, plus Maryland and a few other spots in border and southern states.

This faction is homogeneous and compact under a single outstanding leader, Governor Smith of New York. Its principles and alms are almost, though not quite, as definite as its leadership. Perhaps its most general principle is disapproval of prohibition as it now stands on the statutes.

Another feeling animating it is a suspicion against what it believes to be a spirit of religious discrimination among democrats in other sections of the country. If the present apparent susceptibility of America to acute excitation about questions in the field of religion is to continue to grow, it bodes ill for the democrats.

Somewhat Reactionary.

As regards economic principles, this north and east faction is less homogeneous. Its enemies charge this faction of the party with being reactionary. This is true in the sense that the largest centers of its strength consist of city machines, such as those in New York, Chicago, Pittsburgh and Philadelphia, which unquestionably are more susceptible to domination by conservative interests than other sections of the party.

At the same time, it is impossible to speak of Governor Smith as a reactionary, if justice is conceded to the measure he has successfully urged in the field of social welfare legislation. This faction of the party is very aggressive and very compact. At the same time it is clearly less than a majority and it has a serious weakness in the fact that so much of its strength consists of large city machines that are under such suspicion that any candidate they approve is likely to have, for that reason, the hostility of the rest of the country.

Bryan Led South and West.

The other faction of the democrats consists of the south and west. This is the faction to whom Bryan, if not a formal leader, was at least a hero, an object of sentimental affection, and most important of all, a symbol, such that his approval or disapproval provided a guidance eagerly awaited and gladly accepted. By Bryan's death, unquestionably, this western and southern faction loses some of its spirit, some of its capacity for cohesive action. To this faction Bryan was at least the rallying point.

With Bryan gone, there is no one left who has quite this relation to the southern and western faction. The nearest equivalent is McAdoo, and one result of Bryan's death will be a tendency of the south and west to press closer to McAdoo in the search for a kind of defensive solidarity. This southern and western faction is as uniformly "dry" as the northern and eastern faction is uniformly "wet." Prohibition is the most definite single line of demarcation between the two factions. The southern and western faction is much more definitely progressive than the northern and eastern faction is definitely conservative or reactionary.

This state of the democratic party as Bryan leaves it has a curious similarity to the cleavage which he himself brought upon it when he took the head of it in 1896. Then, as now, the geographic cleavage was the same: North and east versus west and south.

Fought Silver Question.

The line of demarcation now, however, was not the line of demarcation then. There was no "dry" and "wet" cleavage in 1896. National prohibition was not then acute, nor was it an issue that either of the great parties, or any considerable faction of them, would have cared to adopt. Bryan himself resisted the injection of prohibition into the national and state platforms until as late as 1910, and did not become personally an advocate of nationwide prohibition until nearly 1915.

The cleavage in Bryan's time was wholly economic. It was the conservative east and north against the practically wholly radical west and quite generally radical south—the silver west and largely the silver south against the gold north and east. But if the cleavage is on a different set of principles and prejudices, it is geographically the same today, and it is no less deep or wide.

The immediate future history of the democratic party lies in the relation, or, more accurately, the lack of relation, between these two factions. The chasm is deep, and there has been no evidence of any healing tendency since the 1924 convention. Even small incidents that happen to recall the 1924 fight turn out to be as dynamically fruitful of anger as was that convention. In the future, with the leadership of the two factions lying in the same two men who were the antagonists in 1924, the likelihood of healing or of compromise seems no more promising.

Need New Leadership

The hopes of the democratic party as a whole lie in two possibilities. The first is partly within its own control. That is that a new leadership should arise free from association with the 1924 fight, and that each faction should give up some of the satisfaction of revenge for the sake of broader principles and hope of success.

If that does not happen, and if the fight continues, the southern and western faction, being clearly stronger numerically, can probably dominate within the party, but only at the cost of such an alienation of the other faction as will banish success. The other hope of the democratic party lies in the republicans, in the possibility of some such mistake of policy or strategy as would disunite the clear majority of the voters that the republicans now have. Under the leadership of Coolidge, there is no such republican mistake in sight.

Republicans in Danger.

And yet, the curious fact is that the immediate future seems to contain promise for the democrats. We are just at the opening stages of a fight for control of the senate that will last more than a year. Of thirty-four senate seats to be filled, twenty-six are now held by republicans.

Consequently, the republicans must win twenty-six out of these coming thirty-four contests in order even to hold their present dangerously narrow senate majority.

That is almost impossible. The geographical distribution of these thirty-four senate seats is such that only a miracle of misfortune can prevent the democrats from gaining more than they now have. The geographical factor alone is enough practically to guarantee some gains to the democrats. If, added to that, there should be republican mistakes either in broad policy or in the putting up of individual candidates, there might readily result a senate in clear democratic control. Such a taste of success during two years preceding the next presidential election, might be enough to divert the democrats into ignoring their factional animosity against each other.

**

BAPTIST MINISTER DARES DARROW TO DEBATE EVOLUTION

Asbury Park, N.J., Aug. 3 (U.N.)—A challenge to a series of from ten to twenty debates on evolution, to be held throughout the country soon will be issued to Clarence Darrow by Rev. John Roach Straton, pastor of Calvary Baptist church of New York, the fundamentalist leader announced today.

Dr. Straton said that prominent New York men had asked him to accept the leadership of the fundamentalist forces, of which the late William Jennings Bryan was the outstanding figure, and to carry on a nation-wide offensive against the teaching of evolution in tax-supported schools.

"If Mr. Darrow declines the invitation, a similar invitation will be issued to Dudley Field Malone," Dr. Straton said. "An organization has been formed to carry on the battle, but I am not at liberty, at this time, to reveal the name of the organization or the personnel behind it."

**

MRS. W. J. BRYAN ARRIVES AT HER HOME IN FLORIDA

Miami, Fla., Aug. 3. —Mrs. William Jennings Bryan arrived in

Miami at noon today and was met at the station by a party of friends from Coconut Grove, including Rev. Foster W. Taylor, pastor of the Grove Temple church, and F. A. Kent, a close friend of the family, who has been at the Bryan home during the absence of the family.

Mrs. Bryan was bearing up bravely after the strain of the tedious journey from Washington. According to Rev. Mr. Taylor, who called during the afternoon, she seemed in a peaceful frame of mind and apparently well composed, after her week of sorrow.

Mrs. Bryan will begin immediately to finish the memoirs of her husband, using as her material a wealth of notes which Mr. Bryan had prepared for the work. According to Rev. Mr. Taylor, the autobiography is to be called "A Son of Fortune."

Wednesday, August 5, 1925
The Des Moines Register

SCOPES MOVES TO BLOCK LAW ON EVOLUTION

Petitions to Enjoin Enforcement of Statute.

Chattanooga, Tenn., Aug. 4 (A.P.)—With the fanfare of oratory now but a page in the Tennessee evolutionary history, the battle against the anti-evolution law resolved here today into a simple determination of the constitutional questions involved.

The filing of a petition with John Thomas Scopes as plaintiff with the clerk of the southern division of the eastern district of Tennessee federal court, seeking a temporary order enjoining statement of the anti-evolution law, marked the first step.

Even as this brief formally gave voice to a plea from the youthful teacher, "and all others similarly situated," another bill already had been drawn to give vent to a similar prayer for injunction from Robert P. Wilson and four other taxpayers of Rhea county. Filing of the second was delayed until after affidavits could be received from the four additional petitioners.

State Officials Defendants.

The bill filed by Dr. John R. Neal, chief of defense counsel for Scopes, convicted at Dayton for violation of the evolution statute, named as defendants Gov. Austin Peay, Atty. Gen. Frank Thompson and A. T. Stewart, solicitor general of the Rhea county circuit.

It detailed the expense and efforts gone to by the petitioner to procure an education in which scientific subjects predominated.

Allegations of the petition contended that the "theory of evolution is a central feature of science, as taught today throughout the world. It is a feature and an integral part of scientific instruction in every school, college and university.

In part, the petition declares, "It is an inseparable feature of the modern science of zoology, biology, medicine, anatomy, embryology, geology and chemistry. Your petitioner could not honestly, conscientiously or efficiently fulfill the duties to which he had been appointed, and which he has undertaken as an instructor in science, and ignore and fail to expound the theory of evolution as an integral factor and inseparable feature of all modern science.

"Your petitioner further alleges that the theory of evolution denies and is in conflict with the story of divine creation of man, as taught in the bible."

Deprives Defendant of Liberty.

The petition further charges that the plaintiff, through enforcement of the law, would be deprived of his liberty and property without due process of law and would be deprived of the equal protection of the law.

The petition bore the signatures of Dr. John Randolph Neal, Clarence Darrow and Bainbridge Colby.

Dr. Neal prepared tonight to visit Knoxville tomorrow for a conference with Judge Ben Hicks to determine an approximate date for the hearing.

Governor Peay, who only recently returned to the state from Michigan, Attorney General Thompson and Solicitor General Stewart must be notified of the action, after which answer must be made within five days. A definite date for the hearing then will be determined. This will be conducted by three judges, one of whom must be either a justice of the United States Supreme court or a circuit judge, and the other two may be either circuit or district judges.

Thursday, August 6, 1925
The Des Moines Register

FINDS RELIGION OUT OF PULPIT

Minister Starts Life Anew As Oil Salesman.

"A man can find more practical Christianity out in the rough and tumble world of 'he men' than he can in many organized churches today." Declared Rev. Harry H. Koontz, former pastor of the First congregational church at Fremont, Neb., who started work here yesterday as city oil salesman for the Shaffer Oil and Refining company.

Mr. Koontz quit his pulpit when he was beaten in a church fight and a commission of pastors recommended the removal of the pastor and the church board.

"Religion is a matter of salesmanship," Mr. Koontz declared. "A man can learn more religion out in the world practicing salesmanship and bumping up against real people, than he can studying theology for twenty years. And I'm a graduate of two universities, the University of New York and Vanderbilt university at Nashville, Tenn."

Built Up Large Membership

In the two years Mr. Koontz was preaching at Fremont he added 250 members to the church and his preaching filled the church to the doors on many Sundays.

Evolution, the former pastor declared, was the beginning of his differences with certain members of his congregation.

"Away last winter I preached a series of sermons on 'Darwin or Bryan, Which?'

This started the trouble. I'm a modernist and always have been. Evolution is progress," he said.

"The bible is not and never was intended to be a book of science. The apostle Paul, if he thought on the matter at all, went through life thinking the world was flat."

Conceals Christianity.

Referring to the ten commandments, Mr. Koontz said they never were intended to be a set of arbitrary rules governing human conduct, but rather a spirit of conduct.

"The church," he said, "has built up so much paraphernalia surrounding religion that in many cases it has lost the spirit of Christianity.

"I like practical rough and tumble men. I like to buck up against real life as men live it. I like boxing and I used to attend prize fights and this, of course, didn't please some of the members of my church."

Mr. Koontz said he was a church member and probably would preach and lecture occasionally even while he is an oil salesman.

Until he can find a suitable location for his family, Mr. Koontz said, his wife and daughter would remain with relatives in Kansas City.

**

SCOPES COUNSEL SAYS EVOLUTION REFUTES BIBLE

Theory to Be Emphasized in Petition Today.

Chattanooga, Tenn., Aug. 8 (A.P.)—Not only does defense counsel for John T. Scopes, Rhea county teacher convicted of violation of the Tennessee evolution law, hold that the theory of evolution denies and is in conflict with the story of the divine creation of man as taught by the bible, as published yesterday in connection with the filing of a petition for injuction in federal court here, but this theory will be more strongly reiterated in a companion petition to be filed tomorrow.

Such was the statement tonight of Dr. John R. Neal, senior counsel for Scopes in the trial at Dayton, who remained in the city and drafted what he designated as the taxpayer's bill.

Attacks Legality of Law.

The bill will allege the same grounds of complaint as the petition filed yesterday, that the Tennessee law is in conflict with the United States constitution, in that it deprives the plaintiff of liberty to teach his children the truth, and that by barring the teaching of evolution, the money of the taxpayers is being wrongfully used.

Dr. Neal stated that the bill will be predicated on the theory that evolution is in conflict with the story of divine creation of man as taught in the bible. He said that he considered the bill as the most important step in the fight for tolerance, even overshadowing the trial of Scopes at Dayton.

**

State to Fight Scopes.

Battle Creek, Mich., Aug. 5 (By The Associated Press)—Gov. Austin Peay of Tennessee, in a statement here today, announced that the state of Tennessee will employ counsel from this time forward and combat every question that can be raised on appeal of the John T. Scopes case.

The governor and Mrs. Peay left today for Nashville after a six weeks' rest here.

"What the effect of the evolution trial at Dayton will have in the long run is for the future," the governor said. "Surely it will cause a more widespread investigation of the whole theory of evolution that will go a long way to clarify the atmosphere.

"The reckless teaching of a subject, which has been carried on until now and going uncorrected and undigested, has been steadily making agnostics and unbelievers among our youth in shocking number.

Threat to Christianity.

"Ours from the beginning has been a christian nation. Its doom is sealed, and its descent toward oblivion well begun whenever we embrace infidelity and agnosticism as a people.

"The story writers and sensation mongers who crowded Dayton during the trial as though they were having a Roman holiday, made great sport of it and some of them were bitterly unjust and unkind to the people whose hospitality they accepted, and of whose noble qualities they knew little or nothing. The fact is they were among a clear seeing and thinking people, who have no superiors in natural intelligence and excellent qualities in the world."

The people of Tennessee, Governor Peay said, know that evolution is, and in the very nature of things, must always remain a speculation and a theory. They believe that the bible is the revealed and inspired word of the creator of all things and are unwilling for their children to be taught the contrary.

Is Not a Federal Question.

The governor said that there is no federal question in the Scopes case.

"Tennessee is a sovereign state and except as forbidden by the federal constitution, has absolute and exclusive authority to regulate its local concerns and to employ its police powers without any federal interference," he said.

"Whether the law, when properly construed, prohibits in our schools the theory of evolution, remains to be seen. It certainly prohibits its teaching as a fact. No state should permit that. In any event Tennessee would not presume to regulate the schools and methods of instruction in other states and beyond treating with meddlers from elsewhere, who undertake to tell her how to run her own schools, she will give them no attention."

**

They Say They Are.

Ida Grove, Ia.—To The Editor: Knowing that the Register was editorially "evolutionist", I awaited with interest your editorial on "The Dayton Speech" of Mr. Bryan. Now that it has come to us I cannot help but note its manifest weakness in dealing with the argument of the commoner's last words.

It is as difficult to diagnose the causes of personality as of disease, and therefore Mr. Bryan may be right in his conclusions regarding the causes of Darwin's agnosticism, especially in the light of the quotation Mr. Bryan made from Darwin's writings, and The Register wrong. The same with Nietzsche.

The strongest part of the argument of Mr. Bryan The Register overlooks, the part dealing with evolution as undemonstrated, or the part dealing with the philosophy born of evolution which made the Chicago murderers what they were, and who were freed from capital punishment on the ground of the evolutionary hypothesis. Other strong points were evaded.

If the word "evolution" is to be used as the proper characterization of the history of the planet earth as we can know it, without carrying anything with it save the general notion that there has been change during the years of its life, we all can be evolutionists, and no doubt are, if that is the meaning of the word. When it is said that this bishop is an evolutionist and that christian professor is an evolutionist, these men are no doubt that kind of evolutionist which an innocuous conception of it permits them to be. They are not thorough-going evolutionists in the strictest sense of the word, and therefore not real evolutionists at all. The statement that they are is misleading. Daniel L. Eckert.

**

Ask Any Embryologist.

Thompson, Ia.—To the Editor: Will Mr. Darrow or any other well informed evolutionist please tell me what the coming man looked like during the period between the tadpole and monkey? It must of necessity have taken millions of years to develop a tadpole into a monkey, and I am curious to know what kind of looking animals come between.

For my part I glory in the fact that I am a descendant of Adam and Eve, the glorious man and woman that God fashioned with his own hands and in his own image, with promise and hope of life everlasting.

All honor due to William J. Bryan, champion of true Christianity, blessed be his memory! And may God wake up someone to pick up and carry on his standard. Mr. O. B. Johnson.

**

Charlie Bryan's attempt to get into the fundamentalist spotlight after his brother passed out didn't meet with much success.

**

Orthodox.

Sheldahl, Ia.—To the Editor: As you did not print all my letter, some got the impression that I believed in evolution. I do not believe that evolution and Genesis agree. I believe that the bible is the inspired word of God. I also believe that God made Adam, that he fell, and that through Christ we are resurrected from the dead. Mary E. Foster.

Sunday, August 9, 1925
The Des Moines Sunday Register

BRYAN'S WILL GIVES $100,000 TO EDUCATION

Estate Goes to Family and for Promotion of Religious Schools.

(Special Dispatch to The Register.)
(Copyright 1925, by North American Newspaper Alliance.)

New York, Aug. 8. —"In the name of God, farewell." Thus begins the last will and testament of the late William Jennings Bryan, a copy of which was received here today.

The will distributes an estate valued at $860,500 among relatives, friends and institutions. His estate, Marymount, at Cocoanut Grove, Fla., goe4s to his wife, together with one-third of the rest of his estate.

His three children receive approximately $100,000 each, according to his own estimate. Approximately $100,000 goes to educational and religious institutions.

The will, in part, is as follows:

"In the name of God, farewell.

Trusts Salvation to Christ.

"Trusting for my salvation on the blood of Jesus Christ, my lord and redeemer, and relying on his promises for my hope of resurrection, I consign my body to the dust and recommend my spirit to the God who gave it.

"I, William Jennings Bryan, a citizen of Dade county, Fla., being of sound mind and memory but conscious of the uncertainty of life and desiring to make a just disposition of the worldly goods with which an indulgent heavenly father has seen fit to bless me, do make, publish and declare this my last will and testament, hereby revoking annulling all former wills made by me."

The last stipulation in the will is as follows:

"I have saved for the last my bequest for religious education.

While I have devoted a large part of my time to the study and discussion of political questions and have found an abundant reward in the reforms adopted with my humble aid, I feel more interested in religion than in politics because religion is the only influence that controls the heart, out of which are the issues of life.

Interested in Education.

"Next to religion, I am most interested in education, because education can and should increase one's capacity for service.

"But education will not be a benefit to its possessor and a blessing to society unless wisely used.

"I am anxious that each intellectual ship shall be equipped to control its course on life's stormy sea.

"My chief interest is the reform of Christian education, the entwining of the spiritual with the intellectual.

"I had hoped to aid in the establishment of an academy that would embody my idea and serve as a model.

"Fearing that I shall not be able to carry out this plan during the years that remain, I am setting aside a fund equal to each child's share to be used for Christian education."

From this amount, however, Mr. Bryan deducts $50,000, the value of his Nebraska home which he recently gave to the Methodist church for a hospital. The balance of the fund is for the following purposes:

"To establish an academy for boys, which shall be under the control of some unit of government or some evangelical church, Presbyterian preferred but not necessarily, so long as it is controlled by a recognized religious denomination."

Would Symbolize Union.

The gift to the academy for boys includes the unusual clause that Mr. Bryan "would like the boy students to wear a uniform of blue and gray, to symbolize the union of north and south."

If such an academy cannot be founded the funds are to be used for distribution among existing institutions of a similar nature.

The will leaves all publication rights in Mr. Bryan's writings to the widow and three children, who are further authorized to prepare and publish Mr. Bryan's official biography. The will commands that a full sketch of his wife's life be added to his biography, "setting forth particularly the aid which Mrs. Bryan has rendered to her husband in all his work during his life."

Mr. Bryan's sister, Frances Bryan Baird, receives his house in East Lincoln, Neb. He instructs his wife to remember with souvenirs his former law partner, Mr. Talbot, and his former comrade in the army, W. F. Schwind.

Churches throughout the country receive small bequests aggregating $12,000. All persons in Mr. Bryan's employ are to have $100. For each year spent in his service.

The will was drawn and signed at Marymount, Cocoanut Grove, on July 5, 1925.

EPILOGUE

It seems fitting to close our book with the publication of Bryan's will, as one of the outcomes of his will was the establishment of a Christian Liberal Arts college in Dayton, Tennessee.

"During the Scopes Evolution Trial in 1925, William Jennings Bryan expressed the wish that a school might be established in Dayton to teach truth from a Biblical perspective. Following his death on July 26, 1925, a national memorial association was formed to establish such an institution in Bryan's honor.

"William Jennings Bryan University (in 1958 it was designated William Jennings Bryan College, and the name was shortened to Bryan College in 1993) was chartered in 1930 and admitted its first class in the fall of that year. Its stated purpose was, and is, to provide 'for the higher education of men and women under auspices distinctly Christian and spiritual.'

"...Bryan College is founded upon the belief that God is the author of truth; that He has revealed Himself to mankind through nature, conscience, the Bible and Jesus Christ; that it is His will for man to come to a knowledge of truth; and that an integrated study of the arts and sciences and the Bible, with a proper emphasis on the spiritual, mental, social and physical aspects of life, will lead to the balanced development of the whole person."(copied)

"...For further information, contact Bryan College P. O. Box 7000, Dayton, TN 37321-7000; phone 423-775-2041 fax 423-775-7330 or visit their website at www.bryan.edu.**"**

post script:

On February 6, 2000, a fire occurred at the Bryan College administration building destroying the 3rd floor. This building was started in the 1930's and completed twenty years later. Classes resumed on campus the second day after the fire. Plans for rebuilding are in progress. Log on to the above website for further information.